HOLLYWOOD GOES
TO HIGH SCHOOL

SECOND EDITION

HOLLYWOOD GOES TO HIGH SCHOOL

Cinema, Schools, and American Culture

Robert C. Bulman
Saint Mary's College of California

WORTH
PUBLISHERS

A Macmillan Education Imprint
New York

Chapter 3 is an expanded version of a thesis first put forward by the author in *The Urban Review*, Teachers in the 'Hood: Hollywood's Middle-Class Fantasy, 34 (3): 251–276, Bulman, Copyright © 2002, Human Sciences Press, Inc., with kind permission from Springer Science+Business Media.

Publisher: Rachel Losh
Associate Publisher: Jessica Bayne
Senior Associate Editor: Sarah Berger
Development Editor: Katherine Super
Marketing Manager: Kate Nurre
Marketing Assistant: Allison Greco
Editorial Assistant: Kimberly Morgan-Smith
Art Director: Diana Blume
Cover Designer: Blake Logan
Interior Design: Blake Logan
Managing Editor: Lisa Kinne
Photo Editor: Robin Fadool
Director of Editing, Design, and Media Production: Tracey Kuehn
Project Editor: Julio Espin
Production Manager: Susan Wein
Composition: MPS Limited
Printing and Binding: Courier
Cover Photos: manley099/E+/Getty Images

Library of Congress Control Number: 2014959877

ISBN-13: 978-1-4641-7169-7
ISBN-10: 1-4641-7169-6

Worth Publishers
41 Madison Avenue
New York, NY 10010
www.macmillanhighered.com

For Lynne

About the Author

Robert C. Bulman is a professor of sociology at Saint Mary's College of California. He received his BA in sociology from the University of California at Santa Cruz in 1989 and his PhD in sociology from the University of California at Berkeley in 1999. He teaches the sociology of education, the sociology of culture, social stratification, and research methods. In addition to his research on films and American culture, he has published work on educational decision making, the political dynamics of school choice, and masculinity in ballroom dancing.

Contents

Preface

When I was an eleven-year-old boy in 1978, my parents took me and my sister to see *Grease* at a local drive-in movie theater in suburban Southern California. Its sound track became the first album (actually, an eight-track tape) that I ever bought. I remember as a teen catching glimpses of *Fast Times at Ridgemont High*, *Risky Business*, and *Porky's* on cable television late at night. In the last months of my senior year in high school in 1985 I went to the drive-in again, this time with a friend. As suburban high school students, we were impressed by the insights of *The Breakfast Club*. In college, as a burgeoning sociologist, I went to see *Stand and Deliver* and *Dead Poet's Society*. I remember debating the merits of each film with my dorm mates. I recall being skeptical that a charismatic teacher like Jaime Escalante in *Stand and Deliver* could be solely responsible for the intellectual awakening of poor inner-city students. I also criticized *Dead Poet's Society* for its overly romantic depiction of the heroic English teacher Mr. Keating. As an adult, I've enjoyed such classic high school films as *Blackboard Jungle*, *Up the Down Staircase*, *Halls of Anger*, and *To Sir, With Love*.

My interest as a general fan of the high school film genre grew into a serious academic interest as I began to explore ways of teaching the sociology of education using different media. Films such as *Blackboard Jungle* and *Dangerous Minds* nicely offer illustrations of some key concepts in the sociology of education. I further developed this pedagogical method and taught an entire course called "Hollywood Goes to High School" in 2000 at Saint Mary's College of California. The students and I watched and analyzed a dozen or so high school films and compared what was represented on the screen to what we had read in the sociology of education literature and to what we had experienced in our own high schools. As my students worked on their final papers, I began to write up my own observations and analyses of the films. Intrigued by the patterns I began to recognize in the films, I watched as many films about teens and the high school experience as I could get my hands on.

Thus, the first edition of this book in 2005 was the result of a journey that began at a drive-in in 1978. Since 2005 I have continued to watch and analyze films about high school—*Coach Carter*, *Superbad*, *Freedom Writers*, *Easy A*, and so on. While most academic analyses of films are left to scholars in the field of film studies, this book is rooted in sociology. My approach to studying film comes from my training as a sociologist in the areas of social theory, the sociology of education, social stratification, and the sociology of adolescence. Nevertheless, this book will be of interest not only to sociologists, but also to those in the fields of film studies, cultural studies, American studies, communication, anthropology, and education. It will also be of interest to non-academics who have an interest in schools, teenagers, the movies, or American culture in general.

The second edition of *Hollywood Goes to High School* is updated with examples from many of the high school films that have been released in the ten years between the first and second editions. I have also added an analysis on how gender is represented in films about high school and what these gender representations reveal about American culture. This edition of *Hollywood Goes to High School* also includes "A Guide to Conducting Social Science Research with Film" (Appendix A), which offers an overview of the steps students should follow in order to conduct their own research project using film as data.

Finally, since the data for this book come from Hollywood films, it is necessary to tell the story lines, discuss important details, and reveal the endings of many of the movies in the sample. I apologize in advance if in using these films to make arguments about American culture, I spoil your future enjoyment of the films as entertainment. Please consider yourself fairly warned. This potential annoyance, however, can also be seen as an advantage. One of the benefits of doing research with films is that the data are accessible to everyone. Curious or skeptical readers are encouraged to view for themselves these films and others not included in the sample. Readers can easily do their own fieldwork, as it were, in order to confirm or challenge the arguments of this book.

Acknowledgments

Many people read and commented on the manuscript of the first edition of this book in whole or in part. Thanks to Lynne Bartz, J. Schiao, Amy Divine, Carla Koop, Pamela Perry, Jim Elliott, Richard Arum, Bill Domhoff, Joel Devine, Kathy Roper, Valerie Raymond, Paul Stenis, Laura Edwards, Erik Gilg, and an anonymous reviewer at Worth. Thanks to George Ritzer for his helpful comments and for seeing the potential of this project even before I did. Thanks to all of my students at Saint Mary's College of California. In particular, thanks to Bryan Edwards, Christina Hu, Malisa Young, and Samantha Hoffman for research assistance. Thanks to Katie Wilson for research assistance that greatly improved the second edition. Thanks to Sarah Berger and Kate Super for their editorial help and advice regarding the second edition. Thanks to all of my colleagues at Saint Mary's College of California, in particular my sociology colleagues—John Ely, Phylis Martinelli, Cynthia Ganote, Zeynep Atalay, and Ynez Wilson Hirst. Thanks to the Saint Mary's Faculty Development Fund for supporting excellence in both teaching and research—several faculty development grants helped to fund the research for both editions of this book. Thanks to Patty Wade and the other reference librarians at Saint Mary's College. Thanks to Diane Bianchi for her exceptional administrative support. Thanks to Jerry Brunetti for encouraging the research in the project's infancy.

I would like to offer a special thanks to the January Term Program at Saint Mary's College of California. January Term is a four-week intersession program in which faculty are encouraged to step out of their comfort zone and to teach intensive and exciting non-disciplinary courses in innovative ways. *Hollywood Goes to High School* was a January Term class before it was a book. Without the encouragement from Saint Mary's to take chances in the classroom and to learn new things in new ways right alongside our students I would never have pursued this project. January Term is a terribly exciting program that makes Saint Mary's a wonderful place to teach and learn.

Thanks to Thomas Morrione for introducing me to sociology in 1986. Thanks to Bill Domhoff and Rebecca Klatch for giving me the confidence to become a professional sociologist. Thanks to my parents, Bob and Rosemary Bulman, for their continual support and encouragement. Finally, thanks to my wife, Lynne Bartz, and my son, Aron. Their love and support made this book possible.

[one]

Using the Movies to Make Sense of Society

A Sociological Introduction

The fact that film has been the most potent vehicle for the American imagination suggests all the more strongly that movies have something to tell us not just about the surfaces but the mysteries of American life.[1]

—Arthur M. Schlesinger Jr.

Sociologists don't often study films. Most sociological research observes people in social interaction, tracks patterns of social inequality, investigates the workings of social institutions, seeks to understand the process of social change, and studies the distribution of power in society. Generally speaking, sociology is the study of social reality, not fantasy. While many people think that movie images accurately represent something about the way the world really is, they are only presenting an interpretation of reality—an image that resonates with the filmmakers and perhaps the audience, but one that does not necessarily reflect the way things actually are. As bell hooks has written,

> Movies make magic. They change things. They take the real and make it into something else right before your very eyes. . . . They give the reimagined, reinvented version of the real. It may look like something familiar, but in actuality it is a different universe from the world of the real. That's what makes movies so compelling.[2]

Hollywood routinely twists and shapes reality to maximize dramatic or comic effect for commercial purposes. Films must also frame complicated social relationships within two hours and on a two-dimensional canvas, thereby simplifying them.

Yet films *do* reveal a certain truth. While Westerns, mobster films, or high school films (to name just a few genres—clusters of films that share a similar style, form, and content) may not paint an accurate picture about life in the Old West, in the Mafia, or in high school, these films, if viewed systematically, tell us truths about the culture that produces and consumes them. In this sense they are very real and meaningful artifacts of our culture.[3]

What types of stories and characters creative people develop, which film projects make their way through the Hollywood system, how a film is edited and framed, and which films resonate with a popular audience tell us much more about the reality of a particular society than the "reality" of a film's subject. The clustering of films into genres helps us to identify which versions of "reality" are particularly salient to the culture that produces and consumes them. The goal of this book is to help uncover the cultural significance of one particular film genre—the American high school film.

While I am not a film studies scholar per se, I loosely borrow from film studies the tradition of genre analysis—which, in the words of film studies scholar Timothy Shary, attempts to:

> understand cinema based on group and individual representations in (and/or reactions to) films—for example, how films portray a given population or their conditions—under the tacit assumption that films are both aesthetic and cultural documents produced by an industry whose aim is to appeal to (often larger) populations who will find the films worth seeing.[4]

The success of a film genre over time implies that elements of the genre resonate with a large audience. Diana Crane, a noted sociologist of culture, writes that popular texts (books and films, for instance) can help us to understand the cultural worldviews of the members of a society with whom those texts resonate:

> A text is popular if it resonates with readers [or viewers]. For a text to be popular, its message must fit the discourses used by readers to make sense of their experiences. A popular text reassures the readers that their worldviews (discourses) are meaningful. The satisfaction of consuming popular culture is that of being reassured that one's interpretation of the world is congruent with that of others.[5]

In other words, the enjoyment of popular culture such as movies is a *collective* experience. Part of the pleasure of popular culture is that it is popular—that others are experiencing the same cultural product that we are experiencing. This collective process helps to bond members of a society together and to reinforce our collective understanding of the social world we share.

Generally, film studies scholarship is rooted in the humanities, not the social sciences. Film analyses are often based on a small sample of films, and the argument often delves no deeper than the author's interpretation of the "text" of the film. Little effort is made to use the lessons of social science research to help interpret the meaning of a representative sample of films. Powers, Rothman, and Rothman have been critical of this film studies approach.

> [P]oststructuralist theorists and scholars who claim to be interested in politics and society have in no way turned to the social sciences to study society but remain utterly committed to the language of aesthetic critique in the formalist and structuralist traditions. The likes of Weber, C. Wright Mills, and Daniel Bell rarely, if ever, appear in their bibliographies.[6]

In this book I attempt to bring a social science sensibility to a film studies tradition and to bring the rich empirical data of films into the realm of social science.[7]

Films and Culture

What is the relationship between film and society? What do films have to teach us about the societies in which they are produced and consumed? Are films primarily a reflection of a society's culture, or do they in some ways help to shape cultural life independently?[8] I suggest that films both reflect and shape culture. To understand fully the social and cultural significance of films, we need to understand both the production of films and the consumption of films. In other words, we need to understand the social processes that create certain films and film genres, and we need to understand how members of a society interpret and react to those films. Both sides of this equation help us to make sense of the relationship between films and culture.

Genre films, for instance, reflect the culture that produces and consumes them in a variety of ways. First, films reflect the culture to the extent that the creative artists who imagine and make the films are themselves a product of that culture and are attempting to express something about the social world they inhabit. Second, commercial interests (the studios that fund the films) reflect the culture as they strategically select projects, develop them, produce them, and market them to the public. Finally, the audience reaction to the films at the box office reflects the cultural milieu by indicating what resonates with the public. The popularity of certain types of films feeds back to the artistic and commercial interests as they develop new projects. Thus, the genre develops in constant interaction among creative artists, commercial interests, and the audience in a "circuit of culture."[9] As film scholar Thomas Schatz has argued:

> Movies are not produced in creative or cultural isolation, nor are they consumed that way . . . [A genre approach] recognizes the cinema's close contact with its *audience*, whose response to individual films has affected the gradual development of story formulas and standard production practices.[10]

At the same time, films have the cultural power to influence how members of a society make sense of social life. It is important to note that this current study is not a reception study of films. That is, I do not conduct research to see how audiences interpret these films, nor how different groups within society might attach different meanings to the same films. While such a study would shed important light on the social and cultural significance of these films, it is beyond the scope of the present analysis. What I do in this book is treat films as cultural texts. I look for patterns in these texts and I find that they reveal the dominant ways in which American culture views education, adolescents, and class inequality.

Nonetheless, I believe that films do influence how we see the world.[11] The commercial film industry is a socializing institution. Films *teach* us who we are as much as they *reflect* who we are. When we go to the movies, we absorb messages about the social world in which we live. We learn about heroes and villains, about what is possible and impossible, about conflict and resolution, about relationships, and about norms and values. We do not necessarily accept every message we receive without questioning it, but we do learn what messages our culture chooses to convey in its entertainment and we incorporate these lessons into an understanding of ourselves and our society.

Ultimately, it is very difficult to specify exactly how films reflect culture and how they affect it. As sociologist Andrew Tudor has noted, the dynamic relationship between society and the stories society tells about itself is far too complicated to determine causation. Tudor writes,

> . . . the movies participate in a continual and complex social process. They articulate for us the bases of our social lives; they give the underlying regularities our

societies' concrete form. They are both reflection and cause; a link in a closed circle. We act, we create, we form, and even change societies. Our popular culture expresses the irreducibles of these operations.[12]

Films are located at the center of a complex cultural process of production and consumption. Their location within this process provides us with a particularly convenient site in which to conduct a cinematic ethnography to understand something about American culture.

Another reason that it is difficult to pinpoint the precise role that films play in a culture is that culture is complex and messy. As sociologist Kai Erikson argues, every culture is filled with potential contradictions.[13] The symbols and shared values of a society are not seamless. Cultural meanings are not given. People must actively work to make sense of their lives and the complicated social world in which they live. They often must struggle with contradictory notions. I suggest that one way in which we collectively manage to cope with the complexity and confusion of social life is to package reality and to represent it as fiction—to tell stories about our social world that make it more comprehensible. In this sense, films can be viewed as modern-day cultural myths and folktales.

Folktales (or fairy tales) are stories that a culture tells to itself about itself. That is, folktales express elements of a culture (values, norms, beliefs, fears, etc.) in fantastic stories that get told repeatedly in a culture. These tales help individuals to order their social world and to remind members of a society about the common elements of their culture that bind them together. As Jack Zipes, a scholar who studies fairy tales, writes,

> The classical fairy tale makes it appear that we are all part of a universal community with shared values and norms, that we are all striving for the same happiness, that there are certain dreams and wishes which are irrefutable, that a particular type of behavior will produce guaranteed results, like living happily ever after with lots of gold in a marvelous castle . . .[14]

What Zipes points out about fairy tales (particularly as they find expression in the contemporary United States), however, is that they do not necessarily reflect the values and interests of *all* members of society. Fairy tales (and films, as I argue in this book) are more than just entertainment that helps to create social solidarity. They may appear to be politically neutral, but they often reflect the interests of particular segments of society. Zipes continues,

> Yet, amusement is not to be taken lightly, for distraction and divertissement have an important ideological function: almost all the major classical fairy tales that have achieved prominence and are to be enjoyed in the United States can be considered as products that reinforce a patriarchal and middle-class social code.[15]

Similar to Zipes, I argue that Hollywood films convey elements of the dominant ideology in the United States. Specifically, Hollywood films tend to convey the sensibilities of the American middle class: individualism, self-sufficiency, free expression, hard work, and fair play. In many ways the ideology of the middle class is culturally hegemonic in the United States. That is, the middle-class experience is considered to be the "normal" experience in American life. The rich and the poor are usually depicted in Hollywood films as outside the mainstream of society. While I do not disagree with those who argue that Hollywood also privileges the perspective of whites, I find in my analysis of the high school films that a social-class lens better explains the data than a lens of race.[16] Fortunately, the data I analyze in this book are very accessible. Readers are encouraged to conduct their own analysis of the high school film genre to see if my arguments are supported by the evidence and to determine if there are other more persuasive interpretations of the data. I have included an appendix that provides advice for how to conduct such research.

Going to the Movies as a Research Method

To assemble a sample of high school films I surveyed friends, colleagues, students in my sociology classes, the workers at local video stores (I began this research in 2000, when there were still video stores!), and professional movie critics from local newspapers about the high school films with which they were familiar. I collected a list of high school films that have been analyzed by other scholars.[17] I reviewed the weekly television listings of broadcast and cable movies. I ran searches on the Internet Movie Data Base (www.imdb.com) and Netflix and consulted various video guidebooks. From this list I selected the films that use a high school as their primary setting or films whose plots orbit around the life of a high school or high school students. However, it was not enough that the movie feature (even primarily) high school students. In order to be included in the sample, those students had to be connected to a school or to education in some way in the plot. In addition to the classroom, the connection to high school could be based on high-school-related activities, such as dances, parties, football games, student politics, making college plans, or graduation.

To provide some illustration, *Hunger Games* did not fit the criteria because at no time is a school or school-related issue either depicted or referred to. On the other hand, even though most of the action takes place outside of school, *Superbad* was included because the plot revolves around high school students who are coping with their personal relationships and impending graduation. It is not always clear whether a film is a "high school" film or not. Admittedly, the boundary can be fuzzy. Many readers will no doubt remember films they think should have been included in the sample or believe some of the films in the sample should not have been included. This is not meant to be an exhaustive list of all the American films that depict high school and high school students. It is, however, a sample that tries to be inclusive of most of the American high school films of the past few decades. A full listing of the films in the sample can be found in the appendix.

I began this research by asking a simple exploratory question: How are images of high school represented in Hollywood films? I viewed each of the films in my sample at least once (often several times) and noted the major plot elements, the characterizations, and the explicit and implicit lessons each film teaches. I took note of how the films depict curriculum, pedagogy, the role of the teacher, the role of the administration, peer relations among students, relations between students and adults, student attitudes toward schoolwork, extracurricular activities, the role of the family, the resources of the school, the prevalence of violence, the use of drugs, and the expressions of gender and sexuality. I collected the data inductively—that is, I did not at first conduct the research with a hypothesis to test. After careful content analysis of my detailed notes I began to see patterns developing. I then asked an explanatory question of my data: "Do the social demographics of the students in the films affect the ways in which Hollywood tells stories about high school?" It soon became clear that there were significant differences in the ways the students and teachers in the urban public school, suburban public school, and private school films were depicted on screen. My theoretical analysis, therefore, explores the cultural reasons for the differences among these three subgenres of the American high school film.

There are 177 films in the sample. One hundred four films feature middle-class students in mostly suburban public schools (the suburban school sample), thirty-seven films feature poor or working-class students in mostly urban public schools (the urban school sample), and thirty-six films feature a mix of rich and upper-middle-class students in private schools (the private school sample). There are a greater number of suburban school films in the sample because there are simply more high school films made about suburban high schools and middle-class students than there are about urban high schools or private high schools. One reason for this is because the notion of what the high school and adolescent experience is in the United States is wrapped up in middle-class assumptions. A discussion of this hegemonic middle-class worldview in American culture will be explored in chapter 2.

A Brief Review of Other High School Film Analyses

Many studies of the high school film genre treat the genre monolithically, as if all high school films share similar characteristics. Joseph Reed, for instance, narrowly defines the high school film genre as those films based in high school that are told from the point of view of the students, excluding the many important high school films told from the point of view of the teacher.[18] David Considine, however, notes that there are important differences within the high school genre. Considine analyzes films that feature teachers as the main character and argues that between 1935 and 1977 the image of the teacher in film grew progressively more negative.[19] While Considine argues that this change is a function of history, I suggest that he overlooks the important differences between films based in schools with poor or working-class students and those based in schools with middle- or upper-middle-class students. Contrary to Considine's thesis, there has been a resurgence of films that feature the "teacher-hero" since 1977, and most of these films have been based in urban high schools with a poor or working-class student body rather than in suburban high schools with a mostly middle-class student body.

Picking up where Considine left off, Timothy Shary analyzes variants on the teen film genre, focusing on the many teen films released between 1980 and 2000.[20] Shary offers the most in-depth coverage of the teen film genre to date. His discussion of the high school film subgenre constitutes one portion of his overall analysis of the *youth* film genre in general. He maps out the high school genre according to character types—the nerd, the delinquent, the rebel, the popular girl, and the jock—and how these representations have changed over the years. While his discussion of the delinquent overlaps some with my category of the urban school film, he does not make an analytic distinction among urban, suburban, and private high school films, which I find to be the most important distinction to make in the analysis of the high school film genre.

Paul Farber and Gunilla Holm divide the high school films between those that focus on the student and those that focus on the teacher or principal.[21] I agree with their argument that both the students and the "educator-heroes" act independently of the institution of the school. However, their analysis does not highlight the tendency of educator-centered films to be set in urban high schools with poor students while student-centered films tend to take place in suburban high schools with middle-class students. Therefore, they overlook the important theoretical implications about social class, education, and American culture that I highlight in this book. Similarly, both Mary Dalton and David Hill analyze films that focus on teachers.[22] While they recognize differences between films that depict "good teachers" and those that depict "bad teachers," neither of their analyses exploits the tendency of "good teacher" films to be based in schools with poor and working-class students while the "bad teacher" films are most likely to feature middle-class students. The aforementioned authors do not view elite private school films as a subgenre distinct from the urban or suburban school films. In short, most of the existing analyses narrowly focus on the relationship between teacher and student regardless of the school's social context. However, by not analyzing the socioeconomic context in which these movie plots take place, and how the plots and characters differ accordingly, they fail to appreciate the significant lessons about social class and American culture that a sociological analysis reveals.[23]

Hollywood's View of High School: The Three Subgenres

In 2001 the film *Not Another Teen Movie* was released in theaters across the country. It is a satirical movie spoof of the many high school and teen films that had been released in the United States in the preceding two decades. This movie spoof is evidence that the high school film has been successfully established as its own Hollywood genre. The dominant themes of these films are recognizable enough to a general audience to merit the production of a major Hollywood film that pokes fun at the genre. As a

er, Not Another Teen Movie is unoriginal. The reason is clear enough in
g title—*Please, not another teen movie! Aren't there enough already?* Indeed,
r Teen Movie is a redundant film. While its sole purpose is to spoof pre-
exist........gh school films, most of those films are themselves heavily derived from
previous high school films, creating a string of unintended satires. For instance, if
one has seen *Pretty in Pink*, then the themes of *10 Things I Hate About You*, *She's All
That*, and an assortment of other similar films are all too familiar and predictable.

Not Another Teen Movie has a frightfully easy job of satirizing previous teen
films. It often borrows the *exact* same dialogue, sound track, and sometimes even
the same actors from several previous high school films. It is almost more correct
to call *Not Another Teen Movie* a remake of *She's All That*, *10 Things I Hate About
You*, *Pretty In Pink*, and *Varsity Blues* than a satire of those films. *Not Another Teen
Movie* also borrows liberally from *Porky's*, *American Pie*, *Lucas*, *Never Been Kissed*,
Bring It On, *The Breakfast Club*, *Cruel Intentions*, *Can't Hardly Wait*, *Grease*, and
Fast Times at Ridgemont High.

Not Another Teen Movie takes place, appropriately enough, at John Hughes High
School. (John Hughes is the famous writer and director responsible for such teen
classics as *The Breakfast Club*, *Pretty in Pink*, *16 Candles*, *Ferris Bueller's Day Off*,
Weird Science, and *Some Kind of Wonderful.*) It features such common teen film
characters as the popular cool guy, the dumb jock, the bitchy cheerleader, the horny
virgin boys, the misunderstood rebel, the mean football coach, the wise janitor, the
clueless parents, and the nerdy best friend. As with most of the movies it satirizes, its
plot has very little to do with schooling per se. Instead, the story revolves around the
struggles over popularity and dating as the characters figure out who they are, what
is important to them in life, and how to express themselves free of the constraints of
the school, social cliques, and their parents. The moral of the story (and the moral
of most of the movies in the suburban school subgenre) is that you should follow
your heart, regardless of what your friends, your parents, or your teachers advise.

While *Not Another Teen Movie* presents itself as a satire of the teen film genre,
it is, more precisely, a satire of a subgenre of the teen film—the middle-class suburban high school film. The movies that depict poor teens in mostly urban high
schools are *not* satirized in this film. There are no satirical references to movies
such as *Blackboard Jungle*, *Dangerous Minds*, *Lean on Me*, *Stand and Deliver*, *The
Substitute*, *The Principal*, or *Teachers*. In fact, those films have already been satirized
by Hollywood in the 1996 film *High School High*. The fact that Hollywood has
chosen to satirize films that depict poor students in urban high schools separately
from the films that depict middle-class students in suburban high schools suggests
strongly that the urban high school film constitutes its own subgenre with a unique
set of themes, story lines, characters, and messages.

High School High takes place at Marion Barry High School (Marion Barry
was the mayor of Washington, DC, who was caught on videotape smoking crack
cocaine). It is a severely worn-down, vandalized, chaotic, and violent school that
resembles a prison much more than a high school. As with *Not Another Teen
Movie*, *High School High* has an easy time with its satirical poke at Hollywood's
high school film genre. The urban high school film genre, too, has already been
well established with easily recognizable elements common in most of the films.

If one has seen *Blackboard Jungle*, then the plots of *Lean on Me*, *Stand and Deliver*, *Dangerous Minds*, and *Coach Carter*, for instance, are strikingly familiar.

In an exaggerated fashion, *High School High* draws on the plots and characters of the previous urban high school films. In short, a naive new teacher (in this case Mr. Clark) believes he can make a difference in the lives of poor and troubled urban youth. Throughout the film he struggles to "get through" to his students. After several difficult setbacks he ultimately triumphs by getting the students to reject their criminal and apathetic ways and to apply themselves academically. As in most of the urban high school films, the moral of the story is that individual determination and hard work can overcome all obstacles. As Mr. Clark tells the students at the end of *High School High*, "Work as hard as you can. Do a couple hours of homework each night and nothing can stop you." The students, who initially treated the new teacher with skepticism and hostility, ultimately adopt his lessons and learn to love him.

Even as spoofs, *Not Another Teen Movie* and *High School High* reveal important differences about how Hollywood represents poor urban and middle-class suburban high schools in popular films.[24] While there has not yet been a satire of the private school subgenre, Hollywood also has a unique way of representing rich students in private high schools, which will be explored in chapter 6. It is important to note that these different cinematic representations of high schools do not arise because they reflect actual differences between real urban, suburban, and private high schools. The subgenres differ in significant ways because American culture *makes sense of* poor youth, middle-class youth, and wealthy youth (and urban public schools, suburban public schools, and private schools) in very different ways.

These films do have something in common, however. Individualism is the dominant theme in most of the films. Adolescents in these films are expected to transcend the limitations of their communities, the narrow-mindedness of their families, the expectations of their parents, the conformity of their peers, the ineffectiveness of their schools, their poverty or wealth, and the insidious effects of racism or sexism in order to express themselves as individuals apart from social constraints. The source of their academic success and/or personal fulfillment is to be found within the heart and mind of each individual regardless of social context.

There are dramatic differences, however, in the ways in which the theme of individualism plays itself out in the films based in urban high schools, those based in suburban high schools, and those based in private high schools. I suggest that the different expressions of individualism in these three film genres reveal a tension in American culture that is born out of conflicted feelings about social class in the United States.

Outline and Argument of the Book

Chapter 2 is a theoretical overview of certain aspects of American culture. The theoretical issues raised in this chapter lay the groundwork for the arguments presented in the subsequent chapters that deal more explicitly with the films in the sample. Specifically, it outlines the ways that some sociologists have made sense of individualism, the middle class, adolescence, and gender in American society.

In chapter 3 I analyze the films that depict the education of poor and working-class students in mostly urban high school environments.[25] The teacher and principal heroes in the urban school films are selfless outsiders (urban school cowboys) who offer salvation to the students lost in a culture of poverty and despair.[26]

The dominant theme of the urban school films is "utilitarian individualism." As sociologist Robert Bellah and his co-authors in the 1985 best seller *Habits of the Heart: Individualism and Commitment in American Life* explain, utilitarian individualism is that strain of American individualism that celebrates hard work, materialism, and individual self-sufficiency.[27]

In chapters 4 and 5 I analyze the films that depict the education of mostly middle-class students in suburban public high schools. The hero is almost never an adult as in the urban school films, but is usually a student who is able to overcome the conformity of teen society or the authoritarianism of adult society. The dominant theme of the suburban school films is not utilitarian individualism but "expressive individualism." As explained in *Habits of the Heart*, expressive individualism refers to that strain of American individualism that values not material achievements, but the discovery of one's unique identity and the freedom of individual self-expression.

In chapter 6 I analyze the American films that depict the education of private school students. As in the urban school films, the elite private school films focus on academics. However, the narrow focus on academic achievement is often portrayed as an oppressive burden upon students. The hero of these films is often a working- or middle-class outsider who challenges the culture of privilege that pervades the upper-class institution. Individual integrity, well-roundedness, academic merit, and personal happiness are deemed more important than inherited privilege, material gain, social status, or family tradition.[28] Yet these heroes also benefit materially from their affiliation with the school. In these private school films the themes of expressive and utilitarian individualism coexist.

Chapter 7 concludes the analysis with some final thoughts about film, education, and the lessons that these high school films have to teach us about American culture.

In each chapter I lay out my arguments about why Hollywood tends to depict youth and education in these consistently different ways and why they are so predictably patterned by social class. To help make sociological sense of these films and the differences among the urban, suburban, and private school subgenres, however, we must first explore some of the essential characteristics of American culture. Specifically, it is impossible to analyze these high school films as cultural artifacts without understanding the various strains of American individualism, the dominant perspective of the middle class in American culture, and the ways in which American society makes sense of teenagers and gender.

Notes

1. Schlesinger, Arthur M., Jr. 1979. "Foreword." In *American History/American Film: Interpreting the Hollywood Image*. John E. O'Connor and Martin A. Jackson, editors. New York: Continuum.
2. hooks, bell. 1996. *Reel to Real: Race, Sex, and Class at the Movies*. New York: Routledge, p. 1.
3. George Lipsitz argues that films are cultural artifacts in that they are "social-history evidence about the times in which they were made." While I do not disagree with Lipsitz, I do not take a historical approach to the study of films in this book. That is, I find that the themes of the high school films over the past sixty years have been consistent enough across time that I think they tell us as much about American culture in general as they do about any particular time in American history. See Lipsitz, George. 1990. *Time Passages: Collective Memory and American Popular Culture*. Minneapolis: University of Minnesota Press, p. 164.
4. Shary, Timothy. 2002. *Generation Multiplex: The Image of Youth in Contemporary American Cinema*. Austin: University of Texas Press, p. 14.
5. Crane, Diana. 1992. *The Production of Culture: Media and the Urban Arts*. New York: Sage, p. 94.
6. Powers, Stephen, David Rothman, and Stanley Rothman. 1996. *Hollywood's America: Social and Political Themes in Motion Pictures*. Denver: Westview, p. 226.
7. I am indebted to several authors for demonstrating that films can be used successfully as data in sociological research: Wright, Will. 1975. *Sixguns and Society: A Structural Study of the Western*. Berkeley: University of California Press; Tudor, Andrew. 1974. *Image and Influence: Studies in the Sociology of Film*. New York: St. Martin's Press; Denzin, Norman K. 1991. *Hollywood Shot by Shot: Alcoholism in American Cinema*. New York: Aldine de Gruyter; and Vera, Hernan, and Andrew M. Gordon. 2003. *Screen Saviors: Hollywood Fictions of Whiteness*. Lanham, MD: Rowman and Littlefield.
8. See Mukerji, Chandra, and Michael Shudson, editors. 1991. *Rethinking Popular Culture: Contemporary Perspectives in Cultural Studies*. Berkeley: University of California Press, for more discussion about the popular culture debate.
9. See Harrington, C. Lee, and Denise D. Bielby. 2001. "Constructing the Popular: Cultural Production and Consumption." In *Popular Culture: Production and Consumption*. C. Lee Harrington and Denise D. Bielby, editors. Malden, MA: Blackwell.
10. Schatz, Thomas. 1981. *Hollywood Genres: Formulas, Filmmaking, and the Studio System*. Boston: McGraw Hill, pp. vii–viii, emphasis in the original.
11. There are many studies in psychology and communication that show that media have an influence on our thinking and behavior. Among them is an interesting study that finds that teen films tend to support negative stereotypes about women. Behm-Morawitz, Elizabeth, and Dana E. Mastro. 2008. "Mean Girls? The Influence of Gender Portrayals in Teen Movies on Emerging Adults' Gender-Based Attitudes and Beliefs." *Journalism and Mass Communication Quarterly*, 85: 131–146
12. Tudor, *Image and Influence*, p. 218.
13. Erikson, Kai T. 1978. *Everything in Its Path: Destruction of Community in the Buffalo Creek Flood*. New York: Simon and Schuster.

14. Zipes, Jack. 1994. *Fairy Tales as Myth: Myth as Fairy Tales*. Lexington: University of Kentucky Press, p. 5.

15. Ibid., p. 141.

16. See Vera and Gordon, *Screen Saviors*, for a perspective on whiteness in American films. Also see my discussion of this issue in chapter 3.

17. Considine, David M. 1985. *The Cinema of Adolescence*. Jefferson, NC: McFarland and Co.; Reed, Joseph W. 1989. *American Scenarios: The Uses of Film Genre*. Middletown, CT: Wesleyan University Press; Farber, Paul, and Gunilla Holm. 1994. "Adolescent Freedom and the Cinematic High School." In *Schooling in the Light of Popular Culture*. Paul Farber, Eugene F. Provenzo Jr., and Gunilla Holm, editors. Albany: State University of New York Press; Farber, Paul, and Gunilla Holm. 1994. "A Brotherhood of Heroes: The Charismatic Educator in Recent American Movies." In *Schooling in the Light of Popular Culture*. Albany: State University of New York Press; Dalton, Mary. 1999. *The Hollywood Curriculum: Teachers and Teaching in the Movies*. New York: Peter Lang; Hill, David. 1995. "Tinseltown Teachers." *Teacher Magazine* (March): 40–45; Trier, James D. 2001. "The Cinematic Representation of the Personal and Professional Lives of Teachers." *Teacher Education Quarterly* (summer): 127–142; Farhi, Adam. 1999. "Hollywood Goes to School: Recognizing the Superteacher Myth in Film." *The Clearing House* 72, no. 3: 157–159; and Shary, *Generation Multiplex*.

18. Reed, *American Scenario*.

19. Considine, *The Cinema of Adolescence*.

20. Shary, *Generation Multiplex*.

21. Farber and Holm, "Adolescent Freedom and the Cinematic High School" and "A Brotherhood of Heroes."

22. Dalton, *The Hollywood Curriculum;* and Hill, "Tinseltown Teachers."

23. Since the publication of the first edition of *Hollywood Goes to High School* there has been growth in the number of new studies that analyze the cinematic representations of youth and high school. Many of them analyze the films through the lens of social class and some even focus on the role that individualism plays in the depiction of youth and education. See Dalton's second edition (2010) with extensive analysis of films that depict teachers and Shary's updated analysis of teen films (2014). See also Mora, Richard, and Mary Christianakis. 2012. "'No Free Rides, No Excuses': Film Stereotypes of Urban Working-Class Students." In *Blue Collar Pop Culture: From NASCAR to Jersey Shore*. M. Keith Booker, editor. Santa Barbara: Praeger; Yosso, Tara J., and David Gumaro García. 2010. "From Ms. J. to Ms. G.: Analyzing Racial Microaggressions in Hollywood's Urban School Genre." In *Hollywood's Exploited: Public Pedagogy, Corporate Movies, and Cultural Crisis*. Richard Van Heertum et al., editors. New York: Palgrave Macmillan; and Chennault, Ronald E. 2006. *Hollywood Films About Schools: Where Race, Politics, and Education Intersect*. New York: Palgrave.

24. There is an urban teen genre of films that is not represented in this sample of high school films. Films such as *Straight Out of Brooklyn* (1991), *Boyz 'N the Hood* (1991), *Menace II Society* (1993), *South Central* (1992), and *Juice* (1992) are African American urban teen dramas that do not use education or the high school as a central feature of their story. Following Timothy Shary's (2002) genre categorization, I have excluded these films from the high school genre. Furthermore, Hollywood endorses this separate categorization as well—the urban teen genre has its own spoof film, *Don't Be a Menace to South Central When Drinking Your Juice in the Hood* (1996). For the same reasons, I have excluded teen horror and slasher films from this study. Once again, Shary categorizes the genre separately from the school genre—as does Hollywood, which has produced the teen horror spoofs of *Scream* (1996) and its sequels and the *Scary Movie* (2000) series, which is itself a spoof of the *Scream* films.

25. Portions of an earlier version of chapter 3 appeared in Bulman, Robert C. 2002. "Teachers in the 'Hood': Hollywood's Middle-Class Fantasy." *Urban Review* 34, no. 3 (September): 251–276, with kind permission of Kluwer Academic Publishers.

26. A similar point is also made in Considine, *Cinema of Adolescence*; Farhi, "Hollywood Goes to School"; Grant, Peggy A. 2002. "Using Popular Films to Challenge Preservice Teachers' Beliefs About Teaching in Urban Schools." *Urban Education* 37 (January 2002): 77–95; Heilman, Robert B. 1991. "The Great-Teacher Myth." *American Scholar* 60, no. 3: 417–423; Burbach, Harold J., and Margo A. Figgins. 1993. "A Thematic Profile of the Images of Teachers in Film." *Teacher Education Quarterly* (spring): 65–75; Thomsen, Steven R. 1993. "A Worm in the Apple: Hollywood's Influence on the Public's Perception of Teachers." A paper presented at the Southern States Communication Association and Central States Communication Association joint annual meeting, Lexington, KY, April 15; Ayers, William. 1996. "A Teacher Ain't Nothin' but a Hero: Teachers and Teaching in Film." In *City Kids, City Teachers: Reports from the Front Row*. William Ayers and Patricia Ford, editors. New York: The New Press; and Wells, Amy S., and Todd S. Serman, 1998. "Education Against All Odds: What Films Teach Us About Schools." In *Imaging Education: The Media and Schools in America*. Gene Maeroff, editor. New York: Teachers College Press, pp. 181–194.

27. Bellah, Robert N., Richard Madsen, William M. Sullivan, Ann Swidler, and Steven M. Tipton. 1985. *Habits of the Heart: Individualism and Commitment in American Life*. New York: Harper and Row.

28. As will be explored further in chapter 6, the films based in religious private schools operate with a different formula. They tend to mirror the suburban or urban school films, depending upon the social class of the students in the private school.

[two]

Middle-Class Individualism and the Adolescent Frontier

What High School Films Reveal About American Culture

The problem with individualism is not that it is immoral but that it is incorrect. The universe does not consist of a lot of unrelated particles but is an interconnected whole. Pretending that our fortunes are independent of each other may be perfectly ethical, but it's also perfectly stupid.[1]

—Philip Slater

To understand the cultural significance of the high school film, it is necessary first to understand the significance of individualism in American culture. While individualism has many manifestations, at its core is the idea that the individual has autonomy and independence apart from social groups and institutions. To appreciate fully the cultural importance of individualism in the United States, it is necessary to go back in time. In this chapter I first explain the early sociological insights about individualism in modern industrial society. Then I explore the ways in which Protestantism, American democracy, and the western frontier helped to shape utilitarian and expressive individualism in American life. Finally, I outline the important role that the middle class has played in the development of American individualism and how adolescence and gender are understood through the cultural lens of individualism.

Emile Durkheim, one of the earliest sociologists, wrote of the increasing sentiment of individualism in the modern world in his classic work of 1893, *The Division of Labor*. According to Durkheim, there was very little differentiation among individuals in premodern traditional societies. Traditional societies were based on the *similarities* of members. All individuals in a community shared similar beliefs, had similar skills, and lived similar styles of life. These societies based on similarity were held together by what Durkheim called "mechanical solidarity." In effect, the solidarity of traditional societies was automatic. It was taken for granted and held together by the "collective consciousness" of the group. Individuals recognized their membership in the society because of the qualities they shared with all of the other members. Furthermore, such similarity was enforced under the threat of punishment.

As society advanced, however, the population grew, technology developed, urbanization increased, and social life became more complex. Rather than all members sharing similar skills, as in a traditional society, individuals in modern society began to develop specialized skills and unique individualized traits. In other words, individualism was born of modernity:

> As evolution advances, the bonds that attach the individual to his family, to his native heath, to the traditions that the past has bequeathed him, to the collective practices of the group—all become loosened. Being more mobile, the individual changes his environment more easily, leaves his own people to go and live a more autonomous life elsewhere, works out for himself his ideas and sentiments.[2]

The glue that keeps modern society cohesive is not mechanical solidarity based on similarity, as in traditional societies, but "organic solidarity" based on individual *differences*. Because of the specialization of skills, individuals are necessarily interdependent upon each other. While unique and special, modern individuals need others to perform tasks that they cannot. Modern society is like a biological organism: The heart, liver, and lungs, for instance, each have very specific and individual functions, but they each depend upon the other organs in order for the organism (and all the individual organs) to survive.

Durkheim pointed us toward an important irony that is a characteristic of modern society. At just the historical moment when members of modern society feel the sentiments of individualism the strongest (when individuals have skills and characteristics that distinguish them from the crowd), individuals are the most dependent upon others. Individualism, while a product of social life, can ironically prevent individuals from recognizing their connections to the social world. The power of individualism in modern society makes it difficult to exercise what famous twentieth-century American sociologist C. Wright Mills called the "sociological imagination"—the capacity to see the connections that we as individuals have to the larger social landscape.[3]

Durkheim believed that it was a moral duty for individuals to be aware of their social bonds and obligations. A proper equilibrium between the needs of the individual and the needs of society is required for the health of both. The recognition of the "dualism of human nature," however, has proven more difficult in modern life than Durkheim imagined, particularly in a country such as the United States, where the importance of the individual has grown to impressive heights.[4]

While individualism is not a uniquely American trait, it has found particularly fertile ground in the United States. As Bellah et al. note, "Individualism lies at the very core of American culture."[5] While Americans may voluntarily come together to form communities, they believe strongly that each individual is ultimately responsible for his or her self. Americans tend to believe that one's success or failure in life is due almost entirely to the effort, ability, values, and decision making of the individual. There are multiple and complex reasons why individualism is a particularly strong element of American culture. To simplify, however, it can be said that American individualism has its roots in Protestantism, capitalism, democracy, and the history of the western frontier.

The American Development of Utilitarian and Expressive Individualism: The Protestant Ethic, the Capitalist Ethic, and Their Discontents

The United States has inherited much of the individualistic ideology associated with Protestant theology. The Protestant Reformation was predicated on the idea that it is the individual's relationship with God that determines salvation. Departing from the Catholic Church's emphasis on good works, on participation in a religious community, and on a relationship with God that is mediated through a priest, the Protestant Reformation ushered in a powerful cultural emphasis on the role that the individual plays apart from a community. Rather than seeing faith as something that one naturally inherits from one's state or community, Americans tend to see faith as a deeply personal matter to be decided by each and every individual.[6] While Americans *do* come together in groups to celebrate their faith, the decision to do so is ultimately an individual one.

Protestantism also contributes to American individualism in its relationship to capitalism. As Max Weber, an early sociologist, eloquently argued in *The Protestant Ethic and the Spirit of Capitalism*, certain elements of Protestantism contributed to an ethic that fostered the development of capitalism. Without mediation through a religious community, early Protestants were filled with anxiety about their salvation. If faith alone (and not participation in religious rituals or good works) determined one's salvation, how was one to know for certain if one was saved? The Protestant sect of Calvinism offered a solution to this problem by suggesting that salvation was predestined by God. There was nothing believers could do to win salvation. They could, however, determine if they were among the saved by observing certain signs. If they worked hard in a "calling," if they were rational and methodical in specialized work, if they earned money but spent it only on essentials, if they reinvested profits rather than indulging wants, and if they lived ascetic lives, then they might be among the select few who were saved.

Such a powerful incentive to live a rational and methodical life provided important ingredients to capitalism. This ethic of rationality, put into motion by the spiritual needs of the Protestant, quickly became the capitalist ethic. Capitalism, for instance, requires dutiful workers and the reinvestment of capital. The rational way of life of the Protestant soon became the rational way of life for everyone. The Protestant capitalist and the Protestant worker conducted themselves in such a rational and efficient way as to compel even the non-Protestant into methodical and efficient practices in the marketplace and on the job. Otherwise, the non-Protestant would risk losing the economic competition (for profit or for jobs) to the more efficient Protestant.

The new capitalist ethic found its greatest expression in America. Ben Franklin's writing is Weber's favorite example of the capitalist ethic. In his autobiography, Franklin writes about how he managed to succeed in life through hard work, despite his humble origins.[7] Franklin's advice for success is indeed a perfect example of the capitalist ethic, with an emphasis on industry and frugality. It is not the moral content of the ethic (the formerly Protestant but now capitalist ethic) that is valuable, but the material gain that results:

> According to Franklin, those virtues, like all others, are only in so far virtues as they are actually useful to the individual, and the surrogate of mere appearance is always sufficient when it accomplishes the end in view.[8]

In *Poor Richard's Almanac* Franklin writes many pieces of advice that have since become well-ingrained "truths" known to most Americans—"Early to bed and early to rise, makes a man healthy, wealthy, and wise" and "God helps those that help themselves," among many others.[9] The authors of *Habits of the Heart* cite Franklin's lessons as the clearest example of the "utilitarian individualism" that has remained a central part of American culture:

> In short, Franklin gave classic expression to what many felt in the eighteenth century—and many have felt ever since—to be the most important thing about America: the chance for the individual to get ahead of his own initiative.[10]

This utilitarian individualism, however, is not the only form of individualism that has taken root in the United States. As Bellah and his colleagues note, expressive individualism has arisen alongside utilitarian individualism and, in many ways, in opposition to it.

Expressive individualism has its roots not in the capitalist ethic, but in the criticism of an American culture dominated by materialistic values. American philosophers Ralph Waldo Emerson and Henry David Thoreau gave voice to this alternative way of understanding individualism in America. Thoreau, for instance, abandoned the "fool's life" of labor and retreated alone to the wilderness to support himself on the land, to learn about himself, to be conscious of life, and to live as fully as possible. Thoreau was explicitly critical of the work ethic that most Americans accept blindly:

> Most men, even in this comparatively free country, through mere ignorance and mistake, are so occupied with the factitious cares and superfluously coarse labors of life that its finer fruits cannot be plucked by them.[11]

Thoreau condemned the "quiet desperation" suffered by most men and sought out on his own to pluck the finer fruits of life. He recognized the irony that was concealed in the utilitarian individualism of American culture: In effect, to pursue material independence through achievement in mainstream society, one had to conform to certain behaviors and practices of work. In contrast, he valued the *nonconformity* of expressive individualism. He respected the individual who rejected conventional measures of success and social pressures and instead marched to the beat of his or her own drummer:

> Why should we be in such desperate haste to succeed and in such desperate enterprises? If a man does not keep pace with his companions, perhaps it is because he hears a different drummer. Let him step to the music which he hears, however measured or far away.[12]

While Thoreau's expressive individualism is not as dominant in American culture as Franklin's utilitarian individualism, it is, nonetheless, a cultural theme that survives and finds expression in a variety of forms, including, as we shall see, in many Hollywood films.

American individualism grew not only out of the cultural roots of Protestantism and capitalism, but also out of its democratic traditions. It is to these traditions that we now turn.

Individualism and Democracy

Just as Protestantism broke with Catholicism over the issue of the believer's relationship with God, the United States broke with England over the issue of the citizen's relationship to the state. In both cases the rights of the individual challenged the hierarchy of an aristocratic power. In theory, a democratic government values the opinion of each individual citizen. Each citizen, regardless of social status or wealth, is entitled to certain rights under a democratic constitution. Such a belief in the equality of opportunity (whether it is realized or not) is a central part of the picture Americans paint of themselves. It is also what Alexis de Tocqueville, the nineteenth-century French theorist, found to be particularly remarkable about the American experiment. For Tocqueville, democracy created conditions of equality and a belief in the autonomy of the individual. Under such conditions, however, Tocqueville feared that the individual would lose sight of society and social obligations. In fact, it is in Tocqueville's masterpiece *Democracy in America* (based on his travels in the United States near the middle of the nineteenth century) that the term *individualism* was first coined:

> Individualism is a mature and calm feeling, which disposes each member of the community to sever himself from the mass of his fellows and to draw apart with his family and his friends, so that after he has thus formed a little circle of his own, he willingly leaves society at large to itself.[13]

For Tocqueville, the repudiation of aristocratic rule in favor of democracy diminished the social ties that citizens have to the greater community. Democracy, as he wrote, "breaks the chain" that connects everyone from "the peasant to the king." Anticipating Durkheim's concern, Tocqueville feared that individuals in a democracy would begin to see only themselves in the present moment and not their relationship to groups, institutions, or history:[14]

> Thus not only does democracy make every man forget his ancestors, but it hides his descendants and separates his contemporaries from him; it throws him back forever upon himself alone and threatens in the end to confine him entirely within the solitude of his own heart.[15]

Tocqueville's observations of American culture were filled with both admiration and concern. As we shall see in later chapters, the contradictory elements of American culture that Tocqueville noted—the brilliance of equality and individualism and the denial of community—find expression still in Hollywood films.

In addition to its religious, economic, and democratic origins, individualism in the United States was encouraged by the cultural characteristics that developed in the country's expansion into the western frontier.

Individualism and the American Frontier

American individualism also has roots in the particular history of the growth of the United States into the western portions of the North American continent. The expansion of the Union into the frontier helped to create an American character marked by independence, adventure, and endless possibilities for free men. This "rugged individualism" grew out of a political belief that Americans had God-given domain over the North American continent. This "manifest destiny" was embodied in the pioneers who left their homes, moved west, and, with the help of the U.S. government, conquered the Native peoples who lived in the western territories. Such expansionism, and the pioneers who colonized the West, contributed to a particular type of individual character that has become an important part of American culture: the cowboy. Historian Frederick Jackson Turner made the argument that the independent American character was largely shaped by the experiences of frontier life:

> The result is that to the frontier the American intellect owes its striking characteristics. The coarseness and strength combined with acuteness and inquisitiveness; that practical, inventive turn of mind, quick to find expedients; that masterful grasp of material things, lacking in the artistic but powerful to effect great ends; that restless, nervous energy; that dominant individualism, working for good and for evil, and withal that buoyancy and exuberance which comes with freedom—these are the traits of the frontier.[16]

Turner's thesis about the importance of the frontier to the American character has been challenged by new western historians.[17] Nevertheless, even if frontier individualism is a myth, it matters that Americans *believe* the myth. That is, Americans collectively believe that the frontier experience helped to forge the individualism of the American character. This belief, in and of itself, is enough to make frontier individualism a part of the American national culture. As sociologist W. I. Thomas observed, if an actor defines a situation to be real, it is real in its consequences.[18] And those consequences can still be seen. Americans remain a very mobile people. We are not often committed strongly to a geographic place. If opportunities arise elsewhere, we pull up our roots and plant them elsewhere. The frontier is still alive in the hearts of many Americans.

While individualism is characteristic of Americans in every social class, it can be argued that its origins and its purest expression can be found within the American middle class. If one wants to understand the nuances of American culture and individualism, it is perhaps best to start with an inquiry into the nature of the American middle class.

The Middle Class and American Culture

Americans, generally, are not comfortable talking in terms of social class. The individualistic orientation of most Americans leads them to overlook *group* differences based on education, occupation, income, or social prestige. Such differences, to the average American mind, are best explained by looking at the characteristics of the individual. Not surprisingly, most Americans, when forced to characterize their class position, report that they are in the "middle class." What this means to them, however, is not exactly clear. Most likely, it means that they know people who are wealthier than them and they know people who are poorer than them. Therefore, they are, by definition, in the middle. The term *middle class*, however, does have a more precise meaning. While sociologists disagree about how best to measure the middle class, most are in agreement that there are objective criteria that distinguish the middle class from the upper and lower classes (that is, class is not just a matter of subjective identification, but of objective measurement).

I define the middle class broadly as those members of the American population who have attended at least several years of college (and usually have a B.A. degree), are dependent primarily upon their educational skills and credentials to earn a living, work as white-collar managers or professionals, earn most of their income from a salary rather than hourly wages or assets, and have a moderate amount of wealth, usually accumulated in the equity of their homes. They are most likely to live in the suburbs. I estimate that the middle class constitutes approximately 30 percent of the American population.[19]

While not a numerical majority, the middle class has become a hegemonic cultural force in American society. That is, the middle-class experience is generally understood as *the* American experience. As Barbara Ehrenreich notes in her social analysis of American culture, "the professional, and largely white, middle class is taken as a social norm—a bland and neutral mainstream—from which every other group or class is ultimately a kind of deviation."[20] The central place that the middle class occupies in American culture is the result in part of the central place it occupies in the current organization of the American economy.

After World War II, the United States experienced a tremendous period of economic growth, shifting from an industrial-based economy with a strong "blue-collar" (wage laborers) working-class base to a postindustrial, information-based economy with a growing number of "white-collar" (salaried professional) middle-class workers. In the coming decades the computer revolution, together with the increasing export of industrial jobs from the United States to foreign countries (where the cost of labor was cheaper), further increased the prominent position the educated middle class played in the new American economy. These economic transformations were recognized early by such sociologists as David Riesman and C. Wright Mills, who noted that what was developing was a "new" middle class. The independent businessman and the entrepreneur of the "old" middle class were being replaced by the white-collar employee who worked for others in bureaucratic and corporate organizations.[21] Riesman and Mills also noted that the new middle-class worker was emerging not only as an important economic player in the United States, but also as an important cultural player. If you want to understand what it means to be an American in the postwar period, Mills argued, you have to understand the world of the new middle class:

> By examining white-collar life, it is possible to learn something about what is becoming more typically "American" than the frontier character probably ever was. What must be grasped is the picture of society as a great salesroom, an enormous file, and incorporated brain, a new universe of management and

manipulation. By understanding these diverse white-collar worlds, one can also understand better the shape and meaning of modern society as a whole, as well as the simple hopes and complex anxieties that grip all the people who are sweating it out in the middle of the twentieth century.[22]

The most eloquent and persuasive narrators of the American middle-class cultural story are Robert Bellah and his co-authors of *Habits of the Heart*. Interested in exploring the terrain of American culture, Bellah and his colleagues talked to middle-class Americans about their jobs, families, communities, and religious faith.[23] Their interviews touched on the ways in which members of the middle class understand their individual lives and how they relate to their communities. Bellah and company show how the middle-class values of educational and occupational achievement, calculating rationality, and individualism (rather than a commitment to community, tradition, and cooperation) have defined not just the professional lives of middle-class Americans, but also how they govern their lives generally:

> The middle-class is defined not merely by the desire for material benefit but by a conscious calculating effort to move up the ladder of success . . . for middle-class Americans, a calculating attitude toward educational and occupational choice has been essential and has often spilled over into determining criteria for the choice of spouse, friends, and voluntary associations.[24]

While the lower and upper social classes are not as defined by individualism or as dependent upon it as the middle class is, they have been affected by the ethic of individualism nonetheless. In contrast to the middle class, however, these other social classes are oriented more toward community, history, tradition, and ethnicity than individual achievement and calculating rationality. Bellah and co-authors argue that the lower and upper classes find meaning not only in their individualism, but also in their social relationships. These social relationships help to combat the sense of loneliness and emptiness that individualism can otherwise encourage.

Without such ties to a community, history, or tradition, middle-class Americans often feel alienated. Despite its cultural power, there is a tension and an ambiguity that pervade middle-class individualism. The middle class longs for the sense of community and shared meanings that their ethic of individualism denies. The longing is real, but they lack the language to articulate it. As the authors of *Habits of the Heart* put it:

> We deeply feel the emptiness of a life without sustaining social commitments. Yet we are hesitant to articulate our sense that we need one another as much as we need to stand alone, for fear that if we did we would lose our independence altogether.[25]

Hollywood has long represented the middle-class ethic of individualism. As Bellah et al. note, the Western and the hard-boiled detective film genres have depended upon the heroic efforts of a lone outsider who has few social attachments and constraints.

The high school genre, too, depends upon such lone heroes who stand outside society. As we shall see, there is very little use for history, community, or tradition in these high school films. Instead, messages of utilitarian and expressive individualism predominate. Because these high school films are made and largely consumed by members of the middle class, and because middle-class culture is the hegemonic culture in the United States, these high school films tend to reflect middle-class worldviews and assumptions.

Understanding how Hollywood uses such middle-class American values to tell stories about high school, however, requires an understanding of what it means to be an adolescent in the United States and how those meanings vary by the social class of the adolescent.

Teenagers and American Culture

Sociologists tend to see adolescence as socially constructed. That is, even if puberty marks the biological ending of childhood, it is society that determines when one becomes an adult and how the period between childhood and adulthood is socially organized.[26] Therefore, the existence of adolescence is culturally variable. American youth today experience an extended period of adolescence, often well beyond the teenage years. Does adulthood in the United States today begin at age eighteen, when voting is legally permitted in the United States? Or is it at age twenty-one, when drinking alcohol is legally permitted? Perhaps it has nothing to do with age and legal recognition per se, but is marked by the end of formal education and the beginning of full-time work. If that is the case, then adulthood may begin for some people at age seventeen and for others not until the age of thirty or later. The boundaries of adolescence are not always clear. A sociological view suggests that the definition of adolescence and the meanings we attach to it are always shifting, particularly in concert with the shifting of the economic organization of social life.

As a recognized stage of life between childhood and adulthood, adolescence is a relatively recent invention.[27] Before the era of industrialization in Western societies, there was little division of labor between home, work, and school in non-wealthy families. The family was the basic economic unit of production, the site of domestic life, and the place of learning for children. There was little question about the future of the children—they would likely inherit an occupation and social status directly from their parents and live lives similar to those of their parents. There was very little sense of adolescence as a time of preparation for and transition to adulthood because there was very little uncertainty about what the child would be preparing for or transitioning to.[28]

With the spread of industrialization and urbanization, however, there eventually grew a division of labor between home, work, and school. The futures of middle-class children were not as predetermined as they had been in the past. Adolescence became recognized as a stage of life as youth began to prepare for their new and somewhat uncertain adult roles. *Adolescence: Its Psychology and Its Relations to Physiology, Anthropology, Sociology, Sex, Crime, Religion, and Education*, G. Stanley Hall's 1904 publication, became a particularly influential source for the new understanding of adolescence.[29] Hall advocated adult-sponsored institutions to help guide adolescents through this particularly difficult period of life.

A relatively new institution, the high school, became an important incubator for the adult futures of these children. Until the 1930s high school was predominantly an institution for children of the middle class, and it was in the high school years that adolescence became solidified as a distinct stage of life. As historians of adolescence John Modell and Madeline Goodman write:

> Adolescence, as it developed conceptually in the late nineteenth and twentieth centuries, was first and foremost a middle-class creation. It was a notion that initially made sense in those institutional contexts for young people that promoted their socialization as adults able to hold their own in the competitive middle class. Initially, young people not of the middle class were often perceived as having no adolescence.[30]

The high school and notions of adolescence, however, were undergoing profound changes in the early part of the twentieth century. Public high schools gradually expanded to serve a more diverse segment of the population. Capitalists began to demand skilled workers, and members of the working class demanded opportunities for upward social mobility.[31] As a result, public schooling expanded to serve more members of the working class. Around the same time, the United States experienced a dramatic increase in the number of new immigrants to its cities. Many people became concerned that the children of these immigrants would not have American values and would not speak English if they were not properly educated.[32] Concerns about juvenile delinquency, too, spurred efforts to educate and socialize young people of all backgrounds in public schools. By the time of the Great Depression, unemployment forced many more youth out of the workforce and into the high school. As a result of these changes, a record high 65 percent of all American teens were enrolled in high school in 1936.[33]

It is not an accident that the emergence of the adolescent as a social and cultural category in the United States coincided with the profound social and economic changes in the first half of the twentieth century. As a distinct phase of life, adolescence is not "natural." Instead, it is the result of social, cultural, economic, and political developments that have created it and imbue it with certain meanings and expectations. Adolescents are responding not only to their biological development, but also to the social demands placed upon them by the organization of society.

Neither is it a coincidence that the emergence of the "new" white-collar middle class occurred at the same time that "teenagers" were *fully* recognized as a distinct social group in the United States with their own cultural characteristics. In fact, it was not until the Second World War that the term *teenager* was commonly used.[34] Historian Grace Palladino shows how the emergence of the teenage culture in the 1940s and 1950s coincided with the development of an economy that exploited the youthful consumer. She argues that the growth of teen culture was fueled by "a changing economy, a national culture of consumption and individualism, and the age-graded, adolescent world of the high school."[35]

The emergence of the "teenager" as a distinct social, cultural, and economic group in postwar America encouraged the development of the "teenpic," a genre of films specifically directed to an audience of adolescents. In fact, film scholar Thomas Doherty argues that in the 1950s Hollywood films took a distinct marketing turn to capture the new teen audience, thereby "juvenilizing" most filmmaking.[36]

It has been said that James Dean's character in 1955's *Rebel Without a Cause* became the defining image of the American teenager (at least the white male middle-class teenager) and helped to define the age group.[37] In fact, a 1975 television documentary about Dean was titled *The First American Teenager*.

The emergence of the new teenage social group, however, caused a great deal of alarm in the United States. Americans tend to have mixed feelings about young people. While adolescence represents a great deal of creative potential to Americans, it also causes a great deal of anxiety.[38] Fears of juvenile delinquency reached a fevered pitch in the 1950s. Films such as *Blackboard Jungle* (released the same year as *Rebel Without a Cause*) spoke directly to this national hysteria. Academic studies, too, sounded the alarm about this new "adolescent society." In 1961, sociologist James Coleman argued that high school students constituted their own culture, with their own value system that was at odds with the values of adult society.[39] Coleman was particularly concerned that students seemed to care more about athletics and popularity than they cared about academics. Concerns about youth continue today, with some arguing that adolescents have become scapegoats for the ills of the rest of society.[40]

Whether viewed as a promise or a threat, adolescence had arrived as a full-fledged stage of life by the middle of the twentieth century. Furthermore, it was a stage of life that seemed to be expanding. As high school expanded to members of the working class, as the technical requirements for jobs increased, as competition for employment put pressure on youth to pursue more credentials in college and graduate school, and as the average age of marriage increased, the period between sexual maturity and full adult status grew longer and more visible in our culture. Adolescence continues to be the subject of national fascination and anxiety, as the number of teen movies released in the past few decades attests.

If sociologists are correct that adolescence is dependent upon social, cultural, and economic conditions to define its boundaries (rather than biology), then what constitutes the essential features of adolescence in the twentieth and twenty-first centuries in the United States? I would suggest that adolescence today is marked by two distinct social processes. First, the adolescent must search for an identity. Modern American adolescents must make many important decisions about who they are as youth and who they want to be as adults. Nothing is certain in this increasingly postmodern world. Teenagers must decide what their values are, what their interests are, how they should present their "self" to others, what social groups to associate with, what activities to participate in, and what racial, gender, class, and sexual identity to assume. In short, they must come to terms with their expressive individualism. Second, the adolescent must search for independence. They must make plans about their schooling, decide what career to pursue, terminate the dependence on their parents, take responsibility for their individual lives, and figure out how to support themselves materially in a capitalist society. In short, they must in all practical terms exercise their utilitarian individualism.

As will become clear in chapters 3, 4, and 5, however, there are often very different cultural standards applied to American adolescents depending upon their social class. I argue that American culture expects poor youth to exercise utilitarian individualism to climb out of poverty, while it allows more freedom to middle-class youth to exercise their expressive individualism as they search for a meaningful identity.

Finally, it should be noted that adolescence is also a metaphor in American culture for the possibilities of the future. High school films speak directly to an audience of youth, but they also speak indirectly to a middle-aged audience. The theme of possibility is one that the middle-aged American does not want to abandon. Anything is considered possible in our individualistic culture. If you are unhappy in your job, your family, or the way you express yourself, you can always change. The themes and messages of high school films resonate with Americans of all ages on many different levels. They express the possibility that if you work a little harder you can be successful, the possibility that if you follow your heart you can discover your true self, the possibility that you can find true love, and the possibility that your worth as a person is not measured by your performance in competitive capitalism or bureaucratic organizations. In this sense, too, the frontier is still alive in the United States. It is an adolescent frontier. These films permit the exploration of this frontier by audience members of all ages.[41]

Gender and Individualism in American Culture

American society is no different than most in that it is a patriarchy. Patriarchy is a system in which women are subordinate to men economically, politically, socially, and culturally. This subordination can vary in severity, is not always explicit, and is not always recognized. One reason it is often not recognized is because the culture does a good job of concealing it. If a culture successfully represents the experiences and perspectives of men as the *universal* experience and perspective, then patriarchy is hegemonic. That is, it has successfully represented the interests of one group as being in the interest of all. When we speak of the "American" character and the qualities of individualism in American culture we must be careful to ask ourselves this basic question: Are these descriptions of the culture true for women as well as for men? To ignore this question is to make an assumption that men and women have the same experiences. Or worse, it is to assume that only the experiences of men "count" as the measure of society. Canadian sociologist Dorothy Smith criticized sociology for excluding the experience of women from its empirical and theoretical work. Sociology, according to Smith, was no better than society when it came to the inclusion of women. This "eclipsing" of women's experience—this exclusion of women from the cultural frame—harms women and gives us an incomplete picture of social reality.[42]

As the dominant form of individualism in American culture, utilitarian individualism most certainly has a character that is predicated on the experience of men. As Michael Kimmel explains in his cultural history of manhood, the American character of self-sufficiency, of utilitarian individualism, for instance, is of the self-made *man*. For Kimmel, what defines the "Self-Made Man" is

> [s]uccess in the market, individual achievement, mobility, wealth. America expressed political autonomy; the Self-Made Man embodied economic autonomy. . . . Success must be earned, manhood must be proved—and proved constantly.[43]

Being a utilitarian individual means proving your manhood. Proving your manhood means becoming economically independent and providing for your self and your family. It means not being dependent on anyone. Given the meritocracy that is believed to define the American educational system in the post–World War II era, then, proving your manhood means doing well in school in order to earn the skills and credentials that are required for economic success in the marketplace.

Where does this leave women? Have American women been expected to express their individualism in different ways than men? Are they expected to be individuals at all? Since the dramatic social changes of the second half of the twentieth century, American women have certainly entered the workforce in much greater numbers and continue to make progress toward economic and political equality (although there is a long way to go still). These changes, thanks to the women's movement, have certainly opened up doors for women to be as utilitarian and independent as men. However, there are still cultural tensions about the role of women in society. What has it meant traditionally to be an American woman and an American individual?

In the early nineteenth century Tocqueville noted the special place that women played domestically. He observed that love and marriage in the domestic sphere of women would soften the hard edges of utilitarian individualism that characterized American men in the marketplace. Bellah et al. note the irony of this contrast between the hard, cold, and calculating world of the market and the love, interdependence and cooperation of the domestic sphere. Rather than expressing the rugged individualism that was the expectation of men, women in early American society were more likely to be expressive individualists. Bellah et al. write, "As the primary inhabitants of the familial sphere, women were involved with all of those characteristics we noted as part of the expressive, rather than the utilitarian, orientation."[44]

American society has changed much since the early nineteenth century. However, the hegemonic notions of individualism are still quite present. While women's roles in society have shifted and are less defined by the domestic "expressive" sphere of American life, the residue of traditional gender roles persists in our cultural images. Women characters in high school films are more likely to emphasize their "expressive" individualism, often as love interests (and sex objects) for men. In particular, "love" is confusing for Americans. As a part of the expressive domestic sphere that is culturally understood to be the domain of women, love finds a hard time fitting in to the utilitarian individualist's world. As Bellah et al. write, "Love, then creates a dilemma for Americans. In some ways love is the quintessential expression of individuality and freedom. At the same time, it offers intimacy, mutuality, and sharing."[45] Americans are often confused about how to reconcile the contrasting worlds of the "masculine" marketplace and "feminine" domestic sphere. As we will see, the gendered ways in which utilitarian and expressive individualism are represented in popular culture reflect this tension. All too often, this tension is resolved in high school films by privileging the perspective of men.

A Final Note

The themes of American culture introduced in the previous pages will surface again, sometimes explicitly and sometimes implicitly, in the coming chapters. In particular, the various strains of American individualism, the hegemonic perspective of the American middle class, and the search for independence and identity among Americans of all ages will be explored in the analysis of the high school film genres that follows. As will become clear in the coming chapters, the American urban, suburban, and private school films are dominated by the theme of individualism. Whether utilitarian or expressive individualism predominates depends upon the social class of the students who are featured in the film. Regardless of the theme, the movies in all three subgenres are told from the perspective of the middle class. The patterns of each subgenre reveal a particular image that middle-class Americans tend to have about education, adolescence, genders, and inequality.

Films do indeed reflect something real about the cultures that produce and consume them. In the cinematic images of high schools and adolescents, Hollywood reveals some of the characteristics and contradictions of American life. It is my hope that the analysis of the films in the coming pages can help the reader to shed light on some of the mysteries of American culture. Motion pictures provide an entertaining and enlightening laboratory in which to examine culture. However, it must be said that this exploration takes place within the very culture it seeks to understand. My analysis and the reader's interpretation, therefore, may be colored by our own social location and our unique experiences. Therefore, an analysis of these films, these curious cultural artifacts, can help us to understand something not only about American culture, but also, if done attentively, about our selves and our relationships to American culture. Hollywood may not have much of C. Wright Mills's "sociological imagination," but that does not prevent us from exercising our own.

Notes

1. Slater, Philip. 1976. *The Pursuit of Loneliness: American Culture at the Breaking Point*. Boston: Beacon Press, p. 15.
2. Durkheim, Emile. 1984. *The Division of Labor in Society*. Translated by W. D. Halls. New York: Free Press, p. 333.
3. Mills, C. Wright. 1959. *The Sociological Imagination*. New York: Oxford University Press.
4. For more on these issues, see Bellah, Robert N. 1973. "Introduction." In Durkheim, Emile. 1973. "Individualism and the Intellectuals" and "The Dualism of Human Nature and Its Social Conditions." In *Emile Durkheim on Morality and Society*. Chicago: University of Chicago Press; and Durkheim, Emile. 1973. *Moral Education: A Study in the Theory and Application of the Sociology of Education*. Robert N. Bellah, editor. New York: Free Press.
5. Bellah, et al., *Habits of the Heart*, p. 142.
6. See Varenne, Herve. 1977. *Americans Together: Structured Diversity in a Midwestern Town*. New York: Teachers College Press.
7. Franklin, Benjamin. 1964. *The Autobiography of Benjamin Franklin*. Edited by Leonard W. Labaree. New Haven, CT: Yale University Press.
8. Weber, Max. 1985. *The Protestant Ethic and the Spirit of Capitalism*. Translated by Talcott Parsons. London: Counterpoint, p. 52.
9. Cited in Bellah, et al., *Habits of the Heart*, p. 32.
10. Bellah, et al., *Habits of the Heart*, p. 33.
11. Thoreau, Henry David. 1960. *Walden*. New York: Signet, p. 9.
12. Ibid., p. 216.
13. Tocqueville, Alexis de. 1945. *Democracy in America*. Translated by Henry Reeve. New York: Vintage Books, p. 104.
14. There is, however, an antidote to rampant individualism, and that, too, is found in the democratic institutions of America. Tocqueville saw in political freedom and the voluntary associations that constitute civil society opportunities for Americans to exercise their individualism in the direction of the common good. Tocqueville's prescription of participation in voluntary associations is similar to Durkheim's hope that individuals would be integrated in and regulated by social groups. Whether or not Americans avail themselves of this opportunity and contribute to the social good through participation in civil society, however, is still hotly debated today, as illustrated by the wide attention received by Robert Putnam's 2000 national best-selling book *Bowling Alone: The Collapse and Revival of American Community*. New York: Touchstone. While there is great nostalgia in the United States for the values of community, where strong ties of "social capital" help individuals to feel that they are always "at home," the reality is that even when they join groups, Americans remain deeply individualistic.
15. Tocqueville, *Democracy in America*, p. 106.
16. Turner, Frederick Jackson. 1985. *The Frontier in American History*. Malabar, FL: Robert E. Krieger Publishing, p. 37.
17. See, for instance, Hine, Robert V., and John Mack Faragher. 2000. *The American West: A New Interpretive History*. New Haven, CT: Yale University Press.
18. Thomas, W. I. 1928. *The Child in America: Behavior Problems and Programs*. New York: Knopf.

19. While sociologist Martin Marger estimates that the middle class constitutes as much as 50 percent of the American population, social critic Barbara Ehrenreich suggests that the figure is no more than 20 percent of the population.
    Part of the difference is because Ehrenreich excludes from her count the lower middle class (those who may not have a college degree, who earn a lower salary as a result, and who work in lower and mid-level management positions). Marger, Martin M. 2002. *Social Inequality: Pattern and Processes*. Second Edition. Boston: McGraw Hill; and Ehrenreich, Barbara. 1990. *Fear of Falling: The Inner Life of the Middle Class*. New York: Harper Press.
20. Ehrenreich, *Fear of Falling*, p. 3.
21. Riesman, David, with Nathan Glazer and Reuel Denney. 1961. *The Lonely Crowd: A Study of the Changing American Character*. New Haven, CT: Yale University Press.
22. Mills, C. Wright. 1956. *White Collar: The American Middle Classes*. New York: Oxford University Press, p. xv.
23. See also Gans, Herbert J. 1988. *Middle American Individualism: The Future of Liberal Democracy*. New York: Free Press.
24. Bellah, et al., *Habits of the Heart*, p. 148.
25. Ibid., p. 151.
26. See Feldman, Shirley S., and Glen R. Elliott, editors. 1990. *At the Threshold: The Developing Adolescent*. Cambridge, MA: Harvard University Press.
27. See Palladino, Grace. 1996. *Teenagers: An American History*. New York: Basic Books; Hine, Thomas. 1999. *The Rise and Fall of the American Teenager*. New York: Perennial; Kett, Joseph F. 1977. *Rites of Passage: Adolescence in America, 1790 to the Present*. New York: Basic Books; and Modell, John, and Madeline Goodman. 1990. "Historical Perspectives." In *At the Threshold: The Developing Adolescent*. S. Shirley Feldman and Glen R. Elliott, editors. Cambridge, MA: Harvard University Press.
28. See Modell and Goodman, "Historical Perspectives."
29. Hall, Granville Stanley. 1904. *Adolescence: Its Psychology and Its Relations to Physiology, Anthropology, Sociology, Sex, Crime, Religion, and Education*. New York: D. Appleton and Company.
30. Modell and Goodman, "Historical Perspectives," p. 102.
31. See Katznelson, Ira, and Margaret Weir. 1985. *Schooling for All: Class, Race, and the Decline of the Democratic Ideal*. Berkeley: University of California Press.
32. See Katz, Michael B. 1987. *Reconstructing American Education*. Cambridge, MA: Harvard University Press.
33. Palladino, *Teenagers*, p. 5.
34. Ibid.
35. Ibid., p. xxii.
36. Doherty, Thomas. 2002. *Teenagers and Teenpics: The Juvenilization of American Movies in the 1950s*. Philadelphia: Temple University Press.
37. See Lewis, Jon. 1992. *The Road to Romance and Ruin: Teen Films and Youth Culture*. New York: Routledge.
38. See Modell and Goodman, "Historical Perspectives."
39. Coleman, James S. 1961. *The Adolescent Society*. New York: Free Press.
40. Males, Mike A. 1999. *Framing Youth: 10 Myths About the Next Generation*. Monroe, ME: Common Courage Press.
41. According to data from the Motion Picture Association of America (the "2003 U.S. Movie Attendance Study"), 27 percent of all moviegoers in 2003 were between the ages of twelve and twenty, 21 percent were between the ages of twenty-one and twenty-nine, 19 percent were between the ages of thirty and thirty-nine, 14 percent were between the ages of forty and forty-nine, 11 percent were between the ages of fifty and fifty-nine, and 8 percent were over the age

of sixty. While twelve- to twenty-four-year-olds are overrepresented among moviegoers compared with their numbers in the population, it is noteworthy that 61 percent of all moviegoers are twenty-five years of age or older. Despite the "juvenilization of American movies" that film scholar Thomas Doherty, *Teenagers and Teenpics*, writes about, the movies still offer a powerful appeal to moviegoers of all ages.

42. Smith, Dorothy. 1987. *The Everyday World as Problematic*. Boston: Northeastern University Press.
43. Kimmel, Michael. 1996. *Manhood in America: A Cultural History*. New York: The Free Press, p. 23.
44. Bellah, et al., *Habits of the Heart*, p. 89.
45. Ibid., p. 93.

[three]

Fighting the Culture of Poverty: The Teacher as the Urban School Cowboy

I don't want excuses. I know what you are up against. We are all up against something.

—Erin Gruwell in *Freedom Writers*

I look around this room and all I see is choices. Choices waiting to be made.

—Pierre Dulaine in *Take the Lead*

The mind is like a muscle. If you want it to be really powerful you have to work it out. Each new fact gives you another choice.

—Ms. Johnson in *Dangerous Minds*

Generally, the American urban public school films celebrate utilitarian individualism. A middle-class teacher-hero (an urban school cowboy, if you will) rides into the classroom and rescues low-income inner-city students who are wallowing in a culture of poverty. In order to be rescued from academic failure, these students must adopt the middle-class values of hard work, materialism, and individual achievement. These films suggest that if only these "at-risk" students were to adopt a solid work ethic, they could attend college and secure reliable middle-class jobs. While not entirely without merit, the messages of these movies tend to ignore the structural obstacles to academic and occupational success (such as unequal school funding, lack of employment in the inner city, lack of affordable housing, lack of affordable health and child care, poor public transportation, culturally biased curricula, class- and race-based discrimination in the classroom, and so forth). As sociological research has shown, it takes much more than individual effort to succeed under these circumstances.

While utilitarian individualism is celebrated in the urban school films, the films neglect to depict the expressive individualism of these low-income students. That is, the students in the urban school films are not depicted as whole human beings—they are not allowed to express themselves fully as free individuals. Hollywood only gives license to the middle-class students in the suburban school films analyzed in chapters 4 and 5 to express such individuality. The teachers in the urban school films are invariably depicted as the heroes. These patterns in urban and suburban public school films have been in evidence for over half a century.

The now classic 1955 film *Blackboard Jungle* is the granddaddy of urban public school films. It opens with this serious message about juvenile delinquency and American education:

Today we are concerned with juvenile delinquency—its causes and its effects. We are especially concerned when this delinquency boils over into our schools. The scenes and incidents depicted here are fictional. However, we believe that public awareness is a first step towards a remedy for any problem. It is in this spirit and with this faith that *Blackboard Jungle* was produced.

The film, the first set to a rock-and-roll sound track, graphically portrays poor and working-class urban youth assaulting teachers, stealing automobiles, disrespecting authority, and dismissing the importance of an education. It does not exactly represent the peaceful schools and studious youth that many Americans believe to have characterized public education in the 1950s. It is surprising to audiences today, and it was shocking to audiences in 1955. This film is not intended to be mere entertainment. This is a film with a social message. It takes itself very seriously as a social document about real social problems in the nation's real schools. The theatrical trailer advertises the film as "fiction torn from big city modern savagery . . . where teenage savages turn big city schools into jungles." Its negative representation of American schools was of such concern to government authorities that they asked MGM to withdraw the film from the 1955 Venice Film Festival.[1] In the midst of the Cold War, *Blackboard Jungle* did not paint a picture that Americans wanted broadcast to an international audience. It was seen by some as a film that could be used as communist propaganda. Darryl F. Zanuck, the chief of rival film studio Fox, appreciated the quality of the film, but did not think it was politically appropriate to release it:

I felt when I originally saw the picture that in spite of its quality, it could only give an erroneous impression of the American school system to European audiences. I also felt that it would be welcomed with open arms by the Communists.[2]

For many reasons, the film clearly struck a chord with Americans. It also seems to have struck a chord with generations of screenwriters, directors, and producers. *Blackboard Jungle* is the film that establishes the urban high school film genre and is the one from which all of the other urban school films lift their major plot elements and characters. Nearly all of the urban school films discussed in this chapter owe a great debt to *Blackboard Jungle*.

The basic plot of the film is quite simple, and likely familiar even to contemporary film audiences who have never seen the film. Richard Dadier, a World War II navy veteran with a newly minted teaching credential, applies for a job teaching English at a rough-and-tumble New York City public high school that serves an impoverished and racially mixed student population. Mr. Dadier is frustrated with the ineffective school administration, the cynical teachers, and the hostile students. He struggles throughout the film to "get through" to his students. His job is made particularly difficult by a gang of students that disrupts his class, attacks him, and harasses his pregnant wife. Despite these obstacles he is determined to reach these students. He uses unorthodox methods to get the attention of his students, to convince them to care about their education, and to raise their academic expectations. He also establishes a personal relationship with one particularly promising but troubled student. Despite some modest success, however, he nearly quits his job in anger and frustration at his apparent inability to reform these "savage" students. Yet he soon changes his mind after he realizes that he is actually getting through to them and that they truly appreciate his efforts to help them. MGM/UA Home Video describes the film this way:

> Newcomer Richard Dadier can understand why his fellow teachers have given up on their students at North Manual High. Raised in a big city slum, these kids aren't just mischievous teens, but vicious young hoodlums well on their way to careers of crime and violence. Determined to reach them, Dadier stages an uphill battle, defying their threats and brutal beatings until he's forced into a final, winner-take-all confrontation . . . where all he has left to lose is life itself.[3]

By 1995 the Cold War was over, but there was still a tremendous concern about the "crisis" in public education.[4] While the United States, including its public schools, had changed significantly in the forty years since *Blackboard Jungle* was released, Hollywood's representation of urban high schools had not changed at all. *Dangerous Minds* premiered in 1995 and was, in many ways, the same movie as *Blackboard Jungle*. Coolio's "Gangster's Paradise," rather than Bill Haley's "Rock Around the Clock," plays in the background during the opening credits. In nearly all other respects, however, the passage of forty years had not had much of an effect on how Hollywood understood urban education. Hollywood Picture Home Video describes *Dangerous Minds* as follows:

> Former U.S. Marine LouAnne Johnson [is] a first-time high school teacher, assigned to a class of tough-but-smart inner city students. When conventional methods fail to reach them, the feisty Ms. Johnson tries the unconventional—defying the rules and creating her own curriculum! In the process, she instills a new self-confidence in her students—motivating them towards their greatest potential.[5]

Sound familiar? Both Ms. Johnson and Mr. Dadier are military veterans and first-time teachers. They each teach English to a racially diverse classroom of low-income, inner-city students. They are each surprised and frustrated by the hostility they initially encounter in the classroom. Yet neither of them surrenders to cynicism as many of their fellow teachers do. They are each driven to succeed against the odds. Neither of them finds the out-of-touch administrators or the traditional curriculum to be particularly helpful. Therefore, they each use their own unique and unconventional methods to get through to these low-income urban school students. They each try to convince their students that school is valuable and that they have the ability to achieve academic success provided they put their minds to the task. In the climax of each film Ms. Johnson and Mr. Dadier momentarily lose faith in their students and in their ability to reach them effectively. Both Mr. Dadier and Ms. Johnson, however, survive the crisis and decide to continue teaching after their students show academic progress and a sincere appreciation for the efforts of their teacher.[6] However, as I explain later in this chapter, Hollywood's gender double-standard allows only Mr. Dadier to experience both professional success and a supportive domestic life.

Most of the urban school films resemble the basic plot of *Blackboard Jungle* and *Dangerous Minds*. Despite the seriousness with which these urban school films take themselves as documents of real social problems, these films teach us much more about American culture (specifically, how Americans make sense of education and inequality) than they do about the actual condition of public schools and the attitude of urban youth.

I argue in this chapter that the urban school films represent a middle-class American fantasy about the dynamics of social inequality and education. With .the dramatic backdrop of troubled urban public schools, Hollywood reinforces cultural myths about the causes of and prescriptions for poverty. Specifically, these Hollywood films about urban public schools suggest that low-income inner-city students need to believe in themselves, believe in the American dream, believe in the power of an education, work hard, and make better choices in their lives in order to escape their culture of poverty.

In his critique of *Dangerous Minds*, educational theorist Henry Giroux argues that the movie represents "whiteness" as the "archetype of rationality, authority, and cultural standards."[7] While I agree generally with Giroux's critique of *Dangerous Minds* (and, by extension, a critique of many of the other urban school films as well), I believe that these urban school films as a whole are more likely to represent *middle-class* values, not necessarily whiteness, as the archetype of rationality, authority, and cultural standards. While the students in these urban school films are very often African American and Latino, and race is certainly a relevant factor in the story, the social class differences between the students and their teacher-heroes are more significant than the racial differences between them. The middle-class protagonists of *Halls of Anger, Lean on Me, 187, Cooley High, Detention* (1998), *Stand and Deliver, Take the Lead, Coach Carter*, and *Precious*, for instance, are all African American or Latino. Also, there are white working-class students in need of salvation from a middle-class hero in *Blackboard Jungle, Class of 1984, Teachers, The Beat, Summer School, Wildcats, Cheaters, Take the Lead, Coach Carter*, and *Freedom Writers*.

Americans generally lack the cultural language to articulate an understanding of social class. To the extent that they recognize social inequality, they often name it in racial terms. The image of poverty in the United States is the image of urban blackness. However, there are twice as many poor whites in the United States than poor blacks.[8] Because Americans "see" race as the predominant frame when understanding inequality, it often obscures our view of social class. Just as it is in the culture generally, racial differences in these urban high school films are often a proxy for underlying social class differences. In contrast to Giroux's analysis, I agree with the social critic Barbara Ehrenreich when she notes in her review of *The Wild One, Rebel Without a Cause*, and *Blackboard Jungle* that these films deliver "impeccable middle-class messages: Crime doesn't pay; authority figures are usually right; you can get ahead by studying."[9] As I demonstrate in this chapter, Hollywood expects impoverished urban school students of all races to become utilitarian individuals.

A Cinematic Culture of Poverty

In most of the urban high school films, the plot revolves almost exclusively around the activities of one particular classroom of rowdy students and their heroic teacher in a troubled and violent school. The students in this class are depicted homogeneously— they all share similar social class characteristics and similar problems. The audience is rarely offered a glimpse into the complexities of their individual characters, their histories, their identities, or their families (these student complexities are given more flesh in the suburban high school films discussed in the next chapter). The urban high school students, for the most part, are from lower- and working-class homes, are often non-white (but not exclusively so), come from broken families who do not understand or care much about their child's education, have low educational aspirations and expectations, behave poorly in the classroom, and express a great deal of frustration with the formal structure of the school.

The students in these films represent the working- and lower-class populations as they are stereotypically imagined by suburban middle-class Americans. These students represent what middle-class people fear most about low-income urban youth: that they have no family values or work ethic; that they are out of control, loud, disobedient, violent, lazy, and addicted to drugs; and that they reject dominant social institutions. The rejection of the school is particularly offensive to members of the middle class since they are largely dependent upon educational credentials for occupational attainment and because historically schools have served their interests quite well.[10]

Cameron McCarthy and co-authors have argued that such stereotypical notions are the result of psychological projections—that middle-class suburbanites project these images onto the residents of inner cities so as to relieve the burden of carrying such negative characteristics of themselves. In other words, the self-identity of the middle-class suburban resident is formed in opposition to the inner-city resident, who is imagined to be impoverished both economically and morally. The growing social distance between suburban and urban America is reflected in the exaggerated representations of inner-city residents in the popular media:

> As tax-based revenues, resources, and services followed America's fleeing middle classes out of the city, a great gulf opened up between the suburban dweller and America's inner-city resident. Into this void contemporary television, film, and popular culture entered creating the most poignantly sordid fantasies of inner-city degeneracy and moral decrepitude. These representations of urban life would serve as markers of the distance the suburban dweller had traveled away from perdition.[11]

In response to the anxiety they feel about life as they imagine it in the inner city, McCarthy et al., argue that the suburban middle class seeks to impose their particular values and strategies for success upon the residents of the inner city. What prevents inner-city residents from achieving educational and occupational attainment is believed by many to be not a political or economic problem, but an individual problem and a moral problem. Hollywood reinforces these middle-class fantasies about how best to address the problems of the inner city.

Hollywood's depiction of urban life and urban schools generally reflects the "culture of poverty" thesis. This view holds that residents of inner-city neighborhoods are poor not because they face racial and/or class discrimination or because they lack access to stable employment opportunities. Rather, it is argued that the urban poor are impoverished because they have the wrong values and the wrong attitudes about school, work, and family. It is assumed that inner-city residents share a culture of poverty that, as sociologist Christopher Hurn describes it, is

> Characterized by a widespread belief that individuals cannot control their environment, a related belief in fate or luck as determinants of a person's life, a low degree of control over aggressive impulses, a present rather than a future orientation, and low levels of aspiration for educational and occupational achievement.[12]

In contrast to what is considered the "normative" cultural values of the middle class (material goals, rational calculation, and a belief in the efficacy of individual effort), the culture of poverty thesis posits a culture that is lacking in the requisite values to achieve individual success. Edward Banfield has argued that the urban poor (particularly poor African Americans) remain poor because of their failure to adopt middle-class values and to integrate fully into the dominant culture of the United States. While the urban poor may in fact confront significant hardships, Banfield suggests that the adoption of middle-class values and lifestyles by the poor would help them to escape their poverty.[13]

Much social science research, however, has since discredited the idea that cultural values are responsible for either success or failure in life.[14] This research has shown that while cultural values and attitudes do vary, they do so primarily as they adapt to larger historical, social, political, and economic conditions. As sociologists have studied the inner city, they have found that many of the social problems there are less the result of cultural values and more the result of low levels of public investment in infrastructure, poor public housing, inadequate health care, poor schools, and, most importantly, a disappearing employment base.[15] William Julius Wilson has written extensively on the problems of the urban poor. His meticulous research convincingly shows that while many inner-city neighborhoods do exhibit signs of social "pathology" (crime, teen pregnancy, high school dropouts, and so on), these behaviors are not the result of cultural values or individual attitudes. Rather, they emerge out of particular conditions in the social structure. He writes:

> If ghetto underclass minorities have limited aspirations, a hedonistic orientation toward life, or lack of plans for the future, such outlooks ultimately are the result of restricted opportunities and feelings of resignation originating from bitter personal experiences and a bleak future.[16]

The social problems in the inner city, then, cannot be solved through the application of individual-level solutions. Wilson's research has helped to demonstrate that since these problems are inherently structural, they require a structural solution.

Nevertheless, the culture of poverty framework has found its way into the popular imagination, and it is difficult to dislodge. Rather than focusing on the social, political, and economic sources of the problems in the inner city, Americans prefer to place the blame upon the individual moral failings and bad decision making of the residents of the inner city. American culture, rooted in Protestantism and capitalism, suggests that individual failure is often the result of an insufficient work ethic. A national survey in the late 1990s found that a majority of white Americans believe that a lack of personal motivation is the primary reason African Americans, on average, have a lower socioeconomic status than white Americans.[17] Also, in his 1998 study of middle-class Americans, Alan Wolfe found that 65 percent of his respondents believed that "the problems of America's inner cities are largely due to people's lack of personal responsibility for their own problems."[18] Wolfe concludes that "the ideal of personal responsibility is very deeply ingrained in the middle-class mind."[19]

Americans emphasize the importance of equality of opportunity, but they generally explain success or failure in the market as the result of individual effort and ability, not the result of structural obstacles. As President George W. Bush remarked early in his presidency, "Much of today's poverty has more to do with troubled lives than a troubled economy. And often when a life is broken, it can only be restored by another caring, concerned human being."[20] This individualistic perspective is certainly not unique to Republicans. As President Obama said in a 2014 speech about making college more affordable,

> [T]his is a country where opportunity should be available for anybody—the idea that no matter who you are, what you look like, where you come from, how you were raised, who you love, if you're willing to work hard, if you're willing to live up to your responsibilities, you can make it here in America.[21]

Explaining inequality as the result of individual effort helps to relieve the suburban middle class (and upper class) of its share of responsibility for having politically and economically neglected the inner city and the poor. The frame that Hollywood uses to make sense of problems in urban high schools vividly reinforces the culture of poverty thesis and assists the middle and upper classes in their displacement of responsibility from troubled social structures to troubled lives.[22]

There are a handful of urban public school films that reflect a more sociological view of urban education—films that take social forces seriously. These films, however (which I explore in more detail later in the chapter), are in short supply and are not very popular with movie audiences. The most common and most popular urban school films depict a culture of poverty out of which utilitarian individuals are expected to pull themselves up by their bootstraps. The following section outlines the basic structure of most of the films in the urban school genre.

Welcome to the Jungle: The Urban School in Hollywood Films

Most of the urban public school films portray the individual attitude of the students as the *primary* obstacle to their academic achievement. These students don't have the right manners, the right behavior, or the right values to succeed in school. They have low aspirations, have a poor self-image, and believe the odds are stacked against them in school and in the wider society. The schools, therefore, are unable to educate these students effectively, and the reproduction of their disadvantage seems inevitable.

In the classic *Blackboard Jungle*, the 1955 film that was discussed at the beginning of this chapter, a group of working-class New York boys is depicted at first as nothing but a street gang who spend their days causing havoc in their vocational high school: A teacher is nearly raped, a baseball is heaved at a teacher's head, a teacher's wife is harassed, and a newspaper truck is stolen. The metaphor in the film's title is all too literal—these students are seen as working-class animals.[23] These are "beasts" that even music won't soothe—in one scene the students destroy a teacher's priceless collection of jazz records. In *The Principal* one teacher compares the students to animals, only to have another teacher claim that she would prefer to teach animals because at least animals do not carry knives. In *Teachers* the song "In the Jungle" plays while police search student lockers for drugs. In *Lean on Me* the high school is depicted explicitly as an untamed jungle. In the opening moments we see students selling drugs, assaulting teachers, harassing women, and generally running amok. All of this takes place as the movie soundtrack plays Guns N' Roses' angry anthem "Welcome to the Jungle" in the background.

The jungle metaphor conveniently summarizes the imagined difference between middle-class suburban Americans and the low-income urban students portrayed in these films. These are not students as middle-class Americans expect students to act. Their depiction as "animals" suggests that the problems in these schools are rooted in student behavior and, furthermore, that their behavior is rooted in an inferior culture. These "animals" have not been domesticated. The school is nothing but a zoo meant to contain them.

In the opening scenes of *Teachers* one student is stabbed, another student bites a teacher, the school psychologist has a nervous breakdown, and we see a teacher pack a gun in her briefcase. The assistant principal of the school casually explains that these events are typical problems for a Monday. In *The Principal* Rick Latimer single-handedly breaks up a gang fight on his first day on the job as the principal of an inner-city school. In *The Substitute* a gang has such firm control over an urban public high school that members attack a teacher with impunity. In *The Beat* a street gang fights rivals, gets stoned, listens to heavy-metal music, and ignores schoolwork. In *Freedom Writers* Ms. Gruwell contends with a violent fight in her classroom on her first day of teaching and the school is consumed by a gang fight on her second day. In *Dangerous Minds* the middle-class and somewhat naive Ms. Johnson walks into her class for the first time only to walk right back out after encountering nothing but abusive and hostile students who first ignore and then ridicule her. These are the same students who, by the end of the movie, Ms. Johnson (and we the audience) will embrace warmly.

Or is it that by the end of the movie "they" (the at-risk, poor, and inner-city students) will have learned to embrace "us" (the educated, middle-class, and suburban audience, as represented by Ms. Johnson)? This distinction is an important one. Will the audience learn that these students are not animals after all? Have the students simply been misunderstood? Will the audience learn a lesson? Or will the students radically change their behavior as they come under the civilizing influence of the middle-class teacher who will socialize them in the culture of middle-class life? With the exception of a few urban high school films that will be discussed later in this chapter, my viewing of this genre supports the latter interpretation. The films suggest that the students, and sometimes their parents, are to blame for their animal-like behavior and poor academic performance. If there is to be a happy ending (and there almost always is), it is the *students* who must learn and change, not the members of the movie audience. But what about the educators? What role do the teachers and principals play in the transformation of the students in these urban school films?

The School Staff: Inept Bureaucrats and Incompetent Teachers

If the students are portrayed in a negative light, the school administrators and teaching staff are not depicted much more generously. The teachers and staff are generally shown as uncaring, cynical, incompetent, and ineffective educators. In short, the administrative and teaching staffs in these movies represent the worst fears that suburban residents have of urban public school administrators and teachers. These characters represent what many Americans believe is at the heart of the urban public school "crisis"—a selfish, inept, wasteful, and uncaring bureaucracy. These are schools with no soul—just troubled students, failed educational methods, burned-out personnel, too many arcane rules, and too much paperwork. If the harshest critics of public education were to make a movie about the public schools, their fictional schools would look much like the schools in these films.[24]

In *Blackboard Jungle* the stern principal is offended by the suggestion that there are discipline problems in his school. He seems unaware of the obvious problems all around him. In *Dangerous Minds* the soft-spoken principal is so narrowly focused on teaching the students to follow the most minor of rules that he is blind to their real life-and-death problems. Similarly, the administrators in *Up the Down Staircase* are more concerned that teachers follow the strict rules, obey the proper procedures, and fill out the right forms than they are with the welfare and education of their students. The principal in *Teachers* is blissfully ignorant of all the chaotic events in his school. Most of the administrative energy in the school is spent fighting a lawsuit filed by the family of a student who graduated without knowing how to read. The school authorities in *Stand and Deliver* have little faith in their students and do not believe that they could possibly do well in an advanced math class. The school psychologist in *The Beat* doesn't understand the first thing about the problems of alienated, low-income urban youth. In *Lean on Me* the dramatic deterioration of the high school over the years is blamed on the actions of the selfish teachers' union and the corrupt politicians in city hall. In *Here Comes the Boom* the vice-principal is arrested for embezzlement of school funds in an already struggling urban high school.[25] In *The Principal* the teachers complain bitterly when the principal insists that the "thugs" of the school actually attend their classes. In *The Substitute* the principal is actually one of the thugs!

He has established an alliance with the dominant gang in the school to distribute drugs throughout the school district.

The vast majority of the teachers in these films have cynical attitudes about their jobs and seem to believe that most of the students are well beyond the point of hope. They certainly don't believe that the students have the capacity to learn the curriculum of the school. As one teacher from *Up the Down Staircase* summarizes her pedagogical philosophy, "You keep them off the streets and you give them a bit of fun and you've earned your keep." A cynical teacher in *The Substitute 2* offers this advice to a new teacher: "Punch in, punch out, and just try to stay alive." Ms. Campbell, the head of the English Department in *Freedom Writers*, gives this advice to new teacher Erin Gruwell, "You can't make someone want an education. The best you can do is try to get them to obey, to learn discipline. That would be a tremendous accomplishment for them." These veteran teachers are burned out and have nothing left to give but pessimistic appraisals of the potential for each year's class of students. They have failed to do what was assumed to be their professional obligation—to educate these urban school students so that they can find gainful employment or admission to college.

With representations such as these, is it any wonder that a majority of Americans believe that national public schools are failing miserably? In the fall of 2012 only 19 percent of a random national sample of Americans awarded the nation's public schools a grade of A or B. When asked to grade the public schools in their local district, however, 48 percent of the sample awarded a grade of A or a B. Even more dramatically, of the parents in the sample who have children enrolled in the public schools, 77 percent awarded an A or B to the public school that their oldest child attends.[26] It would seem that the closer one is to the public schools and, presumably, the more information one has about them, the more likely one is to evaluate the public schools favorably. Without such firsthand knowledge about particular schools, however, the American public's estimation of the public schools in general may be based upon what they hear in the media, including Hollywood's unflattering representations. Nevertheless, there is one character in these urban school films who makes a difference. An outsider, a representative of the middle-class work ethic, comes to the school to "save" the students by teaching them how to be utilitarian individuals.

The Outsider as the Teacher-Hero

While all of the students, all of the administrators, and most of the teachers are depicted as impediments to education, there is one bright light of hope in these films: the teacher-hero (or, in some cases, the principal-hero or the coach-hero). This lone figure is able to ignore the cynicism of veteran teachers, escape the red tape of the school bureaucracy, and speak directly to the hearts and minds of these troubled youth who are, by the end of the film, transformed from apathetic working-class and poor students into studious and sincere students with bright middle-class futures.

The heroes of these films do not need teacher training, smaller class sizes, a supportive staff, strong administrative leadership, parental participation, technological tools, corporate partnership, school restructuring, a higher salary, a longer school day, charter schools, tuition vouchers, or more financial resources.[27] All they need to bring to the classroom is discipline, tough love, high expectations, and a little good old-fashioned middle-class common sense about individual achievement and personal responsibility.

In each of these movies the hero is someone new to the school, and often new to teaching entirely. The teacher-hero is a mysterious figure who literally becomes the savior of the students.[28] All hope would be lost if not for the intervention of this unconventional new teacher to break the well-established but failed methods of the school and to effectively reach the students with his or her own unique approach. I suggest that the teacher-hero in the urban school films represents a fantasy of the suburban middle-class audience—a character they can identify with goes into a troubled urban high school and single-handedly rectifies its problems. The teacher- or principal-hero can clearly see through the confusion that has bewildered many educators and policy makers for years. He or she can clearly identify the faults in these students and the problems in these schools and knows just what it takes to correct them. The teacher-heroes teach the students to escape the depressing and limiting world of their parents, to appreciate art and poetry, to develop manners and cultural skills, to acquire new study habits, to set high goals for themselves, to have an optimistic attitude, and to believe that hard work pays off. In short, the teacher shows the students how to overcome their culture of poverty. It is through this figure of the heroic outsider that the audience feels some sense of control over an otherwise chaotic and hopeless situation.

We already know Mr. Dadier from *Blackboard Jungle.* He is a white man with plenty of upper-middle-class cultural capital (he recites Shakespeare in his job interview with the principal) who enters the "garbage can of the educational system" (as one cynical teacher puts it). After several thuggish students assault him and a fellow teacher after work one day, Mr. Dadier is tempted to transfer to a middle-class high school where well-dressed and well-behaved students study earnestly and patriotically sing the national anthem. Mr. Dadier, however, is determined to reach the students in his "jungle." He wants them to care about an education, to learn "to think for themselves," and to make something positive of their lives. He takes a special interest in Gregory Miller, an African American student and the charismatic leader of the class, and tells him that he should not settle for being an auto mechanic—that in 1955 racial discrimination and poverty are no longer excuses for blacks not to make something of their lives in the United States. By the end of the film Mr. Dadier has convinced Gregory Miller to stay in school and has reformed his wild jungle into a tame domestic classroom.

In *Take the Lead* Pierre Dulaine is a ballroom dance instructor who suddenly takes an interest in teaching ballroom dance to urban high school students. As a joke, the principal assigns him to teach the "rejects of the school" in detention. She has no doubt that his first day with those students will be his last. After encountering resistance from the students, however, he persists day after day. The students soon look forward to his lessons. As their dancing improves their attitudes toward school improve. The principal eventually endorses the program and offers to help Mr. Dulaine extend his program to other students.

In *Coach Carter* Ken Carter is a successful local businessman who decides to return to his alma mater to coach the troubled men's basketball team. He is not a teacher. He is not a coach. But he wants to give something back to his old school. The players are undisciplined and disrespectful, and many of them struggle in school. Carter insists on strict discipline, respect, and attention to their schoolwork. He is a life coach as much as a basketball coach. While the players resist his demanding rules at first, eventually they grow to love him and appreciate his heavy hand after they start winning basketball games. When they fail to live up to their agreement to keep their grades up he exercises some tough love and locks the players out of the gym and forfeits several games. The players respond by attending class and catching up on their studies. When the lockout ends the team returns to their winning ways and several of the players go on to college. It seems that all they needed was some discipline and to make better choices in their lives.

In *Freedom Writers* Erin Gruwell is an idealistic first year teacher who chose to teach in a racially integrated urban school. At first, her students ignore her and some express outright hatred toward her. Exasperated by their apathetic attitudes toward school, their petty gang turf wars, and their many racial prejudices, she embarks on an unconventional path by teaching them about the Jewish holocaust and requiring them to share their stories in daily journals, just as Anne Frank did. Soon, they learn to shed their racial prejudices, they disengage from gang life, and they blossom as young scholars.

Not all of Hollywood's urban school students, however, are capable of such salvation. Some students are simply beyond even the reach of the middle-class hero. These students, Hollywood suggests, must be run out of town by the good guys.

The Teacher as a Cowboy Vigilante

In some of the urban school films the hero must not only save the students with middle-class values, but also punish and exclude the most dangerous and unredeemable elements of the student population. *Coach Carter* kicks off the team any student not willing to sign a contract agreeing to attend classes regularly and to keep up his grade point average. To enforce his point, he physically slams one student up against the wall after the student challenged his authority by taking a swing at the new coach. In *Lean on Me* Principal Clark's first order of business as the new baseball-bat-wielding principal of a run-down urban high school is to expel 10 percent of the student body. He asks the teachers to compile a list of the students they believe to be involved with gangs and drugs. He gathers these students on stage at a school assembly and announces their immediate expulsion from school. After these most undesirable students are expelled, Principal Clark concentrates on rescuing the remaining students from their troubled, yet redeemable, lives. Principal Clark's relatively peaceful purge, however, is contrasted with the similar, but more violent, methods of exclusion used by the teacher- and principal-heroes in several of the other urban school films. Violence as pedagogy is used centrally as a method of saving the students in *The Principal, The Substitute, The Substitute 2, Class of 1984, Only the Strong, 187,* and *Detention* (2003).

While the educational goals of the teacher- and principal-heroes in these seven films are the same as those in the less violent films (to encourage the students to adopt middle-class values and to achieve high academic goals), their methods are clearly unconventional and often illegal. What these more violent films suggest is that not all "at risk" students in impoverished urban public schools are worth saving. Some students are so far beyond the norms of middle-class life that they must be removed from society before their flawed values and deviant lifestyles corrupt other students. While their methods are extreme, these violent educators ultimately send the same message to viewers as the other teacher- and principal-heroes: The problems in urban public schools are primarily caused by the urban public school students themselves, not larger social structural factors. The solutions, therefore, are located within the individual students (either in their moral conversion to the middle class or in their violent exclusion from civilized society).

In *The Principal* Rick Latimer is a high school teacher who is arrested after lashing out violently against his ex-wife's boyfriend. Rather than firing him, the school board punishes him by making him principal of the most troubled school in the city. As the film studio describes the film,

> Burglary, drugs. Assault. Rape. The students at Brandel High are more than the new principal Rick Latimer bargained for. Gangs fight to control the school using knives—even guns when they have to. When Latimer and the head of security try to clean up the school and stop the narcotics trade, they run up against a teenage mafia. A violent confrontation on the campus leads to a deadly showdown with the drug dealer's gang, and one last chance for Latimer to save his career . . . and his life.[29]

Rick Latimer is a man with a troubled past and no administrative experience. He is a loner, an alcoholic, and a violent man. He rules the school with an iron fist and emphatically declares that he will no longer tolerate drugs or gang activity in his school. He directly challenges the gang leader for control of the school. "No more" becomes his mantra, and he frequently enforces his rules with his fists. Despite his unorthodox methods and violent temper, he is able to sensitively reach several "at risk" students and to get them to reverse their negative attitudes toward school.

Even more dramatically, in *The Substitute* an out-of-work mercenary soldier becomes a substitute teacher at an urban high school in Miami. Using an alias, "Mr. Smith" learns that the principal and the dominant gang, the "Kings of Destruction," run a major drug operation out of the basement of the school. When he is not defending himself against attempts on his life by gang members, the substitute teacher connects emotionally with many of the students in his class and encourages them to reject gangs and drugs. For the first time the students actually begin to pay attention in class. This teacher-hero, however, has far more ambitious goals for the school. In a bloody ending the substitute teacher defeats the "Kings of Destruction" and the thuggish principal. In doing so he nearly destroys the school building, but he makes the school safe for learning and returns it to the students—"at least it's their school again," he says. With his job complete, he and his partner mosey on out of town.[30]

In the *Class of 1984* (based "partially" on real events, as the preface tells us), Andy Norris is a first-time teacher at a violent inner-city high school. A drug-dealing gang, led by the promising but misguided student Pete Stegman, has taken over Mr. Norris's music class. Mr. Norris expels the gang members from his class, but they continue to harass him at school and at home. After a "good" kid dies from the effect of the gang's tainted drugs, Mr. Norris becomes determined to bring the gang to justice. He is frustrated, however, that neither the school administration nor the police take any action against the gang.

Meanwhile, Mr. Norris has been able to "get through" to his music class. Without the distraction of the gang members, he is able to teach the students and to convince them to care about their education. On the night of his class's first school concert, however, Stegman's gang molests the pregnant Mrs. Norris and holds her hostage. Using her as bait, the gang lures Mr. Norris through the empty hallways of the school and into the shop classrooms, where they wait to kill him. In self-defense, Mr. Norris kills one student with a buzz saw in wood shop, burns another to death with gasoline and a blowtorch in auto shop, and kills a third with a wrench. (Note how the working-class tools favored by these violent and rebellious students are used against them as the middle-class outsider, Mr. Norris, enacts his revenge.) Mr. Norris and Stegman face off on the roof of the school for the climactic fight scene. In the midst of their violent altercation Stegman falls through a glass sunroof, gets tangled in the stage ropes, and hangs to death above Mr. Norris's orchestra, in the middle of their brilliant concert performance.

Mr. Norris is the ultimate teacher-hero. He academically inspires his class of troubled youth (as much as Ms. Johnson in *Dangerous Minds*), and he also takes the law into his own hands as he ruthlessly rids the school permanently of its most threatening students. What Principal Joe Clark accomplished in *Lean on Me* by summarily expelling the most troublesome 10 percent of the student population, Mr. Norris accomplishes with righteous violence.

These cowboys of the classroom bring order to the chaos of the urban public schools. As newcomers to their schools, they are asked to deal with problems that are not of their making. Frustrated by lawlessness and the ineffectiveness of the traditional methods available to them, they take matters into their own hands. They use violence to impose righteousness and to clear a path for other students (troubled, yet morally redeemable students) to achieve their full academic potential. As we will see in the following chapter, the tables are dramatically turned on the teachers in the suburban school films. In these films it is the students who sometimes turn violent in order to punish their corrupt teachers.

Hollywood's Lesson Plan: Just Choose Success

Despite the daunting obstacles facing the students and the complexity of urban education, the teacher-heroes present their students with a simple choice. They can *choose* success or *choose* failure. It's that simple. The American ideal of the utilitarian individual who transcends the structural circumstances of their life, makes wise choices, and works hard is promoted heavily in these films. The following exchange between Gregory Miller and Mr. Dadier in *Blackboard Jungle* summarizes Mr. Dadier's (and, by extension, *Blackboard Jungle's*) educational philosophy:

Gregory Miller: I don't need no more schooling. What's wrong with being a mechanic?

Mr. Dadier: You don't want to be, do you?

Gregory Miller: There ain't much choice, is there? Same reason I live in this neighborhood. A Colored neighborhood . . . What's the use? Nobody gives a hoot. Not the other fellahs, not the teachers, not my folks even.

Mr. Dadier: So you quit trying. That's the easy way out, Miller . . .

Gregory Miller: We talking from different sides of the fence. You're not black.

Mr. Dadier: That's not a good enough excuse nowadays and you know it, Miller!

Mr. Dadier expects Miller to choose to stay in school as if the fear of racial discrimination and the lure of a stable auto mechanic's job should not be real considerations in the decision. Similarly, Ms. Johnson tells the impoverished students in her class that they alone are responsible for their success or failure in school and in life: "You have a choice. It may not be a choice you like, but it's a choice . . . there are no victims in this classroom." Louis Stevens, the teacher-hero in *Only the Strong*, tells a low-income, inner-city student, "This world can be about as big as you want it to be, or as small as your tiny little 'hood. I'm showing you some choices. You decide."

In *Take the Lead* Pierre Dulaine takes a special interest in Jason Rockwell. "Rock" is an African American student who is on the edge of being expelled from school. In addition to his academic and behavioral problems at school he must work to support his family. Since his brother was shot and killed his father has sunk deeper into alcoholism and neither his dad nor mom have jobs. There is often no food in the house. After a fight with his parents Rock is kicked out of the house and he becomes homeless. After he is caught sleeping in the basement of the school he is arrested and Mr. Dulaine bails him out. Admiring Mr. Dulaine's apartment, Rock says, "I'm gonna have me a spot like this some day." Mr. Dulaine responds, "You can get whatever you want, Rock." Incredulous, Rock says, "No, only some people get the shit they want." "That's true, replies Mr. Dulaine, "those are the people who show up to get it." According to Mr. Dulaine, if you want nice things in life, you need only show up to claim them. That, and a good foxtrot, is all that he offers these poor inner-city students at an underperforming school in a neighborhood with few jobs. Opportunity, according to Hollywood, is there for the taking—just reach out and grab it. It makes no difference if you are the son of a middle-class college educated professional in the suburbs or the homeless son of an unemployed alcoholic in the inner city. Just show up for success.

At a pivotal moment in *Coach Carter* it is not clear if the players will respond to the lessons of their coach. Ken Carter tells his players, "Go home and look at your lives tonight. Look at your parents' lives and ask yourself, 'Do I want better?' If the answer is yes, I'll see you here tomorrow and I promise you I'll do everything in my power to get you into college and a better life." For Coach Carter, the choice to be successful in school, to get into college, and to live a life better than that of your parents is simple—you have to want it. A poster in *Coach Carter*'s office reads, "Life is full of choices. Choose carefully." But the film glosses over the fact that some people are given more choices than others. Poor youth in the inner city face structural obstacles and have few resources to draw upon as they try to work their way up the ladder. The naïve assumption that success is just a matter of "wanting" it is an insult to the millions who struggle every day to work for a better life and still fall short. Wanting success and working hard for it are certainly necessary steps along the way to a bright future. But to suggest that they are the only steps is to perpetuate the myth of the rugged American individual.

When Erin Gruwell's students in *Freedom Writers* begin to doubt their newfound abilities she declares, "I don't want excuses. I know what you are up against. We are all up against something." Indeed, we are all up against something. But her statement that we are all up against something implies that the challenges she faces as a white, educated, middle-class teacher from Newport Beach are some-how on par with those of her poor, physically abused or threatened, sometimes homeless, non-white students who live in gang-infested neighborhoods. *Freedom Writers* does a better job than most of the films in that it explores the difficult non-school lives of these students. The students are urged to find their voices and to share their stories. Erin Gruwell and the audience do learn about the lives of the students and we come to appreciate the challenges they face. The students in *Freedom Writers* are humanized and the audience begins to understand the pain they feel. At the end of the day, however, the teacher-hero fails to integrate these humanizing lessons in her assessment of their situation. Despite her best efforts, the cinematic Ms. Gruwell becomes Mr. Dadier, Ms. Johnson, Principal Clark, Mr. Escalante, and Coach Carter. The platitudes eventually come to the surface in these urban school films: Work hard. Choose wisely. No excuses. These platitudes prevent Hollywood from representing what it takes to promote real educational achievement in urban high schools.

The assumption (in these movies and too often in actual schools) that aspiring to fix cars or to work on an assembly line is a sign of personal failure serves to condemn those students who, for whatever reason, do not have college in their future. Furthermore, it is disingenuous to assume that the *only* obstacle standing in the way of middle-class occupational attainment for these students is their individual attitude and their failure to exercise their brains or make the right choices. It is not that the middle-class values espoused by the teacher-heroes are without educational merit. However, the implication in these films that the failure or success of these students is reducible to their values and their individual effort, rather than taking into consideration the deep social structural processes also at work, is a pedagogical fallacy. The attitude and behavior of poor and minority students in urban public high schools can have many explanations that these films implicitly (and sometimes explicitly) dismiss. Social science research has found that the source of such attitudes is within structures such as the employment base in urban areas, past and current racial discrimination, and unequal public school funding.

Jay MacLeod, author of the modern sociological classic *Ain't No Makin' It: Aspirations and Attainment in a Low-Income Neighborhood*, studied two groups of high school boys from poor and working-class families in a housing project outside Boston. He found that the group of white boys, the "Hallway Hangers," had come to the conclusion that the American achievement ideology was a lie. They were witness over the years to the failure of their friends and family members in school and the job market. They concluded that for people like themselves, hard work does not pay off. As a result, they lowered their aspirations in life so as not to be disappointed with themselves should they fail to become upwardly mobile. Indeed, the Hallway Hangers failed to achieve much educational or occupational success. They reproduced the impoverished and troubled lives of their parents. But how much of their "failure" was the result of their own actions and how much was beyond their control?

The brilliance of MacLeod's research is that he contrasts the experiences of the Hallway Hangers with those of "the Brothers," a group of African American boys from the same housing project facing the same set of educational and occupational opportunities as the Hallway Hangers. In contrast to the Hallway Hangers, the Brothers believed in the achievement ideology, worked hard in school, and had high aspirations. Hollywood and American culture would expect the Brothers to experience success as a result of their utilitarian individualism. Unfortunately, they did not. MacLeod concludes that both groups of boys faced limited opportunities in school and the workplace because of their social class position and the structure of the American economy. The negative attitude of the Hallway Hangers was not the primary cause of their failure. Rather, their negative attitude was the internalization of grim objective conditions for them in the job market.[31]

Additionally, John Ogbu's research has shown that different minority groups have drastically different orientations toward schooling as a result of the historical legacy of their racial or ethnic group's incorporation into the dominant society. As "involuntary minorities," African American students, for instance, often resist cooperation with the white middle-class standards of the school because the bitter experiences of previous generations and the hardships of the current generation have left them distrustful of the dominant institutions of society. Success in school, seen as "acting white" for many African American students, threatens their identity, which was partly formed in opposition to dominant social institutions.[32] Furthermore, as social psychologist Claude Steele's research has shown, even the minority students who *do* identify and cooperate with the school often perform poorly in school not because they come from a culture of poverty, but because they fear that their performance will confirm the worst stereotypes that others have of their racial or ethnic group. Such "stereotype threat" can insidiously become a self-fulfilling prophecy.[33]

Oppositional identities and stereotype threat are not exclusive to racial minorities, however. Any disadvantaged group can develop oppositional identities that affect performance in school. As Jay MacLeod has shown in his detailed ethnography described earlier, working-class white students also face stereotypes in the wider society and often reject dominant social institutions such as schools because of the low probabilities for success that await them in the middle-class occupational world.[34]

Jonathan Kozol's impassioned work over the years has demonstrated that the severe funding inequities between urban and suburban public schools have an insidious effect on the educational experience of students. While much social science research, starting with the Coleman Report in 1966, has suggested that differential levels of school funding are not *primarily* responsible for differential levels of student academic performance, Kozol's work shows how school funding is nonetheless a factor that contributes to the overall well-being and self-image of students.[35] In his 1991 book *Savage Inequalities: Children in America's Schools*, the inequities Kozol observes between urban and suburban public schools mirror the inequities of Hollywood's urban and suburban high schools. The following description of the urban schools Kozol visited could refer to almost any of the urban schools depicted in Hollywood films:

> [T]hese public schools were, by and large, extraordinarily unhappy places. With few exceptions, they reminded me of "garrisons" or "outposts" in a foreign nation. Housing projects, bleak and tall, surrounded by perimeter walls lined with barbed wire, often stood adjacent to the schools I visited. . . . Their doors were guarded. Police sometimes patrolled the halls. The windows of the schools were sometimes covered with steel grates.[36]

Whereas Hollywood expects students in underfunded public high schools to rise above their depressing circumstances, Kozol sees how such conditions gradually wear a student down and can lead to a fatalistic attitude about school:

> [M]ost adolescents in the poorest of neighborhoods learn very soon that they are getting less than children in the wealthier school districts. They see suburban schools on television and they see them when they travel for athletic competitions. . . . About injustice, most poor children in America cannot be fooled. Children, of course, don't understand at first that they are being cheated. They come to school with a degree of faith and optimism, and they often seem to thrive during the first few years. It is sometimes not until third grade that their teachers start to see the warning signs of failure.[37]

If, as I have suggested, these films present themselves not just as entertainment, but as serious social documents about real social problems, then we must treat seriously what they offer as potential solutions to such problems. Hollywood suggests that all students (with the help of the right teacher) have the power to do whatever they choose to do in life. The only limitation facing students is the limitation within themselves. Unfortunately, the dramatized solutions, while perhaps satisfying as entertainment, fall well short as answers to the social problems they purport to address and leave audiences with misleading impressions about educational inequality.

What Hollywood Could Learn from Social Science

Teachers *can* make a difference in the lives of poor students. Particularly gifted, motivated, and charismatic teachers may be able to inspire some low-income, inner-city students to raise their aspirations and to reorient their attitudes toward school. Establishing personal relationships with students, having high expectations of them, and encouraging them to apply themselves despite their own self-doubt are indeed positive and potentially effective pedagogical methods.[38] However, as an answer to the problems of past and current racial discrimination, lack of economic opportunities in the labor market, and the inequities in funding between urban and suburban public schools, a few highly charismatic teachers can have only a limited impact. Without a depiction of the social, political, and economic context in which these stories take place, the educational lessons of these urban school films are incomplete.

To be convinced to apply themselves in school, students must know that the schoolwork they are asked to do has some relevance to their future lives and that their efforts will likely be rewarded in school and in the wider social structure.[39] The personal attitudes and academic efforts of poor inner-city students will likely change not simply because a middle-class teacher whips them into academic shape, but because the educational, economic, and social opportunities made available to them change.

Short of widespread social and economic changes, however, there are some educational reforms at the level of the school that research has shown can increase student performance.[40] The educational reforms that have shown promise in the real world, however, are not reflected in Hollywood's fantasy about how to improve the academic performance of students in urban schools. What is noteworthy about this research is that it places the responsibility not simply upon the individual student, but upon the coordinated efforts of a community of teachers, students, staff, administrators, and parents. A collective effort is required to succeed in the face of structural inequalities.

There are many ways in which Hollywood's pedagogy is at odds with what educators know about effective schools. For instance,

- While the teachers in these urban school films transform their students despite bad principals, scholarship on effective schools shows that strong school leadership with clearly defined goals is an important element of school success.[41]
- While the teachers in these films transform students despite the apathy of their parents, effective schools' literature suggests that school success requires the cooperation and involvement of parents.[42]
- While the teachers in these films transform their students despite a cynical and uncooperative staff of teachers, the school effectiveness literature suggests that schools with a supportive and cooperative staff can increase student performance.[43]
- While the teachers in these films transform their students by encouraging students to be individually competitive, recent scholarship suggests that collaborative learning can yield high academic results.[44]

- While teachers in these films do not attempt to incorporate pedagogies or curricula that reflect the unique social world and culture of the students in their classes, recent scholarship has shown that attention to cultural differences in the classroom can increase student engagement and performance.[45]
- And, as we saw in a previous section, while some of the teacher- or educator-heroes in these films succeed by excluding the most "at risk" students from their classes, the school effectiveness literature suggests that mixed-ability classes rather than rigidly tracked and exclusive classrooms can raise the achievement level of all students.[46]

The movie *Dangerous Minds* provides a particularly revealing opportunity to analyze Hollywood's lesson plan and compare it to reality. *Dangerous Minds* was based on the nonfiction book *My Posse Don't Do Homework*, by real-life teacher LouAnne Johnson.[47] There are, however, some interesting differences between Johnson's book and Hollywood's "true story" version of it. Despite the cinematic version of Ms. Johnson's speech about personal responsibility, the real Ms. Johnson writes, "I can't help feeling that it's me as a teacher and the school system as a social institution that are, in reality, failing our children and their future."[48] The movie suggests that Ms. Johnson's success was achieved over the course of one semester, but Ms. Johnson's real-life success took several years. Ms. Johnson's most academically successful student, Callie, was actually in an advanced class, not the remedial class depicted in the film. Ms. Johnson received much more help from her teacher friend Hal in real life than the movie depicts. Instead of using the folk lyrics of Bob Dylan (poetry more popular with the middle-aged white middle class than non-white inner-city kids in the 1990s), the real Ms. Johnson used rap lyrics as poetic examples. Finally, and most revealing of Hollywood's bias, the film overlooked many pedagogically important details of Ms. Johnson's "Academy" class. Designed as a program of last resort for troubled but promising students, the real Academy received additional funding from the federal government to lower class sizes and to purchase computers. The students were assigned mentors from the local business community. And the students received personal attention from a team of teachers, not just Ms. Johnson.

Ironically, one of Ms. Johnson's real-life students expresses wisdom that Hollywood actively chose to ignore. After reading Shakespeare's *Taming of the Shrew* and then watching the movie version of the play, the student writes disapprovingly in a classroom journal:

> The movie was all right, but it didn't have as much action as the book and there was some seens [*sic*] in the movie that wasn't in the book and that ain't right. If somebody tells a story and you make a movie out of it, you shouldn't make up your own stuff and put it in the movie because then it isn't the other guy's story anymore.[49]

If Hollywood regularly distorts true stories of urban schools to conform to a generic formula, we need to ask why the formula is more culturally compelling than the reality. The answer, I argue, is that the formula reflects the cultural hegemony of a politically conservative worldview—one that displaces the blame for class inequality from those who benefit from it and places it on the shoulders of those at the bottom of the class structure. But, with the help of compassionate conservatives, there is always the possibility for individual redemption.

Teacher-Heroes as Compassionate Conservatives

As we have seen, in each of these movies the answer to the students' problems is revealed to be primarily an individual one—to reform the individual student, not the educational system or the wider society. In a few of these films the implied solution to the crisis in urban education is to first rid the school of gangs and drugs. Second, and more importantly, the teacher-hero in all of these films must teach students the right values and manners, convince them they have the power to improve their lives, and insist they make better choices and take responsibility for those choices. As Principal Joe Clark in *Lean on Me* tells the students in his high school: "If you fail I want you to blame yourself. The responsibility is yours." Sometimes this message of individual choice and personal responsibility even asks the student to decline assistance from others when they are in desperate circumstances.

For instance, *Precious* is a tragic story of a desperately poor, obese, and illiterate young African American woman who is verbally and physically abused by her mother and raped and impregnated by her father. Upon her second pregnancy the sixteen-year-old is taken out of junior high and sent to an alternative school with other troubled young high school–aged women. The class is taught by Blu Rain, an African American woman who takes a compassionate interest in Precious. Despite Precious's difficult circumstances, Ms. Rain never loses hope for Precious. She tells Precious optimistically, "Get your G.E.D. Go to College. You can do anything, Precious." Ms. Rain teaches Precious to read and write. By the end of the film Precious can read at the seventh-grade level. Ms. Rain also helps Precious get into a halfway house when she is left homeless after her mother tries to kill her. *Precious* is an unconventional high school film, but at its core the film conforms to the basic structure of the urban high school film—a poor, academically weak student from a dysfunctional family is saved in part by the efforts of a heroic teacher. More than most films, *Precious* does explore at great length the home life of Precious, and the audience understands Precious's problems as the result of trauma, not poor personal choices. Nevertheless, the film still has a predominant theme of compassionate conservatism—damaged lives must be helped by other caring individuals, not the government. Despite the fact that Precious is the illiterate and impoverished mother of two children, each the result of rape by her father, Blu Rain urges Precious to eschew welfare benefits. She points to the fraudulent use of welfare by Precious's mother (and her lazy dependency upon it) as an argument against receiving help from the government. Instead, Ms. Rain wants Precious to aspire to and work toward a college education to be a utilitarian individual.

While there is certainly nothing wrong with encouraging personal responsibility and independence among students, these movies, as I have argued, dramatize only a portion of the story when they portray a lack of individual effort as the *only* reason the future of poor students is often limited. The serious business of school reform or revitalization of the inner-city economy takes a distant backseat to the individual reformation of these poor and working-class students. As Erin Gruwell, LouAnne Johnson, Joe Clark, Pierre Dulaine, and Ken Carter make perfectly clear, there are no victims among their students. Success is a *choice* that each individual student must make. In the absence of a portrayal of the social, political, or economic context in which these individual choices are made, however, I argue that there is an implicit (and sometimes explicit) conservative political message conveyed in each of these films.

Near the end of most of these movies the teacher- or principal-hero faces a crisis that almost causes him or her to give up his or her mission. In each case, however, the crisis is heroically dealt with and the teacher or principal stays in the job, having found a true calling in life. I argue that the dilemma facing the hero in the climax of each of these movies tells a significant political story about urban policy choices in late-twentieth- and early-twenty-first-century America. Should the state play an active role in the structural reform of urban schools and urban economies? Should the state retreat and let market forces work the magic of the invisible hand? Or is there a "compassionately conservative" third way in which public policy addresses inequality, but only at the level of the individual?

In *Coach Carter* Ken Carter is disappointed that his students have not lived up to their agreement to do well in classes. He locks the team out of practice and they forfeit several basketball games. This action infuriates much of the community. He's dismayed that the parents and the school board don't support his efforts to help the students achieve academically. Bending to pressure from the community, the school board votes to end the lockout. Coach Carter follows through with his vow to quit if the board undermines his authority. However, when he returns to the gym to clear out his office he finds his players in the gym studying. They have voluntarily continued the lockout until they get their grades back to a GPA of 2.3. One player, the one he previously slammed up against a wall for trying to hit him, says emotionally, "Sir, I just want to say thank you. You saved my life." He abruptly changes his mind and continues to be their coach.

In *Blackboard Jungle* Mr. Dadier also faces doubts and threatens to quit his teaching job. After he is assaulted and his wife is harassed, Mr. Dadier loses the hope he had for these students and nearly takes a teaching job at an elite high school. In a fit of frustration toward the end of the film Mr. Dadier asks, "What's the point of teaching if kids don't care about an education? And make no mistake about it. They don't!" However, Mr. Dadier soon regains faith in his apathetic students when they team up to defeat the most incorrigible troublemakers in class after they threaten Mr. Dadier with a knife. In *Lean on Me* the corrupt fire chief and the politically vulnerable mayor arrest Principal Clark for putting chains on the high school doors (in order to keep the drug dealers out). The students, however, rally to his defense. They surround the jail and demand his release with testaments to how much he has helped them. The news that 75 percent of the students received a passing grade on the state's minimum skills test redeems him. He is released from jail and victoriously returns to lead his flock.[50]

Several crises face Ms. Johnson in *Dangerous Minds*. One of her students, the charismatic leader of the class, is shot and killed by a crack addict. Another gets pregnant and is pressured by the school administration to attend an alternative school. Still other students drop out of school altogether. Ms. Johnson begins to lose hope and announces she will not return to teach the following year. Her students, however, protest vigorously. They literally *need* her. They have grown to rely on her. As several of her students complain:

> "If you love us so much and are so interested in our graduating, why are you leaving?"

> "We've been working hard and we stayed in school. What about us?"

> "Ain't no other teacher going to give me no A."

Callie, the promising student who was encouraged by the administration to leave the school when she became pregnant, returns to school on Ms. Johnson's last day and pleads with her to stay in her job. In reference to one of the poems they had read in class, Callie uses some rather heavy-handed symbolism to make her point:

> I thought you'd always be here for me. . . . I decided, we decided, we aren't going to let you leave like that. . . . [Y]ou have to rage against the dying of the light. . . . [W]e see you as being our light. You are our teacher. You got what we need.

They feel angry and, ironically, victimized by Ms. Johnson's apparent betrayal. Their emotional appeal works. Moved by her students' testimonies, Ms. Johnson decides to continue teaching at the school. How can she abandon them now?

In each of these moments of crisis, teachers are at the end of their rope. They are disappointed that they have failed as teachers, angry that the students have not responded to their lessons, or frustrated that the administration has tied their hands. This moment epitomizes the anxiety and frustration with urban schools expressed by politicians and many middle-class suburbanites. I understand this pivotal moment to be a representation of the neoconservative impulse to retreat from state efforts to solve social problems. It is as if the teacher-hero says, "Well, I've done my best to help these people but it failed. Let's cut school funding, eliminate affirmative action, cut back on welfare, and insist upon personal accountability. Their failure is no longer my responsibility."

Hollywood, however, does not let the story end with such a laissez-faire message. In Hollywood, the well-intentioned middle-class reformer ultimately succeeds just when failure seems imminent. Success, however, is measured not by any institutional or social changes, but by the adoration of the students for the teacher-hero.[51] With such admiration from the students, the "compassionately conservative" teacher-hero continues to work with the students. This is the moment of truth in these movies—proof to the teacher-hero that the students have been successfully reformed. They have progressed from lower-class animals to respectable middle-class students who finally understand and appreciate the efforts of their middle-class teacher- or principal-hero. Their troubled lives have been compassionately transformed by a caring and concerned human being. This familiar story that a middle-class hero can convince poor students to finally get their act together and become upwardly mobile is a fairy tale that eases the psychic burden of the middle and upper-middle classes. These stories tell them that they are not to blame for inequality. The fairy tale allows those who have achieved at least a middle-class status to congratulate themselves—not only for their own success, but also for the potential salvation they can provide for people who continue to make the wrong choices.

A Cultural Contradiction

Despite an emphasis on the value of individual transformation and self-reliance (utilitarian individualism), the students in these films continue to express a need for a relationship with their teacher. This is a need that the teacher-hero, in all good conscience, can't ignore. Without their work, who else will save these students?

There is an implicit assumption in most of these movies that if the middle-class hero does not agree to stay on at the school, the students would quickly jettison the lessons they have learned and return to their apathetic underperformance and violent behavior. There is no other teacher (and certainly no school reform) that can reach these students. Ms. Campbell, the head of the English Department in *Freedom Writers*, hits the nail on the head when she objects to Erin Gruwell's request to continue teaching her students for another year: "If your students have made the progress you say they have they should be ready to move on. They might even learn something from more experienced teachers." But Ms. Campbell is not the hero of this film. She is the antagonist. The students don't need her like they need Ms. Gruwell. There is a *dependence* upon the middle-class teacher by these lower-class students, which points to an inherent contradiction in these movies—a contradiction that stems from the ambiguities of American individualism itself.

The teachers encourage their students to transcend their dysfunctional families, their rotten peers, their lousy schools, and their culture of poverty. The teachers encourage their students to use their power as individuals to compete successfully and to attain a higher social status. Yet to reach this goal, the students are necessarily placed in a position of dependence upon the teacher- or principal-hero. For all of the rhetoric about independence and individual achievement, we never see the students in these urban high school films fully express their autonomy. Rather, their individualism is embedded in their relationship with the teacher-hero. The authors of *Habits of the Heart* make exactly this point when they discuss one of the ironies of American individualism. In short, they argue, the individual needs attachment with society in order to be fulfilled. Individualism requires community for it to have meaning:

> This ambivalence shows up particularly clearly at the level of myth in our litera-
> ture and our popular culture. There we find the fear that society may overwhelm
> the individual and destroy any chance of autonomy unless he stands against it,

but also recognition that it is only in relation to society that the individual can fulfill himself and that if the break with society is too radical, life has no meaning at all.[52]

Similarly, the lessons that these urban school films teach about autonomy, competition, and individual achievement ironically require a relationship of interdependence, cooperation, and shared goals. The utilitarian individualism of independence and achievement is heralded explicitly, while the lessons about interdependence, cooperation, and shared goals are left implicit. This may reflect American culture's lack of a language to articulate (or an unwillingness to acknowledge) our reliance on community. Nonetheless, these films seem to hint that such social connections may ironically be an important element in the constitution of American individualism. As anthropologist Claude Levi-Strauss has argued, folktales and myths can help to resolve cultural contradictions.[53] They help to ease cultural tension and make coherent sense out of the world. Perhaps these urban school folktales provide American audiences with an opportunity to reconcile some apparent cultural contradictions between individualism and community.

Learning from the Anomalies

As noted earlier, there are a few urban school films that do not conform to the major themes discussed thus far. While small in number, their exceptionalism reveals all the more strongly Hollywood's tendency to interpret urban education from the perspective of middle-class individualism.

Cheaters, *Light It Up*, and *Chalk* are noteworthy as anomalies in this sample of urban high school films because they are similar to other urban high school films in form, but their content directly challenges the central features of the genre. In their departure from the genre formula, they highlight the predictability of the messages conveyed in most of the other urban high school films.[54]

Cheaters is based on a true story of working-class students in an underfunded and gritty Chicago public high school who cheat in order to win the Illinois State Academic Decathlon contest. What is remarkable about this film is that while it initially appears to follow in the footsteps of all the urban school films (a classroom of poor and troubled urban students is poised to be "saved" by a middle-class teacher-hero), its moral message is radically different. Rather than inspiring the students to work hard and achieve their full potential honestly, the teacher-"hero" actually encourages the students to cheat, facilitates their cheating, and helps them to conceal their cheating from the authorities.

The teacher-"hero," Mr. Plecki, recruits the brightest students at the school to be part of the Academic Decathlon team. He has a hard time finding enough students to participate. The students are not willing to put in the time it would take to be successful. Nor are the working-class students impressed by a promotional video that boasts that the Academic Decathlon is "building skills that work in corporate America." After all, what future do *they* have in corporate America? Nevertheless, he is able to organize a team, and they begin to compete against other schools. They do moderately well at first, exceeding expectations by placing fifth in the citywide competition. As a result, they narrowly qualify for the state championship. Knowing that they stand little chance of success at the state level, however, few students are interested in continuing to compete. As one student remarks, "I love the dream you gave to us, but at a certain point you have to realize it's just a fucking dream." With an assortment of work and family obligations, the time to prepare for the competition at the state level is simply too consuming for the students. Their attitude soon changes, however, after one of the students finds the test book for the state competition. They all agree, with Mr. Plecki's support, to cheat.

Mr. Plecki rationalizes the cheating as an act of civil disobedience—a collective effort to strip away the built-in advantages of social class and social connections enjoyed by the upper-middle-class students at a very prestigious and well-funded public magnet school across town, Whitney Young. Whitney Young has abundant resources and has dominated the State Academic Decathlon championships for years. Mr. Plecki and his students believe there is a suspiciously cozy relationship between Whitney Young and the Academic Decathlon authorities. The administrative offices of the national Academic Decathlon are even located on the grounds of Whitney Young High School.

Mr. Plecki wishes to level the playing field for his working-class students not for learning's sake, but for the sake of winning. Mr. Plecki cannot in good conscience spout platitudes to his students about playing by the rules and working hard. He knows through bitter personal experience that the achievement ideology and meritocracy are myths. His working-class immigrant father played by the rules and worked hard his entire life only to be cruelly laid off by his lifelong employer when he contracted cancer late in his career. Mr. Plecki has learned that in the United States it is winning that ultimately counts, not integrity. He feels unrewarded as a dedicated and talented schoolteacher while many of his less worthy peers have prospered. Mr. Plecki encourages his students to work cooperatively in order to challenge the system—to rebel against a structure that further benefits the advantaged and impedes the upward mobility of the disadvantaged.

One of the things that makes this film remarkable is that the teacher, the students, and the film do not apologize for the blatant breaking of the rules. The students are eventually caught and Mr. Plecki loses his job. Yet there are no regrets. As Jolie, a bright student who actively participated in the scheme and serves as the narrator of the story, remarks at the end of the film, "I learned more about the way the world really works from my nine months on the Decathlon team than most people will learn in a lifetime." By consciously not conforming to the common formula of the urban school film genre, *Cheaters* is almost refreshing in its cynicism. One need not condone the cheating to respect the film for its unidealized portrayal of an urban school and for its attempt to portray the elements of the wider social structure within which the students must act.

Light It Up is also an exceptional film in the urban high school genre. The heroes of this film are the students themselves, not middle-class adults. The students in Mr. Knowles's class are mostly good-intentioned and motivated kids who show a lot of promise. However, they are poor, they have troubled home lives, and there are few opportunities for them at school. There is no heat in their classroom, the ceiling leaks, and the windows are broken. Fed up with these inferior conditions, Mr. Knowles takes his class to a local restaurant during school hours. As a result of breaking school policy, the principal suspends Mr. Knowles.

Angry that their favorite teacher was suspended, several of the students stage an impromptu protest in the principal's office. A police officer is called to break up the protest and the principal suspends several students, including Ziggy, a troubled but sensitive student and talented artist who is often beaten by his father. Desperate to avoid more trouble at home, Ziggy tries to run. In a struggle with the police officer, Ziggy grabs the officer's gun and accidentally shoots the officer. Lester, a football player with a solid grade point average whose dad was shot and killed by the police three months earlier, picks up the gun and threatens the officer and the principal. Lester, Ziggy, Rodney (a gang member), Stephanie (an honor student with a bright future), Lynn (a good-natured but troubled white student who just learned she is pregnant), and Rivers (a slick con artist with a good heart) take the police officer hostage, barricade themselves in the school, and create a list of demands. They demand that the school rehire Mr. Knowles, buy more textbooks, fix the broken windows and leaks in the school, establish a career day, and routinely test all the teachers in the school.

This film does not present student attitudes, middle-class values, or individual achievement as the solution to the problems in inner-city schools. Rather, it tackles head-on the structural and social problems that these students are faced with on a daily basis. These students consciously struggle against racism, poverty, an underfunded school, and the stereotype that they are violent thugs who don't care about (and therefore don't deserve) an education. These students have been victimized by the system and misunderstood by society (including, as this film explicitly portrays, by the media). Ultimately, the story ends in tragedy as Ziggy is shot to death by the police.

While Mr. Knowles is a favorite teacher who cares about the students, he does *not* become anyone's savior in this film. Mr. Knowles is merely a secondary character. The help that these students need is beyond that which a single teacher can provide. Rather than looking exclusively to Mr. Knowles, the students look to themselves for answers, and they take action (as flawed as it may be). They do not eventually adopt new values and attitudes. Instead, the audience begins to learn more about who these students are as individuals and sympathetically understands why they took such drastic actions. Even the wounded police officer testifies on behalf of the students at the criminal trial.

Chalk is a "mockumentary" about several teachers at an urban high school. It follows them over the course of a year, showing in comic detail how difficult, frustrating, and, at times, rewarding their jobs can be. The teachers are, for the most part, well meaning but ineffectual. Ultimately, there is no salvation of the students and the ending is ambiguous. For instance, we don't know if the first year teacher will be back for another year or if he has given up on the profession. The film is an anomaly in the honest and sometimes uncomfortable way it depicts the daily grind of trying to teach teenagers. Unlike the other urban school films, it does have a refreshing scene that shows the teachers reaching out to the students to try to understand *their* world. Rather than a student spelling bee, Harrison High has a teacher "spelling hornet" in which teachers and administrators compete to spell slang words that the students use on a daily basis—words that otherwise separate the worlds of teacher and student. Such an attempt to acknowledge and value the cultural world of the urban students—and not just the cultural world of the middle-class hero—is rare in the genre.

It is doubtful that these films represent a major change in the cultural understanding of urban high schools. Tellingly, these films are also unique in that they are among the least commercially successful films in the sample. *Light It Up* played in 1,252 theaters and it grossed only $5.8 million.[55] By comparison, *Dangerous Minds* played in 1,783 theaters and grossed nearly $85 million. *Cheaters* was produced by and shown only on HBO. *Chalk* is a low-budget independent film that grossed only $300,000. These films clearly break the mold of the urban high school film genre and offer the viewer something new to consider about urban high schools. Nevertheless, they do not seem to resonate with a wider audience as the other films in the sample do. Their uniqueness only serves to reinforce the dominant theme of most urban school films—that utilitarian individualism can help the students to escape their culture of poverty.

Not All Teacher-Heroes Are Created Equal: The Persistence of Gender Inequity

While the central argument in this book is about the ways in which American culture distorts an understanding of social class in order to privilege the position of the middle class, I conducted a preliminary analysis to see what these films also tell us about gender in American culture. Since the heroes of the urban school films are teachers, I focused my analysis on the ways in which gender affects the representation of the teacher-hero (in chapter 5 I analyze the ways gender influences the representation of student-heroes). I argue that just as these urban school films privilege the position of the middle class, they also privilege the position of men. While there are many similarities between teacher-heroes regardless of their gender, there are also important differences that reveal the cultural assumptions Americans still have about the role of men and women in society. All teacher-heroes ultimately convince a class of poor students to care about their education and to aspire to become obedient and conforming middle-class citizens. However, the price that these teacher-heroes pay for their professional success is patterned by their gender.

My analysis supports the assertion made by Mary M. Dalton in *The Hollywood Curriculum: Teachers in the Movies* that in Hollywood films teachers who are women are not allowed to live full lives with a healthy balance between home and work. I too found that women must sacrifice domestic happiness in order to succeed as teachers, while men tend to succeed in the classroom and simultaneously maintaining happy home lives. I argue that this is the result of the residue of an American cultural assumption that as individuals, women are best suited for the domestic "expressive" sphere while men are best suited for the "utilitarian" world of work.

For instance, in *Up the Down Staircase*, Sylvia Barrett is a young single woman without any apparent private life. She devotes herself to her job and laments the loneliness she feels at home: "I have a telephone, but it only rings once a week on Sunday. When my mother calls long distance to remind me of all the recent murders in the city." Sylvia Barrett's life is consumed by her job. Her unhappiness is, in part, because of the imbalance between her work and domestic life. In contrast, Richard Dadier in *Blackboard Jungle* has the full support of his loving wife, Anne. Anne spends most of the film at home, pregnant, and fretting that her husband is having an affair. After her husband is beaten up by students and after she is tormented by a student, she wants her husband to quit. However, after she sees the good that he can accomplish in the classroom she has a turn of heart. She encourages her husband to continue teaching. She supports him unconditionally: "No matter what happens, I love you. . . . I wanted you to quit teaching at that school. I understand now why you wanted to keep trying. I'm glad you didn't quit." Anne is the stereotypical image of a wife whose primary job is to support the work of her husband.

In *Dangerous Minds*, as in *Up the Down Staircase*, Louanne Johnson devotes her entire life to her new job. She is recently divorced (having been physically abused by her husband) and it is implied that because of the divorce she now must teach in order to support herself. She has no apparent social life outside of her friendship with fellow teacher Hal. The only scenes of her at home are scenes of her working late at night in preparation for the next day at school. She commiserates with Hal about her unhappy personal life. In contrast, Jaime Escalante in *Stand and Deliver* has a rich domestic life. He is happily married with children and several scenes depict him as a husband and father. Just as in *Blackboard Jungle*, his wife, Fabiola, expresses frustration with the demands of his job but ultimately offers unconditional support of his work. For instance, when he is discouraged by accusations that his class cheated on the Advanced Placement calculus test he goes home to his wife. He is bitterly dejected. She sits down with him and lovingly supports him by saying, "Regardless of whether they passed that test or not, they learned." Glumly, he says he may quit and take a higher paying job elsewhere. His wife changes his mind by reminding him how important he is to the students: "Jaime, those kids love you."

Coach Ken Carter is another hero with a supportive domestic life. Ken Carter is dedicated to his job, but *Coach Carter* also depicts the healthy relationships he has outside of school with both his loving girlfriend and his son. His girlfriend Tonya is irritated that Ken is going to take a job he doesn't have time for. "You promised to take your girlfriend to Mexico in January," she reminds him. He replies, "There's no way I'm not going to Mexico and hanging out on the beach with you and your bikini. I can't take that job." And, yet, she knows that he will take the job regardless. "So when do you start?" she replies. Later in the film Tonya is shown supportively sitting with Ken Carter at the school board meeting when they vote to end the lockout. He relies on her support to get him through that tough time.

Erin Gruwell in *Freedom Writers*, however, has no such domestic support to help her through the tough times at work. Her husband Scott is initially supportive of her new teaching job, but he quickly grows irritated with the amount of time it takes away from the rest of her life. When she takes on part-time jobs to help pay for school supplies he withdraws all of his domestic support and divorces her. She pays the ultimate price for professional dedication and success—the loss of her husband and support at home. The following exchange between Erin and Scott speaks volumes not only about the gender double standard in urban school films but in American culture as well. "I finally realize what I'm supposed to be doing and I love it," says Erin. "Then what do you need me for?" Scott asks. Erin responds, "Why can't you stand by me and be a part of it the way wives support husbands?" Scott's answer sums up the assumptions about gender roles that continue to perpetuate inequality in American society: "Because I can't be your wife."

He can't be her wife. In other words, he can't be supportive of her professional achievements. He can't be a domestic support for her work outside the home. He can't, as a man in American culture, find a role for himself that is both true to himself and true to the woman he loves. He can't be Anne in *Blackboard Jungle* or Fabiola in *Stand and Deliver*. Despite the work of the women's movement and the growing professional achievements of women, there is still in American culture an assumption that the professional sphere is for men and the domestic sphere is for women. It is noteworthy that Richard Dadier, Ken Carter, and Jaime Escalante not only have supportive wives or girlfriends, but also have their own children. Sylvia Barrett, Louanne Johnson, and Erin Gruwell, on the other hand, are childless. It is as if in their dedication to teaching their students they have no maternal energy left for a family of their own. The men, however, can have it both ways—they are allowed to fully exercise both their expressive and utilitarian individuality. They have satisfying work and domestic lives. The women must choose one or the other.

Conclusion: The Urban School Frontier

With a small handful of exceptions, these urban high school films are a celebration of the middle-class values of rational calculation and individual achievement. The low-income students in urban public schools must become autonomous utilitarian individuals if they are to achieve any measure of mainstream success. In true Hollywood fashion, the middle-class teachers and principals have saved the day as solitary heroes. These educators—mysterious, well intentioned, selfless, and heroic—are the cowboys of the dangerous and untamed urban high school frontier. They represent the essence of American rugged individualism: They stand outside society in order to save it.[56] The students, meanwhile, are explicitly grateful for their salvation. However, the salvation the teacher-heroes offer is inevitably tangled up with the contradictions of American individualism: The independence they demand of students requires a relationship of dependence to achieve.

Certainly, a high score on a test, an emotional tribute to a beloved teacher, and happy and optimistic students make for a good dramatic conclusion. But what do these endings imply for the public's image of urban schools? The audience is left feeling triumphant and optimistic about the potential for improvement in urban public schools. By simplifying the many problems of urban public education and turning inner-city students and public school teachers into caricatures of their respective social classes, however, Hollywood is doing nothing but reflecting middle-class anxiety about the problems of inner-city schools and the naïve hope that such problems need not a sustained political commitment from all members of society, but merely the individual moral conversion of poor students.

When Hollywood turns the lens on middle-class students in suburban public schools, however, the stories change dramatically. The next chapter outlines the ways in which Hollywood and American culture make very different sense of middle-class suburban adolescents than they do of poor adolescents in urban areas.

Notes

1. See Considine, David M. 1985. *The Cinema of Adolescence*. Jefferson, NC: McFarland and Co.
2. Ibid., p. 122.
3. Quoted from the back of the 1996 MGM/UA Home Entertainment and Turner Entertainment Company Vintage Classics VHS packaging.
4. See Berliner, David C., and Bruce J. Biddle. 1995. *The Manufactured Crisis*. Reading, MA: Addison Wesley, for a good discussion of the perceived crisis in American public education.
5. Quoted from the back of the 1995 Hollywood Pictures Home Video VHS packaging.
6. For an elementary school version of *Dangerous Minds* and *Blackboard Jungle*, see 1999's *Music of the Heart*. As the promotional material for the video says, "A single mother with little more than talent and the determination to make a difference, Roberta Guaspari overcame the skepticism of everyone who didn't think she should be teaching violin to students in a tough inner-city neighborhood."
7. Giroux, Henry. 1996. "Race, Pedagogy and Whiteness in 'Dangerous Minds.'" *Cineaste* 22, no. 4: 46–50.
8. Macartney, Suzanne, and Alemayehu Bishaw. 2013. "Poverty Rates for Selected Detailed Race and Hispanic Groups by State and Place, 2007–2011." www.census.gov.
9. Ehrenreich, Barbara. 1989. *Fear of Falling: The Inner Life of the Middle Class*. New York: Harper Press. p. 94.
10. See Eckert, Penelope. 1989. *Jocks and Burnouts: Social Categories and Identity in High School*. New York: Teachers College Press.
11. McCarthy, Cameron, et al. 1996. "Race, Suburban Resentment, and the Representation of the Inner City in Contemporary Film and Television." In *Off White*. Michelle Fine et al., editors. New York: Routledge, p. 230.
12. Hurn, Christopher. 1993. *The Limits and Possibilities of Schooling*. Boston: Allyn and Bacon, p. 151.
13. Banfield, Edward. 1968. *The Unheavenly City*. Boston: Little, Brown.
14. See, for instance, Wilson, William Julius. 1996. *When Work Disappears*. New York: Knopf; Bourdieu, Pierre. 1977. "Cultural Reproduction and Social Reproduction." In *Power and Ideology in Education*. Jerome Karabel and A. H. Halsey, editors. New York: Oxford University Press; Swidler, Ann. 1986. "Culture in Action: Symbols and Strategies." *American Sociological Review* 51: 273–286; Lareau, Annette. 1987. "Social Class Differences in Family–School Relationships: The Importance of Cultural Capital." *Sociology of Education* 60: 73–85; Willis, Paul. 1981. *Learning to Labor*. New York: Columbia University Press; Gibson, Margaret A., and John U. Ogbu, editors. 1991. *Minority Status and Schooling: A Comparative Study of Immigrants and Involuntary Minorities*. New York: Garland; and MacLeod, Jay. 1995. *Ain't No Makin' It: Aspirations and Attainment in a Low-Income Neighborhood*. Boulder, CO: Westview Press.
15. Wilson, *When Work Disappears*.
16. Wilson, William J. 1987. *The Truly Disadvantaged: The Inner City, the Underclass, and Public Policy*. Chicago: University of Chicago Press, pp. 158–159.

17. Schuman, Howard, Charlotte Steeh, Lawrence Bobo, and Maria Krysan. 1998. *Racial Attitudes in America: Trends and Interpretations*. Cambridge, MA: Harvard University Press.

18. Wolfe, Alan. 1998. *One Nation, After All.* New York: Viking, p. 205.

19. Ibid., p. 204.

20. Hutcheson, Ron. 2001. "Bush Calls for Faith-Based 'Assault on Poverty.'" *Sacramento Bee* (May 21): A15.

21. "Remarks by the President on Opportunity for All: Making College More Affordable" June 9, 2014. www.whitehouse.gov.

22. Todd Gitlin, too, notes in his study of television that Hollywood prefers to depict individual-level solutions to social problems rather than collective ones. See Gitlin, Todd. 1983. *Inside Prime Time*. New York: Pantheon.

23. While the word *jungle* in the title might suggest a racist overtone regarding which students are truly wild, it is important to note that *Blackboard Jungle* depicts a racially mixed classroom of working-class students. In fact, the African American student turns out to be the most amenable to Mr. Dadier's lessons, while an Irish American student is the most incorrigible.

24. For critics of public education, see Lieberman, Myron. 1993. *Public Education: An Autopsy.* Cambridge, MA: Harvard University Press; and Chubb, John E., and Terry M. Moe. 1990. *Politics, Markets, and America's Schools*. Washington, DC: Brookings Institution Press.

25. *Here Comes the Boom* is somewhat different from the other urban high school films. Scott Voss is not a new teacher to the school. He is a former teacher of the year. However, he's lost his passion for teaching and his students are bored and passive. Neither Mr. Voss nor his students think that school matters in their lives. When the school's music program is threatened because of budget cuts, however, Mr. Voss vows to raise the funds to save the program and the job of the music teacher. He becomes a cage-fighter and raises the money through his victories in the ring. Through this process he rediscovers the joy of teaching and ignites the intellectual interest of his students.

26. PDK/Gallup Organization. 2012. "44th Annual Phi Delta Kappan/Gallup Poll of the Public's Attitudes Toward the Public Schools" (September).

27. One exception to this is the 2012 movie *Won't Back Down*. It is not a part of my sample because it is about an elementary school. Nonetheless, the movie takes a decidedly political turn in advocating for the rights of parents to seize control of their underperforming local public schools from the district and turn them into semi-autonomous charter schools.

28. For a good discussion of the teacher as savior, see Ayers, William. 1996. "A Teacher Ain't Nothin' but a Hero: Teachers and Teaching in Film." In *City Kids, City Teachers: Reports from the Front Row*. William Ayers and Patricia Ford, editors. New York: The New Press.

29. Quoted from the back of the 1988 RCA/Columbia Pictures Home Video VHS packaging.

30. In a strikingly similar sequel, the violent teacher-hero of *The Substitute 2* achieves the same sort of victory. High school members of the carjacking gang The Brotherhood kill a popular teacher. The slain teacher's brother, a mercenary soldier, is hired as a substitute teacher in Lenthrop High, a violent New York City high school. Under the alias "Mr. Perakowski," he discovers (no surprise here) that the ringleader of the gang is a well-respected teacher at the high school. With the help of a former mercenary colleague and the school janitor (a shell-shocked veteran of the Vietnam War), the substitute kills the evil teacher, defeats The Brotherhood, and rescues the school from the grips of a criminal conspiracy.

31. MacLeod, *Ain't No Makin' It;* see also Bourdieu, "Cultural Reproduction and Social Reproduction"; and Wilson, *When Work Disappears* and *The Truly Disadvantaged.*

32. For a good overview of Ogbu's research and similar research by others, see Gibson and Ogbu, *Minority Status and Schooling.*

33. Steele, Claude M. 1997. "A Threat in the Air: How Stereotypes Shape the Intellectual Identities and Performance of Women and African Americans." *American Psychologist* 52: 613–629.

34. MacLeod, *Ain't No Makin' It;* see also Willis, Paul. 1981. *Learning to Labor.* New York: Columbia University Press.

35. Coleman, James, et al. 1966. *Equality of Educational Opportunity.* Washington, DC: U.S. Government.

36. Kozol, Jonathan. 1991. *Savage Inequalities: Children in America's Schools.* New York: Crown Publishers, p. 5.

37. Ibid., p. 57.

38. See Rosenthal, Robert, and Lenore Jacobson. 1968. *Pygmalion in the Classroom.* New York: Holt, Rinehart, and Winston; and Sewell, William H., Robert M. Hauser, and David L. Featherman, editors. 1976. *Schooling and Achievement in American Society.* New York: Academic Press.

39. See Natriello, G., Aaron M. Pallas, and E. L. McDill. 1986. *Community Resources for Responding to the Dropout Problem.* New Brunswick, NJ: Rutgers University Press; and Fine, Michelle. 1991. *Framing Dropouts: Notes on the Politics of an Urban High School.* Albany: State University of New York Press.

40. See Bryk, Anthony S., and Valerie E. Lee. 1993. *Catholic Schools and the Common Good.* Cambridge, MA: Harvard University Press; Natriello, Gary, Edward L. McDill, and Aaron M. Pallas. 1990. *Schooling the Disadvantaged: Racing Against Catastrophe.* New York: Teachers College Press; Darling-Hammond, Linda. 1997. *The Right to Learn: A Blueprint for Creating Schools That Work.* San Francisco: Jossey-Bass; Corbett, Dick, Bruce Wilson, and Belinda Williams. 2002. *Effort and Excellence in Urban Classrooms: Expecting and Getting Success with All Students.* New York: Teachers College Press; and Lee, Valerie E. 2001. *Restructuring High Schools for Equity and Excellence: What Works.* New York: Teachers College Press.

41. Purkey, Stewart C., and Marshall S. Smith. 1983. "Effective Schools: A Review." *Elementary School Journal* 83: 427–452.

42. Epstein, Joyce L. 1987. "Parent Involvement: What Research Says to Administrators." *Education and Urban Society* 19, no. 2: 119–136; and Epstein, Joyce L. 1996. "Perspectives and Previews on Research and Policy for School, Family, and Community Partnerships." In *Family–School Links: How Do They Affect Educational Outcomes?* A. Booth and J. Dunn, editors. Mahwah, NJ: Lawrence Erlbaum Associates.

43. Lee, *Restructuring High Schools.*

44. Darling-Hammond, *The Right to Learn.*

45. Deschenes, S., David Tyack, and Larry Cuban. 2001. "Mismatch: Historical Perspectives on Schools and Students Who Don't Fit Them." *Teachers College Record* 103, no. 4: 525–547.

46. Oakes, Jeannine. 1985. *Keeping Track: How Schools Structure Inequality.* New Haven, CT: Yale University Press.

47. Johnson, LouAnne. 1992. *Dangerous Minds.* New York: St. Martin's Paperback.

48. Ibid., p. 117.

49. Ibid., p. 189.

50. Before *Lean on Me* was filmed, real-life principal Joe Clark was praised publicly by President George Bush and his conservative secretary of education, William Bennett, for his no-nonsense approach to expelling the "bad" students and holding the other students responsible for their educational achievement.

Principal Clark received a great deal of media attention, including a cover story in *Time* magazine as well as the major motion picture based on his experiences at East Side High. It is noteworthy that Principal Clark's methods were publicized by both the Bush administration as well as by Hollywood. It is not enough to analyze *how* Hollywood depicts stories about schooling. We must also ask how Hollywood *chooses* which school stories to tell. As a principal of an inner-city high school not far from East Side High told Jonathan Kozol, "There is a notion out there that the fate of all these children is determined from their birth. If they fail, it's something in themselves. That, I believe, is why Joe Clark got so much praise from the white media." Kozol, *Savage Inequalities*, p. 142.

51. For more on this point, see Grant, Peggy A. 2002. "Using Popular Films to Challenge Preservice Teachers' Beliefs About Teaching in Urban Schools." *Urban Education* 37 (January 2002): 77–95.

52. Bellah, Robert N., Richard Madsen, William M. Sullivan, Ann Swidler, and Steven M. Tipton. 1985. *Habits of the Heart: Individualism and Commitment in American Life*. New York: Harper and Row. p. 144.

53. Levi-Strauss, Claude. 1978. *Myth and Meaning: Cracking the Code of Culture*. Toronto: University of Toronto Press.

54. While nearly 75 percent of the urban school films in this sample have remarkably similar plots and messages, there are a few exceptions in addition to *Cheaters* and *Light It Up*. Several of the urban school films do not have an adult teacher or principal hero as the central character. Among them, *Cooley High, Class Act,* and *Love Don't Cost a Thing* are also unique as three of the six comedies in the urban school sample. *Fame*, as much a musical as it is a drama, is primarily a series of vignettes about students at a selective performing arts high school. While *Zebrahead* and *Save the Last Dance* take place in urban high school settings, their stories more closely resemble the themes of the suburban school films analyzed in the next chapter. This is perhaps the case because their central characters are white middle-class students who fall in love with poor African American students. *Love Don't Cost a Thing* is a remake of the 1987 suburban school film *Can't Buy Me Love*. The 2003 remake is set in a mixed-race and mixed-class Long Beach, California, public high school. Its theme is the same as that in the suburban school original: The division between the popular and unpopular students is artificial and ultimately destructive—it's best just to be yourself (*then* you will be popular!). One of the most interesting anomalies is the remarkable independent film *Half Nelson* (2006). Since it takes place in a junior high school it does not meet the criteria for inclusion in my sample. Nonetheless, it is noteworthy because the would-be middle-class teacher-hero (Dan Dunne) is revealed to be a cocaine addict and is ultimately cared for and "saved" by Drey, one of the poor urban African American students in the school. As with the other anomalies, it is an independent film that grossed less than $3 million.

55. *187*, it should be noted, grossed about the same amount as *Light It Up*. Figures are from www.imbd.com and www.boxofficeguru.com.

56. A point made by Wright, Will. 1975. *Sixguns and Society: A Structural Study of the Western*. Berkeley: University of California Press.

four

We Don't Need No Education

The Rejection of Utilitarian Individualism in Suburban School Films

Whoso would be a man, must be a nonconformist. . . . Nothing is at last sacred but the integrity of your own mind.[1]

—Ralph Waldo Emerson

How could youths better learn to live than by at once trying the experiment of living? Methinks this would exercise their minds as much as mathematics.[2]

—Henry David Thoreau

Maybe there is more to a person than being valedictorian and class president.

—Nova in *Prom*

Not all high school films are created equal. The suburban high school film differs significantly from the urban high school film. While this might not be terribly surprising, it is important to note that the differences between these two subgenres are not primarily a reflection of the real-life differences between urban and suburban high schools. The dramatization and sensationalism of Hollywood films make them poor documents of social reality. However, it is Hollywood's predictable tendency to dramatize and sensationalize particular elements of urban and suburban high schools that makes these films relevant for critical social analysis. The urban and suburban high school films are consistently told from different points of view, have different moods, have different heroes and villains, tell different stories, and teach different lessons. The American cultural value of individualism is at the heart of both subgenres, but it is expressed in very different ways in each. While the urban high school films highlight the hard work and self-sufficiency of utilitarian individualism, the suburban high school films emphasize the identity formation and freedom of expressive individualism. The differences between these two subgenres are the result of the ways in which American culture makes sense of adolescents from different social classes. When poor students are represented on screen, Hollywood portrays utilitarian individualism as their key out of the culture of poverty. When middle-class students are represented, Hollywood portrays expressive individualism as their key out of the culture of popularity and conformity.

This chapter will show that while adults are nearly always the heroes in the urban school films, they are absent from or are antagonists in the suburban school films. Also, in dramatic contrast to the urban school films, the suburban school films are only tangentially related to the school *as a school*. That is, in the suburban school films the high schools are not recognized primarily as places of learning. In fact, academic content plays almost no role in the suburban school films, but it is the central feature of nearly all the urban school films.[3] While the students in the urban school films must conform to middle-class values and adult authority in order to transcend the culture of poverty, I argue in this chapter that the students in the suburban school films must reject peer conformity and the authority of adults (teachers and parents) in order to realize and freely express their true individual identities.

Being a White Upper-Middle-Class Suburban Teenager Sucks

Consider the life of a teenager. You have parents and teachers telling you what to do. You have movies, magazines and TV telling you what to do. But you know what you have to do. Your job, your purpose, is to get accepted, get a girlfriend and think up something great to do for the rest of your life.

—"Hard Harry" in *Pump Up the Volume*

Oh, the life of a middle-class suburban teenager! As Hard Harry notes, American teens are oppressed by their high school, by their families, by the popular culture, by pressures to conform, and by career expectations. The middle-class suburban teenager in the United States has no freedom and no voice. Hard Harry (meek high school student Mark Hunter by day and raunchy pirate radio DJ by night) is not concerned about developing positive study habits, earning good grades, achieving high SAT scores, or making college plans. Instead, he devotes his energies to saving the soul of the American teenager from the stultifying effects of adult society. He, like J. D. Salinger's adolescent hero Holden Caulfield, desperately wants to be the "catcher in the rye"—to help prevent adolescents from growing up, selling out, and becoming phonies. Hard Harry epitomizes the independent hero of the suburban high school film.

In his radio broadcasts to the students of Hubert Humphrey High School, an orderly, bland, and mostly white suburban high school with a good academic reputation and the highest SAT scores in Arizona, Hard Harry rages against the generation of his parents (the baby boomers), against suburbia, against the teachers and guidance counselors at the school, and against the middle-class conformity he sees as the oppression his generation must overcome. His parents are ex-hippies from the 1960s, and his father is now a school commissioner in the local district. Having moved from town to town as his father moved up the professional ranks, Harry is bitter that his parents sold out in pursuit of conventionally defined success. His parents, however, are unaware of his rage. Mark Hunter is a quiet, shy, and studious boy who gets good grades and lacks much of a social life. His parents are worried that he is not making friends at his new school, but he brushes aside their attempts to help: "The deal is I get decent grades and you guys leave me alone."

Despite Mark Hunter's quiet and obedient demeanor, Hard Harry is an angry and loquacious spokesperson for all the disaffected youth at his school. He encourages his adolescent listeners to throw off the shackles of their repression at home and school, to stand up to authority, to rebel, to deviate from the norm, to find their true identity, and to turn their anger, boredom, frustration, and depression into creative self-expression. Unfortunately, one of his listeners, a depressed, lonely, and nerdy teenage boy, commits suicide shortly after calling in to Harry's radio show. The school authorities, in particular the rigid principal, Miss Cresswood, blame the suicide on Harry's illegal broadcasts. The Federal Communications Commission (FCC) begins an investigation to find him and shut down his pirate radio broadcasts. The angry and scared parents in the community meet with school officials to discuss the threat that Harry poses to their children. Meanwhile, the students increasingly look to Harry as their hero and role model.

While Harry speaks directly to the social outcasts at the school (the assortment of nerds, social misfits, low achievers, and punks that occupies the margins of many schools) he also finds a receptive audience in the students at the center of the school—the popular and high-achieving students. Paige Woodward is one of the beautiful, popular, and high-achieving girls at Hubert Humphrey High School. She, too, however, suffers under the oppression of conformity enforced by the pressure of parents, peers, and the school. While popular and successful, she is never truly happy. Yet she suffers in silence until Harry's broadcasts inspire her to reject the expectations everyone has of her and to just be herself. In the community meeting to address the parental concerns about Harry's broadcasts, Paige defends Harry: "He's trying to tell you there is something wrong with this school. We are all really scared to be who we really are. I'm not perfect . . . inside I'm screaming!"

The authorities eventually catch up to Harry. As the FCC zeroes in to shut down Harry's broadcast, he urges his listeners not to let the authorities win. He pleads with the youth of his generation not to give up, not to commit suicide: "High school is the bottom. Being a teenager sucks. But that's the point. Surviving it is the whole point. Quitting is not going to make you stronger. Living will!" As Hard Harry's career as a pirate DJ nears its end, he urges others to pick up his mantle and to exercise freedom of speech. He urges students to "find your voice and use it!"

Harry is the hero of the movie, but he is no martyr. Upon his arrest it is learned that Principal Cresswood was illegally expelling the "losers and troublemakers" in order to maintain the school's high scores on the Scholastic Aptitude Test. Harry's crusade reveals that the narrow middle-class focus on academic achievement is soulless and corrupt. Even Harry's school commissioner father is disgusted and promises to have the principal fired. And Harry (now simply Mark Hunter) finally, and ironically, ends up with a girlfriend.

In the same vein as *Pump Up the Volume*, 2007's *Charlie Bartlett* explores the themes of teenage angst and the inability of adults to address their problems. Charlie Bartlett is a privileged kid who keeps getting kicked out of private schools. He finally has no choice but to attend the local suburban public school. Charlie has a hard time fitting in at the new school. His dress and demeanor are out of the norm, and he's harassed and picked on. The school bully beats him up in the bathroom. Because of his difficulties fitting in, Charlie goes to a therapist who prescribes Ritalin to help him with his "concentration problems." Charlie knows that he is not the only one with feelings of insecurity, doubt, and fear. He has a recurrent fantasy that he is speaking to a large crowd of teenagers:

> If there is one thing I want you to walk away with tonight it's that the sky is the limit! For those of you with troubles, for those of you feeling scared or confused or angry—Remember, you are not alone!

In contrast to Charlie's insights about adolescents, the principal of the school does not understand the needs of his students. He is an alcoholic who is ineffectual in a job that he hates. Rather than seeking to understand the students, he announces that the district will be installing security cameras in the student lounge, the one area of campus where the students have some freedom and autonomy. The students begin circulating a petition to oppose the cameras. However, the political action against the cameras is not the primary focus of the film. Instead, Charlie partners with the school bully to sell to students the drugs that he has been prescribed by his therapist. Soon, students from every clique are coming to Charlie seeking prescriptions for anxiety, depression, and obsessive-compulsive behaviors. More importantly, Charlie becomes a therapist to these students—talking to them about their problems in his "office," the boy's bathroom. Only Charlie, not their parents, teachers, or counselors, can understand their problems and help them.

One of the students under the psychiatric "care" of Charlie is Kip, a depressed and lonely young man. Kip attempts suicide with an overdose of the sedatives prescribed by Charlie. As in *Pump Up the Volume*, Charlie is blamed for Kip's attempted suicide. But Charlie knows that he is not the problem—there is an undercurrent of dissatisfaction at the school, and he has the power to help these kids. As he tells the principal, "I'm helping these kids. Nobody else is listening to them." Nevertheless, Charlie agrees to stop selling the drugs to students, but continues to conduct therapy sessions with them in the bathroom. He takes a particular interest in Kip and helps Kip to express his feelings in a more productive way. Charlie convinces the principal to allow Kip to produce a play he's writing, "Hell Comes with Your Own Locker." It's a play, as Kip says, "about us and the way we see things."

Meanwhile, the students opposed to the security cameras in the student lounge stage a protest rally. The students look to Charlie for guidance and inspiration. Charlie addresses the crowd:

> You guys don't need me. . . . [Y]ou think I'm any less screwed up than you are? I get up every morning and I look in the mirror and I try and figure out just where I fit in. And I draw a complete blank. You guys are looking to me to tell you what to do? You need to stop listening to me. Stop listening to people telling you who you should be. Stop listening to the people telling you that you aren't good enough to do the things you want to do.

A chant of "Charlie, Charlie" erupts from the crowd as the kids begin to destroy the security cameras. As a result of his inability to control his school, the principal is fired by the superintendent. Charlie and the drunk principal have a confrontation at the principal's house, where, ultimately, they have a heart-to-heart discussion and attend Kip's play together. Charlie, as confused and screwed up as he is, is the hero of the film. The film ends not with Charlie getting into college, but with him getting a summer internship at a psychiatric institute.

In contrast to the problems of the students in the urban school films—underfunded schools, drug dealing, violence, academic failure, dropping out, racism, poverty, unemployment, homelessness, prison, death, and so on—the teen angst of the suburban school students, as illustrated in *Pump Up the Volume* and *Charlie Bartlett*, appears to be nothing but the cries of spoiled children who live comfortable lives, have bright futures, but chafe under the vaguely defined "oppression" of their parents and teachers. They are rebels without much of a cause.

Compared with the urban high school films discussed in the previous chapter, *Pump Up the Volume* and *Charlie Bartlett* are very different sorts of high school films. But they are not anomalies. They conveniently summarize the major themes of most of the films based in middle-class suburban high schools. The heroes are independent and free-thinking students. The antagonists are narrow-minded achievement-oriented adults (and often narrow-minded popular students). Obedience to authority and conformity to peer pressure are criticized. Mild disobedience and creative self-expression are rewarded. Individualism is celebrated, but it is not utilitarian independence from poverty that defines it, as in the urban school films. Rather, it is an independence from peer pressure and the constraints of adult authority that allows students to express their true identities.

As the next section demonstrates, the expressive individualism of the middle-class suburban school film rejects the characters who offered such salvation in the urban school films—the teachers. While the middle-class teachers offered utilitarian salvation to the urban poor, in the suburban school films these cowboys wear black hats. Teachers are once again representatives of middle-class American culture, but this time that culture offers not salvation, but oppression. It is up to the student-hero (the expressive individual) to defeat this symbol of conventional, utilitarian, and conformist authority.

Middle-Class Teachers as Antagonists

Far from representing the middle-class civility and values of the urban school teacher-heroes, teachers are depicted in many of the suburban school films as, at best, benign fools or, at worst, ruthless enemies. As representatives of a stale and oppressive middle-class future of corporate, bureaucratic, and suburban conformity, the middle-class teachers in the suburban school films are definitely *not* characters to be emulated.

Rather than offering needed assistance to the students, the teachers in the suburban school films (to the extent to which teachers are featured at all) are often depicted as a direct threat to the students. In contrast to the songs that refer to the urban high school students as dangerous jungle animals, the film sound tracks to *Disturbing Behavior* and *The Faculty* feature Pink Floyd's song of adolescent rebellion, "Another Brick in the Wall (Part II)," with its evocative lyrics, "We don't need no education . . . teachers, leave them kids alone!" The suburban school films suggest that the teachers are dangerous, not the students. There are several nefarious authority figures in the suburban school films. For instance, in *Easy A* the school counselor is having an affair with a student and refuses to come to the aid of another student for fear it will reveal her own moral failings. The coach of the women's soccer team in *Palo Alto* sleeps with one of his players. Students in the suburban school films do not work with an adult authority figure in order to achieve academic goals. Instead, the students must form their adult identities *in opposition to* adult figures. One of the most explicit examples is *Teaching Mrs. Tingle*.

Far removed from the teacher-hero role in the urban school films, Mrs. Tingle is a mean-spirited, bitter, and terrifying presence in her history classroom. She routinely insults and humiliates her students, grades them harshly, and delights in the abuse of her power. Leigh Ann Watson is a bright lower-middle-class student from a single-parent home. She is one of the best students in school, but she has not been able to impress the stubborn Mrs. Tingle. In order to escape her small town and to attend college, Leigh Ann is in desperate need of an academic scholarship. To win the scholarship, she needs to graduate first in her class. All that stands in her way is Mrs. Tingle. Leigh Ann's final history project, an impressively detailed re-creation of a diary of a seventeenth-century accused Salem witch, is assessed brutally by Mrs. Tingle, who favors the sycophantic Trudie (Leigh Ann's academic rival). Leigh Ann's hopes for a college education seem dashed. Meanwhile, Luke, an academically challenged burnout, steals a copy of Mrs. Tingle's final exam and offers it to Leigh Ann. Leigh Ann refuses to accept the exam, but Luke stuffs it into her backpack just before Mrs. Tingle walks into the room. Mrs. Tingle discovers the exam and seems pleased to have caught the "smartest girl in school" cheating.

In order to help set things straight, Luke, Leigh Ann, and Leigh Ann's best friend, Jo Lynn, go to Mrs. Tingle's house that night to plead on Leigh Ann's behalf. Nevertheless, Mrs. Tingle has no sympathy for Leigh Ann. In desperation, Luke raises a crossbow (the final history project of another student in class) to threaten Mrs. Tingle. He yells, "Time to teach Tingle a lesson. . . . You can't keep treating people the way you do!" Mrs. Tingle struggles with Luke, the crossbow drops, and Jo Lynn picks it up and fires it at Mrs. Tingle, who is knocked unconscious. The three students then tie Mrs. Tingle to her bed, conspire to frame her in a sex scandal, and plan to use the incriminating photographs as blackmail against her. Mrs. Tingle spends most of the movie tied up as she and her student captors wage psychological warfare on each other.

Eventually, Leigh Ann finds Mrs. Tingle's grade book and changes Trudie's final grade to a B and her own to an A. She delivers the grade book to the counselor's office, and the grades are posted. When Trudie sees the grades, she is incredulous about her B. Meanwhile, Mrs. Tingle manages to escape from the bed and ties Luke to the bedposts. After a violent struggle with Leigh Ann, Mrs. Tingle attempts to kill her with the crossbow. Rather than hitting Leigh Ann, however, Mrs. Tingle accidentally shoots Trudie, who had come to Mrs. Tingle's house to complain about her B in history. As a result of this violent outburst, the principal fires Mrs. Tingle. Mrs. Tingle finally learns her lesson.

Ultimately, none of the students are punished for their behavior. Leigh Ann graduates first in her class and wins the academic scholarship that allows her to attend college. Assaulting your teacher, holding her captive, and blackmailing her seem to have the desired effect. Contrasted with the tragic outcome for the students who held a policeman hostage in the urban school film *Light It Up*, the happy ending of *Teaching Mrs. Tingle* speaks volumes about Hollywood's representation of urban and suburban school students.

The Evil High School Football Coach

In addition to the occasional rogue history teacher, high school football coaches are often portrayed as antagonists in the suburban school films (see *Lucas, All the Right Moves, Dazed and Confused, Varsity Blues*, and, to a certain extent, *Friday Night Lights*[4]). Rather than an adult figure who cares for the players and mentors them into adulthood, the typical coach in the suburban school film is a cruel and heartless man (frustrated by his own limitations in life) who crushes the spirit of his players and is ultimately defeated by a heroic student unafraid to stand up for himself. (*Remember the Titans* and *Radio*, which play more like urban school films with a coach-hero, are exceptions to this trend.) These high school football films reject adult authority and celebrate the personal growth of adolescents as they learn to express their emerging adult identities.

Varsity Blues depicts football as a sacred activity that binds together a small Texas town and its high school.[5] The quarterback is revered around town as a larger-than-life hero (he even has his own billboard), the players are granted many entitlements as local celebrities, the players' fathers live vicariously through their sons, and the coach is an obnoxious egotist who cares only about winning. Despite the American middle-class respect for tradition, authority, adherence to rules, and achievement, *Varsity Blues* suggests that sometimes you have to disobey authority, break with tradition, learn that winning is not everything that matters, and, as the promotional material for the film states, "make your own rules."

Moxon (Mox) is the brainy backup quarterback for the West Canaan Coyotes under the leadership of Coach Bud Kilmer, a local legend who has twenty-two district championships under his belt. Disliked by the coach, Mox rides the bench for most of the season with little interest in the game. (During one game he surreptitiously reads Kurt Vonnegut's *Slaughterhouse Five*, the paperback slipped within his football playbook.) His father, like most of the players' fathers, is a former Coyote who is obsessed with football and with his son's performance on the field. He asks Mox to pray for playing time each week. Mox, however, couldn't care any less about playing in the games. He is counting down the last games of the season and anxiously awaiting a hoped-for acceptance to Brown University. Mox loves football for the purity of the game, but he despises what it has become—a system that values winning at any cost and that eats up players and spits them out without regard for their best interests. He hates that football means more to the residents of West Canaan than it means to the players. And he hates that Coach Kilmer cares only for his own glory.

Coach Kilmer is a hard-nosed coach who demands the strict obedience of his players and ruthlessness on the field. "Don't show weakness!" he exclaims to his players. "Inflict pain!" He inflicts his own pain upon the players by coercing them to play hurt. Despite several concussions, he insists that Billy Bob continue to play as a key offensive lineman. Lance Harbor, the star quarterback with an athletic scholarship waiting for him at Florida State, has an injured knee. Rather than letting his knee heal, however, Coach Kilmer has been injecting painkillers to keep Lance playing. Coach Kilmer is so driven to win that he disregards the long-term health consequences to Lance. Inevitably, Lance's knee is badly damaged in a game (jeopardizing his athletic scholarship to Florida State and his future football career). With Lance sidelined, Mox is required to play in his place. Mox plays well and wins game after game, although he does so by calling his own plays and not Coach Kilmer's. Kilmer, however, threatens to tamper with Mox's transcripts and to block his academic scholarship to Brown if he doesn't obey.

In the game that will decide the district championship, the running back Wendell injures his leg. At halftime Coach Kilmer tells the trainer to do anything he can to get Wendell back in the game. Mox is livid that Kilmer would sacrifice Wendell's health for Kilmer's glory. Mox stands up to Kilmer and threatens to quit playing if Wendell receives the painkiller. The rest of the players rally around Mox. "The only way we are going back on that field is without you," says Mox. Coach Kilmer, in humiliation, leaves the locker room and does not return for the second half of one of the most important games of his career. Meanwhile, inspired by Mox's locker room speech that asks them to play "like gods" for the love of the game, the players return to the field. Without Coach Kilmer, the team wins in dramatic fashion. It is the last football game that Mox ever plays. He receives the academic scholarship and enrolls in Brown University in the fall. The football legend Kilmer, thoroughly defeated, never coaches football again.

As the student-hero, Mox rejects adult authority, rebels against the expectations that his parents and the rest of town have of him, and breaks free from the shackles of the school to emerge as an independent hero. However, rather than being punished for his mutiny, Mox is rewarded for it. Under Mox's leadership the team triumphs, independent from school authority. The triumph, however, is the winning of the championship. Winning, Coach Kilmer's goal, is also the goal of the players. The triumph is not in their rejection of Kilmer, but in their winning without him. While poor urban school students need a middle-class adult as a guide in order to achieve their goals, middle-class suburban students (and, in this case, middle-class rural students) achieve their goals independently. Rather than challenging the status quo, however, these goals are often consistent with the goals the rejected adult authorities had for these students in the first place. The middle-class youth don't invent new goals. Rather, they travel their own path to achieve conventional ones. In the words of sociologist Robert Merton, these suburban school student-heroes are "innovators"—deviants who accept culturally defined goals, but pursue unconventional paths to achieve them.[6]

Adults as Fools

Adults are not antagonists in every suburban school film. They are often simply absent. The personal development of teens in many suburban school films often *requires* the absence of adults—just think of the countless films that depict adolescent identity formation at parties, once the parents have left town (*Project X, Superbad, Risky Business, Can't Hardly Wait,* and so on). In many cases, however, adults play the fool. Adults are often amusing secondary characters who suffer humiliation as the smooth-operating adolescents run circles around them. Whether adults are absent, antagonists, or fools, however, the resulting message is the same: Adults are not required for middle-class suburban school students to discover their identity.

In *Ferris Bueller's Day Off,* Ferris Bueller is a confident, charming, and charismatic upper-middle-class high school senior who, from time to time, takes a day off from school because, as he says, "life moves pretty fast. If you don't stop and look around once and a while, you could miss it." Ferris is not about to miss out on life. And life, apparently, does not happen in high school, which, according to Ferris, is "a little childish and stupid." The only two teachers depicted in the film deliver their lectures in such a monotonous drone that it takes all the life out of their subjects and makes the school day nearly unendurable for the bored-to-death students. Ferris, however, is loved by nearly everyone—his parents, all the students and teachers in the school, and many others in the community at large. He is a bit of an operator at the school (he hacks into the school computer to change his record, he can get kids out of summer school, etc.), but he never gets caught. His sister, however, is frustrated that everyone is fooled by Ferris's charms.

Ferris is pushing the limits on his school absences (nine so far in his final semester). One morning Ferris fools his gullible parents into believing he is sick. They forbid him to attend school, ignoring his mock protestations that he needs to attend school because it is an investment in his future: "I want to go to a good college so I can have a fruitful life." It is clear through his sarcasm that Ferris does not believe that his high school experiences will play any role in his future success, of which he has little doubt.

Mr. Rooney, the dean of students, is skeptical of Ferris's illness. Fed up with the student's cons, he makes it his mission to reveal Ferris as the "dangerous character" that he is. Mr. Rooney complains to his secretary that Ferris "jeopardizes my ability to effectively govern the student body." At each step of the way, however, Ferris thwarts Mr. Rooney's attempts to catch him.

Ferris orchestrates the release of his girlfriend from school (by faking the death of her grandmother) and convinces his neurotic friend Cameron to "borrow" his father's 1961 Ferrari. Ferris and his friends make the most of their day off. They go to the top of the Sears Tower and gaze out at the city. They observe the manic gestures of the traders at the Chicago Board of Trade. They con their way into a reservation for lunch at an exclusive French restaurant. They attend a Cubs game (where Ferris catches a foul ball). They lovingly absorb the masterpieces at the Art Institute of Chicago. They watch the German American Day parade (and Ferris takes center stage on one of the floats). Meanwhile, Mr. Rooney hunts the city for Ferris.

While Mr. Rooney searches for him unsuccessfully at the teen-filled video arcade of a local pizza parlor, Ferris and his friends are partaking in very adult (and upper-middle-class) activities in fancy restaurants, art museums, skyscrapers, expensive cars, and financial markets. Ferris and his friends will soon be successful upper-middle-class adults, but on this day off from high school they are simply rehearsing for that inevitability. While they act like adults with ease and confidence, however, Mr. Rooney acts like a childish fool. Mr. Rooney plays the bumbling slapstick fool to Ferris's cool and controlled hero. In the course of searching for Ferris, Mr. Rooney suffers the indignities of soda spit in his face, an attack by a dog, the loss of a shoe in a puddle of mud, ripped pants, a kick to the face, a towed car, and a lost wallet. Ferris, on the other hand, escapes all consequences for his faked illness, lies to his parents, absence from school, and the eventual destruction of the priceless Ferrari.

After leaving the pizza parlor, Mr. Rooney goes to Ferris's home, drugs their attack dog, breaks in, and is assaulted by Ferris's startled sister. Injured and humiliated, Mr. Rooney waits outside the home for Ferris's return from truancy. Meanwhile, on an adventure of her own, Ferris's long-suffering sister is also struggling to prove that Ferris is conning his parents. Ferris races home to beat his parents' return from work, only to find Mr. Rooney waiting at the door. Ferris's sister, inside the house, faces a choice either to let Ferris be caught and punished by Mr. Rooney or to let him in the house before his parents learn of his ruse. Almost incredibly (perhaps because of her anger at Mr. Rooney's corrupt authority), Ferris's sister allies with Ferris and lets him off the hook at the last minute. Score one for the adolescents. All the adults are either fooled or defeated in humiliation. Without passion, soul, or wisdom, the adults are mere pawns in Ferris's game. Ferris is the untarnished adolescent hero whose confidence and charm transcend the limitations of his youth. In part, Ferris's convincing success is because of the talents of the actor who portrayed him, Matthew Broderick. In an ironic but rather predictable turn of cinematic events, however, thirteen years after *Ferris Bueller's Day Off* Matthew Broderick played the role of the bumbling, foolish, and humiliated teacher with a student nemesis in the 1999 suburban school film *Election*.

The Irrelevance of Academics in the Suburban School Films

Since teachers are often absent, antagonists, or fools, it is not surprising that academic achievement does not figure prominently in suburban school films. While academic achievement is offered as a solution to the problems facing the students in the urban school films, academic achievement is ignored, criticized, or even depicted as dangerous to the students in the suburban school films. For most of the suburban school films the school is central to the plot, but primarily as a social space within which the drama of teen angst is played out. The dramatic questions in the suburban school films are not about passing or failing, graduating or not graduating, going to college or not going to college.[7] The students in the suburban high school films may do well in school or they may do poorly in school, but it matters very little to the story. In either case, the students don't seem to care about learning or academic achievement. While disinterest in school was enough to drive the adult characters of the urban school films into heroic action, it raises very little notice in the suburban school films.

Whether it is Ferris Bueller's wildly successful efforts to avoid class during a "day off" from his suburban Chicago high school, the conspicuous absence of the classroom in *The Breakfast Club*, Cher's shameless bargaining with her gullible teachers for higher grades in *Clueless*, Hard Harry's disgust with the hypocrisy of the school in *Pump Up the Volume*, Jeffrey Spicolli's amused contempt for Mr. Hand's history class in *Fast Times at Ridgemont High*, the obsessive focus on parties at the expense of studies in *Project X* and *Superbad*, or the angry and bitter resentment of school by nearly all of the students in *Rock and Roll High School*, academic matters are consistently downplayed in these films.

Unlike the students in the urban school films, the middle-class students in the suburban school films tend to take their education for granted. These students attend schools with plenty of resources, have parents who have been to college, and have peers who are headed to college as well. These characters know they will likely graduate from high school, attend college, and at least reproduce their parents' middle-class status. The rough social trajectory of their lives has essentially been predetermined, independent of their effort in school. They merely need to go through the motions. Therefore, the education of the suburban school students is not a central feature of the plot in these films. What matters most in these films is not academic achievement, but the achievement of one's independent identity.

For instance, in *She's All That* Zach is the student body president, a star athlete, and the most popular guy in school. He is apparently a gifted student as well (he has the fourth highest grade point average in his class), although that part of his life is never depicted on screen. He has been accepted to Yale, Harvard, and Dartmouth colleges. But Zach has problems. His dad, a wealthy Dartmouth alumnus, is putting pressure on him to choose Dartmouth: "[My dad says] pick a college, Zach. Pick a future. But what he's really saying is pick *my* college. Pick *my* future." Zach, however, finally wants to make his own decisions in life, to be independent. While most of the film tells the familiar story of the rich and beautiful popular student falling unexpectedly in love with the lower-middle-class or working-class rebel or oddball (see also *Pretty in Pink, The Breakfast Club, Say Anything, Can't Buy Me Love, Some Kind of Wonderful, Cry Baby, 10 Things I Hate About You, Crazy/Beautiful, A Cinderella Story,* and *Prom*), Zach is tortured throughout the film by the decision of which elite private college to attend. Only in this context can his final decision to choose Yale over Dartmouth be seen as an act of independence and rebellion.

Zach's acceptance to Yale University is never legitimated for the audience. Any schoolwork or learning that justifies acceptance at such competitive colleges takes place backstage, out of the audience's view. Even though schoolwork plays no role in the plot, the last scene of the movie takes place at graduation. While participation in graduation was an achievement in and of itself for the students in the urban school films, for Zach participation takes on an entirely different meaning.

Expressing his newly discovered individuality (and making good on a bet), he accepts his diploma in the nude—his individuality and self-confidence on view for all.

Similarly, in *10 Things I Hate About You* Kat is an intelligent, beautiful, and angry young woman who desperately tries not to live up to others' expectations of her. She charts her own path, even if that means the loss of popularity at school. She does not date boys and she does not seek the popularity that her peers, including her sister, value so highly. The focus of the movie is Kat's efforts to assert her independence from her father. She must choose between two high-status colleges—Sarah Lawrence (her first choice) and the University of Washington (her medical doctor dad's alma mater and preferred choice). As in *She's All That*, the battle between her and her father about which school she will attend becomes symbolic of her developing adult identity. The academic path she traveled to be in a position to choose between such elite colleges, however, is never revealed to the audience. Apparently, Kat's upper-middle-class home life and her experiences in a high-quality Seattle public high school are enough for the audience to believe that she could follow in the successful professional footsteps of her father. In an act of adolescent "rebellion" and identity formation, however, she will do so at Sarah Lawrence and not at the University of Washington.

If there is any action directly related to academic achievement in the suburban school films, it is usually heroic action by students *against* the achievement ideology and against the authorities of the school. In a stunning reversal of the messages conveyed in the urban school films, Hollywood can be quite critical of academic achievement when the plot takes place in a middle-class suburban high school. For instance, in *Disturbing Behavior* conformity to the expectations of the school (academic achievement, obedience to adult authority, and joining the "right" crowd) is depicted as a serious threat to individuality and adolescent freedom. The adult authorities of the school and the "successful" mainstream students are defeated by the heroic actions of an unlikely collection of disobedient students who reject the authority of the school and resist the pressure to conform to the expectations of their teachers, parents, or peers.

The Threat of Academic Achievement

In *Disturbing Behavior* something is very wrong at Cradle Bay High School. It is a typical suburban high school in an upper-middle-class community in Washington State. It is populated by a typical grouping of student cliques—the "geeks," the "freaks," the "burnouts," and a special group called the Blue Ribbons. The Blue Ribbons are the jocks and the academic achievers of the school. They have high self-esteem, they identify with the school, they work hard, they are polite to others, they are respectful of adults, they are accomplished athletes and students, they are civic minded, and they are involved in school activities. They hang out innocently at the yogurt shop, dress modestly, and stay out of trouble.

While few teachers are featured in the film, the school psychologist is a prominent character. He is the supervisor of this elite club. The teachers and administrators *love* the Blue Ribbons. Parents, too, love the Blue Ribbons, and many try to get their children to join the club. The obedience, conformity, and high achievement that the club seems to foster are seen by most parents and school personnel as key to overcoming adolescent rebellion, drug use, and poor academic performance. Imagine how the urban school films would celebrate such a club!

And yet there is something not quite right about the Blue Ribbons. While they seem to be the ideal students, they are like robots. They dress alike, act alike, and, oddly, they explode in bursts of rage and violence from time to time. Their targets, however, are usually the burnouts of the school. These occasional transgressions are generally dismissed by school authorities. What is even more odd, however, is that many of the burnouts of the school become mysteriously converted to the Blue Ribbons—they suddenly become model students. Soon most of the school is filled with obedient high achievers. Rather than being celebrated, however, this sudden transformation from adolescent miscreant to honor student is a cause for grave concern. What is at stake is the individuality of the students. As the promotional material for the video version of the film states:

> "Achieve, be excellent . . . and be afraid." When the esteemed Blue Ribbon club of Cradle Bay High takes its slogans too far, things in the small coastal town begin to go wrong. Newcomer Steve Clark finds fast allies in Gavin, an overly imaginative paranoid and Rachel, a "bad girl" with a razor-sharp tongue and a body to match. But when some "dark sinister force" begins turning the school's curricularly challenged into the soulless, academic elite, these three "outsiders" join in a desperate, dizzying race to avoid becoming insiders—and losing their individuality forever.[8]

The only ones who are worried about such "strange" behavior of peer conformity and academic achievement, however, are the remaining burnouts and rebels at the school. The parents, teachers, and administrators are more than happy to see the troubled students finally get their acts together, join school activities, and apply themselves academically. The only adult character to suspect that something is terribly wrong with the Blue Ribbons is the school janitor. (While in the urban school films a student who aspired to be a janitor would be resoundingly criticized, it is not uncommon for school janitors to be the wisest and most admired adult characters in the suburban school films; see also *The Breakfast Club, 17 Again,* and *Not Another Teen Movie*.) Most of the Blue Ribbons, however, dismiss the janitor as a worthless laborer. His concerns are not taken at all seriously, except by the student-hero Steve Clark.

As a moody adolescent who is having a tough time adjusting to his new life in Cradle Bay, Steve Clark resists the efforts by his parents and the school psychologist to become a Blue Ribbon. As it turns out, he is right to be suspicious. The Blue Ribbons are a creation of the school psychologist, who implants computer chips into the students' eyes and brainwashes them to behave like perfect little students who never rebel, never question authority, never make mistakes, and never fail.

Unable to recruit Steve and his girlfriend voluntarily, the Blue Ribbons capture them and take them to the psychologist's clinic. As the psychologist tells Steve moments before he attempts to implant a computer chip into his eyes: "Adolescence is a mine field. But soon you'll be fully equipped to walk right through. . . . It's time to leave mediocrity behind." Steve and his girlfriend manage to escape from the clinic before the psychologist can implant the computer chips. They meet up with another uninfected student who is worried that they have already been brainwashed into Blue Ribbons. To be sure, he gives them a test—"What is the capital of North Dakota?" He is relieved when they don't know the answer. Their ignorance is a sure sign that they are not Blue Ribbons.

Meanwhile, the janitor has learned that a mechanical device that emits a high-pitched noise in order to repel rats also happens to torture the Blue Ribbons (because of a malfunction of their implanted computer chip). The janitor collects dozens of the devices, loads them into the back of his truck, turns them on, and drives to the psychologist's clinic, where the Blue Ribbons have gathered. The Blue Ribbons begin screaming in agony as the noise emitters disrupt their programming. They climb onto the truck to destroy the devices and the janitor sacrificially drives his truck over a cliff, killing them all.

All, that is, except one. One Blue Ribbon somehow survives. In the last scene of the film we see him again years later. He is training to become a teacher so that he can continue the psychologist's original project to implant the devices and change the behavior of disaffected and rebellious high school students. His teacher training takes him to a high school where Hollywood filmmakers just might approve of such behavior modification—an impoverished inner-city public high school.

In *Disturbing Behavior* (and many other suburban school films) academic success is the last thing on the minds of the student-heroes. Obedience to authority, conformity to the expectations of parents, teachers, and peers, and academic achievement clearly do *not* provide a solution to the problems in their lives. Rather, obedience, conformity, and academic achievement pose a direct threat to their identities.

There is also a fear among the characters in many of these movies that a narrow-minded focus on achievement prevents the fun and carefree enjoyment of life. For instance, In *Project X* Thomas's parents allow him to host a small party for his birthday while they are out of town. The father is not at all concerned about the party because Thomas, as he sees him, is "a loser," nerdy and unpopular. Nonetheless, the party grows out of control into epic proportions. Not only is the house destroyed, but much of the neighborhood is destroyed as well. Thomas's dad is angry, but not as angry as one would expect. In fact, his dad inquires about the party with a hint of pride:

Dad: Do you have any idea how much all of this will cost, Thomas? Your college fund is gone, I can tell you that. You had so much going for you and you just pissed it all away for one night? I just didn't think you had it in you.

Thomas: I know, I'm sorry I let you down.

Dad: No, I literally didn't think you had this in you. So how many people were here?

Thomas: 1,500. A couple thousand maybe. You should have seen it. It was awesome.

Thomas' academic and financial future is cast into doubt, but Thomas is proud of the party and his father is a little bit proud of his son, despite the damage. Had a low-income student in an urban high school film expressed pride at having sacrificed his financial and academic future by hosting a party that destroyed his parents' house, I doubt it would have been cast in a positive light! We have turned 180 degrees from the lessons of the urban school films.

If the students in the urban school films were to treat academic achievement with the disinterest or contempt expressed by the students in the suburban school films, they would be promptly kicked out of school (and out of the movies) and continue to suffer in their culture of poverty. The students in the suburban school films, however, are *rewarded* for such behavior. They win acclaim for their heroic action, they become popular in school, and they win the attention of their love interest. Furthermore, despite their lack of attention to academic matters, the middle-class suburban students tend to maintain their middle-class status.

American culture has very different conceptions of poor urban and middle-class suburban youth. Because of these different conceptions of adolescence and social class, the school plays a much different role in the urban and suburban school films. What middle-class American culture wants most for poor urban adolescents is a rejection of the culture of poverty and the attainment of a middle-class lifestyle and financial independence through hard work. Therefore, the school is central to this project of turning urban adolescents into responsible and gainfully employed adults. The occupational future of the "at risk" youth in the urban school films is in jeopardy if they do not abide by the lessons of their middle-class teachers.

On the other hand, because future gainful employment is generally assumed for the middle-class youth, what middle-class American culture wants most for the middle-class suburban adolescent is a stable and self-assured adult identity that is strong enough to resist peer pressure, thoughtless conformity, and self-destructive impulses. Since the ability of the students in the suburban school films to attain a middle-class lifestyle is rarely questioned (even when they reject the school), academic achievement is rarely a feature of the plot as it is in the urban school films.

Furthermore, the hostile attitude toward academic achievement in the suburban school films is representative of an ambivalence that middle-class Americans feel about utilitarian individualism. While there are cultural expectations that Americans should be rational, responsible, hardworking, and achievement-oriented, there is also a sense that the personal costs of taking such a narrow path to achievement can be too great. There is a fear that pursuing utilitarian individualism not only means that you sacrifice a carefree existence in the moment, but it jeopardizes your potential for happiness in the future as well. For instance, a geometry teacher in *The Spectacular Now* attempts to tutor the apathetic Sutter, a student with a D+ average in the class. "Don't you want to graduate?" he asks Sutter. Sutter responds, "I don't know. I'm just being honest with you. Everyone's telling me I've got to move on. I don't know what's so great about being an adult. Are *you* happy?" The teacher responds with silence.

Similarly, while not a high school film, 1967's classic film about cultural alienation, *The Graduate*, reflects this perspective beautifully. Ben, the recent college graduate in the film, confesses to his very conventional and financially successful father that he has doubts about what he should do next in life, "I'm just worried . . . about my future. I want it to be . . . different." It is not surprising, then, that in several of these suburban school films the heroes are dissatisfied middle-aged adults who, in one way or another, wish their lives were different. They are unhappy. They long to go back to high school in order to do it over again—to get it right this time by following their heart and being true to themselves and, hopefully, to avoid the problems they face in their middle-aged, middle-class lives.

The High School Do-Over: Getting a Second Chance to Find Yourself

There are a handful of suburban school films in which the adult characters express a longing to go back to high school. These characters, often caught up in the rat race, bogged down by family responsibilities, or filled with regret about how their lives have turned out, fantasize about a chance to go back and do it all over. It's hard to imagine any adult characters in the urban school films longing to return to their troubled high schools. While the major theme of the urban school films is to get *out* of high school, often in the suburban school films the theme is to *return* to high school. For instance, in *Friday Night Lights* a middle-aged man with a small child runs into a few of the local high school football players at a diner. He tells the boys, "You remember every minute of this. I'm telling you right now. You are only 17, but it goes fast. Don't waste a second of it. Before you know it [snaps fingers], it's done. Nothin' but babies and memories."

In *Napoleon Dynamite* Napoleon's naïve middle-aged Uncle Rico lives a sad existence—living out of his van and selling a variety of products door-to-door. He desperately wants to go back to high school to relive his glory days and to somehow reshape his future. He asks Napoleon's older brother, "Do you ever wish you could go back, with all the knowledge you have now?" He optimistically buys a "time machine" online only to be disappointed that it, like the products he sells, is a fraud. But in some of the movies time machines are not a hoax. Middle-aged characters, unsatisfied with some aspect of their lives, magically travel back to high school in *Peggy Sue Got Married, Touchback, Freaky Friday,* and *17 Again*. Middle-aged characters in other movies disguise themselves to go back to high school in *Never Been Kissed* and *21 Jump Street*. In most of these cases, the adult characters are searching for themselves in the past, eager to find out—and to correct—what is ailing them in the present.

In *17 Again* Mike O'Donnell is a high school basketball star with a beautiful girlfriend and a bright future. In his senior year of high school Mike has a chance to impress basketball scouts from major colleges in order to win an athletic scholarship. "My whole future is riding on this game," he says. However, his girlfriend approaches him before the game to tell him she is pregnant. Rattled by the news, he plays poorly and then leaves the court to be with his girlfriend. They marry and have a family, but Mike's life does not go as he had planned. He's unhappy as a salesperson for a pharmaceutical company and, much to his surprise, he's passed over for a promotion. He and his wife are separated, awaiting divorce proceedings, and he has a rocky relationship with his children. "I am extremely disappointed with my life," he laments.

He goes back to his old high school, where his children now attend, and runs into a mysterious old janitor who finds him staring nostalgically at old pictures of his high school basketball days. The janitor asks him if he would rather live in the past. "Of course I want to live in the past. It was better there," he answers. Later that day Mike is transformed into his seventeen-year-old self. He quickly is enamored by the change. "I'm going back to high school!" he says excitedly. "This is my chance to have my life over but to do it right."

He earns a spot on the basketball team again and hopes to impress the scouts so he can go to college and live his life over, without making the mistakes he made before. Presumably, those mistakes included abandoning basketball in order to marry his pregnant girlfriend. While in high school as a seventeen-year-old again he spends much of his time befriending and helping his son and daughter, who are both unaware of his identity. Befriending them entails spending some awkward moments with their mother, his soon-to-be ex-wife. The time spent with his wife, undercover as a seventeen-year-old, reminds him of what it is he loves about her. He realizes that she is not the reason he is unhappy and begins to regret the impending divorce. He attends the divorce hearing, as a seventeen-year-old, and reads a letter he says is written by the adult Mike O'Donnell: "I grew up and lost my way. And I blamed you for my failure."

The movie comes full circle with another big basketball game. Mike is the star. The scouts are in the audience. His wife, confused by the touching letter read by Mike at the divorce hearing, attends the basketball game. Faced with the same choice he had twenty years ago, he makes the same choice. He leaves the game to be with his wife. But this time he gives the ball to his son as he leaves the court. He says to his wife, "You are the best decision I ever made. I just forgot. . . . I thought I wanted a second chance at life, but I just want a second chance with you." He and his wife reunite and Mike gets a new job—as the high school basketball coach.

While Mike O'Donnell ultimately decides that he made the right choices in life, he has to go back in time to convince himself of that. While a seventeen-year-old again he is able to get the perspective on his life that he is unable to get as an adult. Stuck in a bad job and a bad marriage, the adult Mike O'Donnell is powerless either to make the necessary changes or to learn to live with his decisions. He must return to his youth in order to get back in touch with who he is and what he wants. He goes back in time not to change history, but to find himself. In order to fully realize and express his individual identity Mike O'Donnell must become a teenager. The adult Mike O'Donnell was too stuck in the utilitarian rat race and too hobbled by adult responsibilities to understand who he was. Released from those concerns, the seventeen-year-old Mike O'Donnell thrives.[9]

Middle-Class Conformity in American Culture

Don't you find it ridiculous that from day one they tell us to be unique. They tell us to be individuals. Then they give us a standardized test that makes us one faceless herd?

—Kyle in *The Perfect Score* (2004)

I suggest that these suburban school films reflect an American middle-class fear that conformity to the expectations of an achievement-oriented culture will eclipse the expressiveness and creativity of individuality. In the 1950s sociological classic *The Lonely Crowd* David Riesman warned against the new American cultural and psychological character developing in the ascendant "new" middle class of corporate managers and bureaucrats. Riesman worried that the "other-directed" character of the new middle class depends upon others for approval and guidance rather than looking inward and charting an autonomous course:

> What is common to all the other-directed people is that their contemporaries are the source of direction for the individual—either those known to him or those with whom he is indirectly acquainted, through friends and through the mass media.[10]

Similarly, C. Wright Mills wrote a withering critique of the new "white-collar" middle classes that were emerging as the dominant American social class in the postindustrial era. Mills argued that conformity is the hallmark of life in the corporate and bureaucratic world of employment. Unlike the earlier entrepreneur or farmer, the white-collar employee lives a drab life of suburban conformity and a lack of individuality:

> The twentieth-century white-collar man has never been independent as the farmer used to be, nor as hopeful of the main chance as the businessman. He is always somebody's man, the corporation's, the government's, the army's; and he is seen as the man who does not rise. The decline of the free entrepreneur and the rise of the dependent employee on the American scene has paralleled the decline of the independent individual and the rise of the little man in the American mind.[11]

Riesman and Mills shared a fear that such cultural trends brought on by the rise of the new middle class implied that Americans were becoming a different sort of people—less autonomous, less competent, and less free. A middle class that is dependent upon corporate bosses and bureaucratic rules, that is passionate only about their status vis-à-vis their middle-class neighbors, and that looks to others for approval and direction is a middle class in trouble. In other words, the new middle class is caught up in the "rat race," trapped against its will in the "red tape" of bureaucracy, and preoccupied with "keeping up with the Joneses." Such cultural clichés capture the middle-class existence that developed in the middle of the twentieth century. However, this is not a cultural critique relevant only to the 1950s. While the protest movements of the 1960s and 1970s encouraged the growth of nonconformity and the critical questioning of many middle-class values, the middle class in the 1980s and 1990s returned the national culture to values similar to those that were criticized by Mills and Riesman. For instance, a more recent cultural critic, Barbara Ehrenreich, notes that the middle-class "yuppies" of the 1980s, while they believed themselves to be unique individuals, unexpectedly found themselves to be conformists:

> But many in the middle-class could see some part of themselves, some emerging constellation of tastes (for coarse-grain mustard, linen suits, or frequent work-outs), and realize that they themselves had been labeled, caricatured, and fingered as part of some larger conformity emanating from beyond their individual will and judgment.[12]

While Mills bemoaned the possibility that the white-collar workers were content with such a life of conformity, that they were "cheerful robots," Riesman argued that the overwhelming psychological state of the new middle class was one of anxiety. Indeed, the cultural contradictions in the new middle class are enough to cause a severe case of diffuse anxiety. On the one hand, the spirit of American individualism and free expression remain cultural values, yet the work and domestic lives of the middle class seem to encourage conformity, obedience to authority, competition for status among peers, and the censorship of unpopular ideas.

I suggest that this anxious tension is still a problem facing today's middle class. Despite (or perhaps because of) the corporate rat race, the red tape of bureaucracy, and the quest to match the consumption of the Joneses, there is, among the middle class, a powerful underlying longing for independence, creative self-expression, and rebellion. In other words, there is also a tendency in American culture to express Riesman's "inner-directed" character type—one who has a strong sense of individuality, autonomy, and creativity. Perhaps this tension finds some measure of at least temporary resolution in entertainment, such as Hollywood films. The middle class can live vicariously through these films, films in which the middle-class heroes can shed their anxiety and express themselves freely without concern for their future. This fantasy diminishes the importance of academic achievement and professional success. As I show in the next chapter, this vicarious fantasy also challenges the importance of social popularity, conformity to peers, and obedience to authority. However, the ways in which the student heroes of the suburban school films accomplish their goals reveal contradictions about individualism in American culture.

Notes

1. Emerson, Ralph Waldo. 1883. "Self Reliance." In *Essays*. Boston: Houghton, Mifflin, and Co., pp. 51–52.
2. Thoreau, Henry David. 1960. *Walden*. New York: Signet, p. 39.
3. One of the few exceptions to this is *Bill and Ted's Excellent Adventure*. The plot revolves entirely around Bill and Ted's travels through time so that they can bring historical figures back to 1988 to help them with their oral history report.
4. The coach in *Friday Night Lights* is a more complex character with glints of humanity and compassion for his players. Yet, as with the other football coach characters, he has his moments of verbally abusing his players.
5. In many ways the film echoes Douglas Foley's observations about the symbolic role high school football plays in defining American culture. Foley argues that the "great American football ritual" symbolizes the ways in which Americans learn contradictory messages about race, class, and gender that are embedded in our culture. Foley, Douglas. 1990. *Learning Capitalist Culture: Deep in the Heart of Tejas*. Philadelphia: University of Pennsylvania Press. Merton, Robert. 1968. *Social Theory and Social Structure*. New York: Free Press.
6. Merton, *Social Theory and Social Structure*.
7. One notable exception is *The Perfect Score* (2004). The plot revolves around six high school seniors who break into the headquarters of the Educational Testing Service in order to steal the answers to the SAT exam. This is a rare suburban school film in that it acknowledges the importance of academic achievement. However, the movie does so by criticizing standardized testing and celebrating the creative deviance of middle-class students who find a way to beat the system. In their deviance, the students come to terms with their identities and discover what is truly important in their lives—and it turns out that the SAT is not one of those things. None of the six decides to use the stolen answers.
8. Quoted from the back of the 1998 MGM Home Entertainment VHS packaging for *Disturbing Behavior*.
9. *Peggy Sue Got Married* and *Touchback* are very similar to *17 Again*. In each case dissatisfied middle-aged characters returns to high school, intent to change the future, but ultimately learn, as reborn adolescents, who they really are and what they are meant to be. The characters return to the present, ready to face their lives with renewed energy and a positive attitude following the rediscovery of their expressive identities in their second adolescence.
10. Riesman, David, with Nathan Glazer and Reuel Denney. 1961. *The Lonely Crowd: A Study of the Changing American Character*. New Haven, CT: Yale University Press, p. 21.
11. Mills, C. Wright. 1956. *White Collar: The American Middle Classes*. New York: Oxford University Press, p. xii.
12. Ehrenreich, Barbara. 1989. *Fear of Falling: The Inner Life of the Middle Class*. New York: Harper Press, p. 238.

five

Students as Heroes
Expressing Oneself in a Culture of Conformity

One of our duties as teenagers is to occasionally piss off our parents.
—Charlie in *Charlie Bartlett*

You've got to do everything you can to blend in or decide not to care.
—Olive in *Easy A*

Look at me now, bitches! . . . My party is legendary!
—Thomas in *Project X*

Students as Heroes: The Possibilities of Youth

In contrast to the antagonistic and foolish roles that teachers and parents play in suburban school films, the students almost universally play the role of the hero. These student-heroes express themselves in opposition to the tyranny of the middle-aged and middle-class establishment. The endless possibilities of youth, creativity, and freedom are alive in the hearts of the student-heroes as they battle the forces of conformity, status hierarchy, and restrictive social conventions. The students are heroes when they discover and express their individuality regardless of what their parents, their school, or their friends expect of them.

In the 2011 movie *Prom* we see most elements of the typical suburban school film. It is two weeks before the Prom at Brookside High. The prom organizer, Nova, is an overachieving student who already has secured a full scholarship to Georgetown University. Of course, we never see evidence of her academic accomplishment. As we saw in the previous chapter, academic achievement is taken for granted. The focus of the movie is on Nova's growth as a young woman as she develops a relationship with a "rebellious" boy and as she stands up to her father.

Nova works feverishly to make the prom as perfect as possible. She sees the prom as a magical night in which all of the school's cliques come together and celebrate their time together as they prepare for the future. However, not everyone at school sees it the same way. Jesse Richter is a rebellious kid from a working-class family who dresses in black, rides a motorcycle, has long hair, and often gets into trouble at school. He thinks the prom is a silly tradition and ridicules Nova for taking it so seriously.

Principal Dunnan is an unlikable character who has a particular dislike for Jesse. After Jesse is absent from his last class of the day yet again, Principal Dunnan threatens him with the possibility of not graduating. He has nothing but contempt for Jesse and tells him so: "You and I both know it. You are going nowhere." After the prom decorations are destroyed in a fire, Principal Dunnan assigns Jesse to help Nova rebuild them. Neither Jesse nor Nova is happy about this turn of events. But Jesse complies because his graduation is contingent on his cooperation.

As they work together, however, they begin to get to know each other. Even though they belong to drastically different social groups at the school and seem to be on very different life paths, they begin to develop an admiration for each other. Jesse is impressed with Nova's many accomplishments. Nova is impressed that Jesse helps to care for his younger brother (that's why he often misses class).

Jesse and Nova break into a rival school to spy on its prom decorations. While this is expected behavior by Jesse, it's quite an unexpected deviation from the rules for Nova. A security guard spots them and they run, but are eventually caught. When Nova's dad comes to take her home he is furious that she is with Jesse. "That kid's a loser," he says. But he's wrong, and only Nova knows it. She can now see that Jesse has a heart of gold. As she tells Jesse, "A lot of people are wrong about you. And I was one of them."

Nova's dad, however, is determined to keep Jesse away from his daughter. He doesn't trust him. He believes that he will derail Nova's plans to go to Georgetown and undermine all that she has worked so hard for. He goes to Jesse and tells him to stay away from Nova. He tells Jesse that Nova has worked hard and achieved a lot and "she's in the home stretch now. And that's where you came in. Right at the end. . . . If you care about her . . . you won't be the thing that holds her back." Jesse gets the message. A part of him believes what others think of him—that he's a loser who is going nowhere. When he tells Nova this she responds, "None of that matters as long as you feel the same about me as I feel about you." He lies and says that he does not.

Devastated, Nova learns that her dad had a talk with Jesse and that is why Jesse has had a change of heart. She confronts her dad about it. He explains to Nova, "I didn't want him to ruin all the great things you had ahead of you." She replies, "I know you think you were doing what's best for me. But tonight could have been one of those great things." Nova, depressed, goes to the prom and goes through the motions, clearly unmoved by the "one special night." Meanwhile, Jesse's mom gives him a pep talk and encourages him to go after Nova. He dresses in a tuxedo and goes to find Nova at the prom. They meet up, dance, and kiss in a stereotypically magical prom moment. As happens often in suburban school films, love conquers all. At the end of the film Nova narrates the moral of the story, "Prom: a night when . . . maybe you find what you are looking for. Or maybe you just find yourself."

Prom nicely summarizes the ways in which youth are the heroes of the suburban school films. They aren't heroes because they get scholarships to Georgetown. Instead, they are heroes because they find themselves. Their journey is a journey to find and express their identities, independent of their family and school. More specifically, the heroes of the suburban school films are heroes

1. when they break down the social barriers of race or social class.
2. when they criticize and escape the culture of popularity at their high school.
3. when they stand up to parents and teachers and prevail as independent youth.

1. Breaking Down the Walls of Race and Class

A number of suburban school films depict students who cross the boundaries of race or class in the pursuit of romantic love (or, in the case of *Remember the Titans*, in the pursuit of friendship).[1] These films suggest that no social divide is strong enough to keep two adolescents from expressing their love for each other. These student-heroes transcend the barriers of the social world to express their true feelings, regardless of the social consequences. No film better represents this dynamic than *Pretty in Pink*.

Andie Walsh lives on the wrong side of the tracks. In fact, the train runs right by her house. Her mom left the family years ago, and her dad is unemployed. She attends Meadowbrook High, a large high school that serves the students of a very wealthy community. However, the school reserves some spaces for the working- and lower-middle-class kids on the other side of town. There is a severe social divide between the "richies" and the students who are bused to the school. At lunch the rich students hang out inside the school wearing clean, tailored, pressed, and bright preppy pastels. The kids from the wrong side of town hang out in the courtyard, smoke cigarettes, and wear grungy, baggy, and dark clothing. Andie and her working-class friends withstand abuse and ridicule from the wealthy students in the school.

Despite the social divide, Andie develops a crush on Blane, a rich guy who doesn't act as aloof as the other "richies." Blane's friend Steff, however, can't believe that Blane would stoop to date such a "mutant" as Andie. Andie's devoted friend Duckie (also from the wrong side of the tracks) has a secret crush on Andie. He is devastated that Andie would date Blane, whom he considers to be as conceited and selfish as the other rich students. On the night of Blane and Andie's first date, they attend a party at Steff's house. They are not received warmly. Blane's rich and snobby friends ridicule Andie and criticize Blane for bringing her into their social world. Frustrated, Andie and Blane leave the party and attend a club frequented by Andie's friends. Their reception at the club, however, is not friendly, either. Blane offers to drive Andie home, but she is ashamed to reveal to Blane the modesty of her house: "I *don't* want you to take me home. . . . I don't want you to see where I live!"

Despite her shame, he does drive her home. While dropping her off he surprises her by asking her to the prom (she had been waiting for *someone* to ask her). They kiss passionately before Andie goes inside to talk to her dad, who observed the kiss through the window. Despite her feelings for Blane, Andie is cautious about their ability to overcome the chasm between their social class positions. Andie's dad quizzes her when she enters the house:

Mr. Walsh: Who is this guy?

Andie: His name's Blane. He's a senior. He's so beautiful. Umm. He's a . . . richie.

Mr. Walsh: A whatie?

Andie: A richie. It's kind of stupid. It's just, his family has a lot of money.

Mr. Walsh: Is that a problem?

Andie: No. It's just weird. His friends have a lot of money. He has a lot of money. He drives a BMW. I am not really sure they can accept me.

Mr. Walsh: What does that mean? You like him. He likes you. What his friends think shouldn't make a difference.

Andie: Yeah, but it's not just his friends. It's my friends, too. It's everybody. I'm not real secure about it.

Mr. Walsh: So take the heat. . . . It's worth it.

Andie: Is it?

Mr. Walsh: Well, isn't it?

Thanks to the pep talk from her dad, Andie forges ahead with her emotional investment in the relationship with Blane. Blane, however, is getting more resistance from his friends. Steff gives Blane an ultimatum: "If you want your little piece of low-grade ass, fine. Take it. But if you do, you are not going to have a friend." Confused, Blane stops calling Andie and breaks off their date to the prom. Andie, however, is not about to let the rich snobs ruin her prom. She stitches together a homemade pink dress and goes to the prom by herself. Just before entering the dance she runs into the heartbroken Duckie, who is also attending alone. Happy to find each other, they pair up and enter the dance together. Blane, looking glum and sitting by himself, brightens when he sees Andie. As he goes to talk to her, the insufferable Steff intercepts him, but Blane finally stands up to Steff and follows his heart.

Blane apologizes to Andie and, in front of the long-suffering and lovesick Duckie, confesses his love for her: "I always believed in you. I just didn't believe in me. I love you. Always." Blane walks away and Andie is left speechless. Duckie, the poor sap, urges her to follow Blane and to take advantage of this romantic moment. "You're right." Duckie admits. "He's not like the others."

The movie ends happily ever after with Blane and Andie embracing in the parking lot. They are both depicted as heroes for dismissing the class-based concerns and prejudices of their friends and listening to their own hearts. The courage to express their feelings honestly despite the rigid social and economic barriers between them demonstrates that the power of individuals can overcome the obstacles of social class. It is worth noting that racial and class inequality only become issues in these suburban school films when they interfere with romantic attachments. Once the barriers of irrational prejudice and clannish balkanization are broken—once love prevails—the issues of race and class in the suburban school films disappear. As in the urban school films, Hollywood once again privileges individual-level solutions to social problems rather than addressing them structurally. This, too, is typical of American culture in general.

2. Overcoming the Culture of Popularity

I really think it's in my best interest if I went out with someone more popular.
—Beth in *Better Off Dead*

In addition to shattering the barriers of race and class, the students in the suburban school films are heroes when they attack the culture of popularity that governs the social organization of their schools. The resentment of a status hierarchy is a rich theme in these suburban school films. The social divide between the popular and the unpopular students is even more gaping than the social divide between different races and social classes. In these films the hierarchical organization and exclusivity of student cliques, the mindless conformity to the expectations of the "leading crowd,"[2] and the cruelty inflicted upon the less popular students are resoundingly criticized. The student antagonists of these films judge people according to their level of social popularity. The student-heroes demand that students be judged not by the social clique they belong to but by the content of their individual character. The less popular nerdy characters almost always prevail over the popular kids. Hollywood is telling us that there is hope for all—even the social misfits can find their voices and freely express their identities without fear of ridicule or marginalization. In *I Love You, Beth Cooper* the nerdy Denis prevails when he wins the affection of the beautiful and popular Beth Cooper. Beth Cooper, meanwhile, confesses that her days of power and privilege are over: "High School was great for me. I had a great, great ride. Now it's over. . . . [E]verything from here on out in my life is going to be ordinary." Perhaps the film that best represents this attack on the culture of popularity is the dark comedy *Heathers*.

The three most popular girls at Westerbrook High School are all named Heather. They are wealthy, they're snobby, and they rule the school. Their popular male counterparts are the football jocks Kurt and Ram. Veronica Sawyer is also a "Heather," although she has mixed feelings about her own popularity and the way it has separated her from her old friends. For instance, the Heathers ask Veronica to write a forged love letter to the fat and lonely Martha "Dumptruck." When Martha approaches the football player whose signature Veronica forged on the fake love note, she is humiliated in front of everyone in the lunchroom. Ashamed of herself, Veronica begins to wonder why she associates with such a cruel crowd.

Jason Dean (J.D.), a new student at the school, stands up to the harassment of Kurt and Ram. He pulls a gun on them in the lunchroom and fires blanks, scaring them nearly to death. Veronica takes an immediate liking to J.D., and the two of them begin a romance. J.D. is incredulous about the crowd with whom she associates. Veronica explains to J.D., "I don't really like my friends. . . . It's like they're people I work with and our job is being popular and shit." Increasingly frustrated with her friends and feeling trapped in the conformity to their expectations, Veronica begins to have fantasies of killing Heather #1. As she confesses to her diary, "Tomorrow I'll be kissing her aerobicized ass, but tonight let me dream of a world without Heather, a world where I am free."

J.D. and Veronica plot to make Heather #1 suffer. They break into her house the morning after a big party and concoct a hangover "cure" that will make her vomit. J.D. suggests giving her a mug of drain cleaner, which Veronica dismisses as a bad joke. Nevertheless, J.D. pours the poison into one mug as Veronica mixes milk and orange juice in another. Veronica mistakenly takes the poisoned mug up to Heather's room. Heather drinks the drain cleaner, collapses, and dies. To cover their crime, J.D. and Veronica compose a suicide note.

Heather's "suicide" becomes big news at the school, and she becomes even more popular in death. In the meantime, Kurt and Ram have been spreading lurid rumors about Veronica. Veronica and J.D. plot their revenge against the popular jocks. They plan to lure the two to a clearing in the woods, have them remove their clothes (under the impression that they are about to have sex with Veronica), shoot them with what Veronica thinks will be bullets that only stun them (when, in fact, J.D. knows they are lethal), and then plant a note framing them in a gay suicide pact. After unwittingly killing them, Veronica begins to develop a guilty conscience: "Dear diary, my teen angst bullshit has a body count. The most popular people in school are dead." She decides that her "Bonny and Clyde days are over" and she breaks up with J.D.

J.D., however, has a lust for killing his high school peers. In fact, he hatches a plan to kill all of the students in the school in a mass "suicide." After the death of Heather #1, J.D. convinces Heather #2 to take her place in the power structure of the school's social world. He blackmails her into starting a petition to gather the signatures of all the students in the high school (ostensibly to get a popular band to play at their prom). Heather #2 takes to her new role with relish. She wears in her hair Heather #1's red scrunchie, the symbol of social power and popularity. She also inherits Heather #1's cruelty. After Martha Dumptruck attempts, but fails, to kill herself by walking into auto traffic, Heather #2 jokes, "Just another case of a geek trying to imitate the popular people of the school and failing miserably."

J.D. plans to blow up the entire school and to frame it as a mass suicide, using the faked petition as a collective suicide note. (J.D.'s attempt to plant bombs in the school while wearing a black trench coat is eerily prescient of the Columbine tragedy.) As J.D. tells Veronica, "The only place different social types can get along together is in heaven." Veronica, however, foils J.D.'s plans. She shoots him and prevents the bombs from detonating beneath all of the students gathered for a pep rally in the school gym. J.D., hurt and bleeding, stumbles outside and detonates a bomb strapped to his chest.

In the final scene of the film, Veronica approaches Heather #2, takes away her red scrunchie, and ties it into her own hair, announcing that there is a "new sheriff in town." It doesn't take us long to figure out how Veronica will use her new power. She approaches Martha Dumptruck, now in a wheelchair, and says:

My date for the prom kind of flaked out on me, so I thought if you weren't doing anything that night we could go to the video store and rent some new releases or something. Maybe pop some popcorn.

"I'd like that," says Martha. "So would I," replies Veronica.

In an earlier version of the script the school is destroyed and the jocks and the nerds finally commingle in a heavenly prom, with their petty earthly cliques finally dissolved.[3] In the actual ending, however, Veronica, as the student-hero, begins a new social regime at the school without divisions between different social groups. She garners the individual strength to stand up to the toxic popularity of the Heathers, the homophobia of the jocks, and the cynical destructiveness of J.D. She finally discovers her true self and resists the pressures to conform to any social group. She is finally in a world where she is free of Heathers, a world where individuals are valued for their personality, not their popularity.

In a more recent example, *Mean Girls* has the same theme as *Heathers*, but it is told less darkly. Cady Heron is the new girl in a suburban public high school. She makes friends with the "plastics," the beautiful, popular, and "mean" girls of the school. She simultaneously is friendly with the less popular outcasts of the school. She conspires with the outcasts to infiltrate the plastics in order to learn their secrets and to use these secrets against them. She successfully defeats the "queen bee," is seduced by the powerful status of the plastics, and becomes the new queen bee herself. She neglects her studies and becomes consumed with appearances, popularity, and being cruel to others. Predictably, she realizes the error of her ways at the homecoming dance. She is elected queen, but she uses the opportunity to make a speech denouncing cliques and popularity. She breaks her tiara into many pieces and says, "Everybody looks like royalty tonight." She distributes the broken pieces of the crown to all sorts of students—popular, pretty, and otherwise. By the next semester there are no cliques at the school and students of different social categories get along with each other. I almost expected to see Cady invite Martha Dumptruck over to watch movies.

3. The Triumph of Youth: "When You Grow Up, Your Heart Dies"

Finally, the students of the suburban school films are heroes when they stand up to parents and teachers and prevail as youth. We have seen evidence of this in *Pump Up the Volume, Teaching Mrs. Tingle, Disturbing Behavior, Varsity Blues, Prom,* and *Ferris Bueller's Day Off*. No movie better dramatizes this heroism of youth against the adult world than John Hughes's 1985 classic, *The Breakfast Club*. In fact, *The Breakfast Club* is perhaps the quintessential suburban school film. It expresses all of the suburban school film themes discussed so far: The heroes are students, parents are mostly absent, school officials are depicted as antagonists and fools, the walls of social class and social cliques are torn down, and academic and athletic achievement are criticized.

The film begins with the following voice-over, the reading of an essay written to the dean of students, Mr. Vernon, as punishment during a Saturday detention at Shermer High School in a wealthy suburb of Chicago:

> We accept the fact that we had to sacrifice a whole Saturday in detention for whatever it was we did wrong—and what we did was wrong—but we think you're crazy to make us write an essay telling you who we think we are. What do you care? You see us as you want to see us . . . as a brain, an athlete, a basket case, a princess, and a criminal. Correct? That's the way we saw each other at 7:00 this morning. We were brainwashed.

The five students who report for Saturday detention are Claire, the rich and popular "princess"; Andrew, the popular "athlete"; Brian, the nerdy "brain"; Bender, the gruff and burned-out "criminal"; and Allison, the enigmatic "basket case." Claire and Andrew seem to know and like each other, but for the most part the five students don't understand and don't like each other. As Brian notes in the essay he wrote for the dean of students, they had been brainwashed. They'd been falsely led to believe that the differences between them as students were greater than the differences between young people and adults.

They each belong to a different social group at school, and they are forced against their will to spend this day together for transgressions they each have committed against the authority of the school. Their hostility for each other is palpable from the beginning. Bender in particular is the lightning rod for disputes between the students. He antagonizes Claire and Andrew by provocatively inquiring about their sexual experiences. Andrew, in turn, attacks Bender by suggesting that he is nothing but a worthless burnout.

There is no adult savior in this film to help the students to find themselves, to realize their personal potential, or to usher them into adulthood. Over the course of the film the five students discover their own identities and the identities of their peers *despite* the authority of the school. Set entirely in the high school library during one day's detention, the movie is essentially group therapy that helps the students to tear down the differences that divide them and to come to terms with their own personal problems—problems that are a different sort entirely from those of students in the urban school films. While the urban school students all had to overcome their culture of poverty and prove themselves academically, these suburban students have to deal with the problems of popularity, peer pressure, virginity, bad parents, high academic expectations, and personal identity.

Mr. Vernon has absolutely no legitimate authority in the eyes of these students. His rants against their worthlessness only serve to bond them together as students, despite their differences. Richard Vernon's character is deliberately portrayed as an antagonist and a fool. For instance, immediately after declaring that he will "not be made a fool of," he turns to reveal to the students that a sanitary toilet seat cover is hanging out of the back of his pants. Richard Vernon believes that the students in his high school have turned on him. He complains to Carl, the wise janitor, that the students in his school get more and more arrogant each year. Carl, who knows better, responds, "Bullshit, man. . . . The kids haven't changed, you have."

Slowly, the students begin to overcome their differences and unite in opposition to the corrupt and buffoonish Mr. Vernon. Their bonding is cemented over their collective use of illicit drugs. The five escape from their library prison briefly to travel to Bender's locker, where he has a stash of marijuana. After they bond over the drugs, the five students begin to share their intimate secrets and reveal their souls to each other. Mostly, they vent their anger toward their parents. Brian reveals the intense pressure he feels to keep a high grade point average. A failing grade in shop class drove him to consider suicide with a flare gun. Andrew confesses that he hates his father for the pressure he puts on him to excel at sports. Allison confesses to being a compulsive liar and to having parents who ignore her. Claire complains that her parents hate each other and use her as a pawn to hurt each other. Bender reveals that his father abuses him physically. In exasperation, Andrew asks if they will all end up like their parents. Allison's answer summarizes the fear that they all have of the future, as adulthood inevitably overtakes them: "It's unavoidable. It just happens. . . . [W]hen you grow up, your heart dies."

In addition to complaints about their parents, the students complain about the pressures they feel from their friends and the rigidity of social cliques at school. When Claire confesses that she probably won't be friendly to the "weird" Brian and Allison in school on Monday, Bender attacks her. Claire, however, says it isn't so simple: "I hate having to go along with everything my friends say. . . . [Y]ou just don't understand the pressure they can put on you." The collective confessional continues and soon, with their anger, fears, and frustration purged, they begin to understand each other and themselves a little better.

By the end of their detention the students like each other much more than they had eight hours earlier. They *will*, it seems, all be friends in school on Monday morning. After Claire gives Allison a beauty makeover, Allison and Andrew become romantically involved. Despite her initial animosity toward him, Claire approaches Bender, kisses him, and gives him her diamond earring. Brian, as the "brain," agrees to write the punishment essay for all of them. He concludes with a statement that summarizes their newfound solidarity and identity as youth who challenge the expectations of adults: "What we found out is that each one of us is a brain, and an athlete, and a basket-case, a princess, and a criminal. Does that answer your question?"

Gender Variations

Allison's beauty makeover in *The Breakfast Club* is an all-too-common scene in suburban high school films that suggests that women must conform to standard measures of beauty in order to attract men (see also *Clueless, Jawbreaker, She's All That,* and *Not Another Teen Movie*). Furthermore, it points to a larger theme in many of these films that young women characters are defined primarily by their romantic relationships with young men. Generally speaking, love and sex, as expressive qualities of the individual, are much more present in the suburban school films than they are in the urban school films. However, Hollywood does not depict young men and women expressing themselves in this sphere equally. Young men in the suburban school films tend to pursue sex (often by objectifying women) and still are given latitude to pursue other aspects of their identity (in school, sports, friendships, etc.). Young women characters in the suburban school films pursue love, but do so by limiting their own expressiveness in ways that are pleasing to men, not in ways that allow them to express their identities in full.

We have seen in *Ferris Bueller's Day Off* how Ferris has it all. He's smart, confident, and popular. He has a beautiful girlfriend, a best friend, supportive parents, and a bright future. He also violates many rules without suffering any consequences. Jeanie, his high school–aged sister, however, can't believe he gets away with it all. She does not enjoy the privileges that Ferris takes for granted as a young man. While he is enjoying his deceitful "day off," she is at school, simmering with resentment over her brother's ability to get what he wants. She complains, "Why should he get to do whatever he wants whenever he wants? Why should everything work out for him? What makes him so god-damn special?" What makes him special, in part, is his gender. Few women protagonists in the suburban school films get to enjoy such a wide array of privileges as Ferris.

In some ways, Kat in *10 Things I Hate About You* is similar to Ferris. She is smart, charismatic, and strong-willed. In contrast to Ferris, however, she is limited in how she expresses her identity. For much of the film Kat accepts her reputation at school as a "heinous bitch" and she actively avoids any sort of relationship with boys. She spends most of the film as a strong independent woman who is not defined by men (either her father or a boy-friend). "Why should I live up to other people's expectations instead of my own?" she asks. Kat's character is poised to be a rare one in high school films: a woman who defines herself and acts with confidence in pursuit of her goals without a concern about her heterosexual attractiveness. When, for convoluted reasons, a mysterious rebel at the school is paid to date her, however, she is slowly won over by his charms. Even after she learns that his initial interest in her was fabricated, she falls in love with him. Toward the end of the film she is no longer the strong independent woman she was in the beginning. She acts out of character in English class and recites a gooey love poem to the boy with whom she's fallen in love. The very last scene of the film depicts the two of them talking to each other about their new relationship. Kat attempts to make a point, only to be interrupted by his kiss. The strong young woman she was at the beginning of the film is juxtaposed harshly with her literally being silenced by her new boyfriend. Ferris is allowed to be a friend, a boyfriend, a rebel, and an intelligent student with a promising future. Kat, however, is limited in the ways in which she can express her individualism. She still is going to Sarah Lawrence and has a promising future. Nevertheless, the film emphasizes that the most important development for Kat is that she is in love with a boy and is no longer a "heinous bitch."

The boys in *Project X* are certainly heinous, but they never have to make amends for it. *Project X* epitomizes the degrading ways in which many young men in suburban high school films relate to women. Their epic party is staged, in part, so that the three relatively unpopular boys can have sex with young women. They advertise the party with misogynist statements such as: "Epic party at Thomas Kub's house. Hot bitches dress like it. Ugly bitches stay home." The party is filled with gratuitous scenes of young women swimming topless and crude young men objectifying them. This is typical in many suburban school films (see my discussion of *Porky's* and *American Pie* in the next section) in which sex becomes a rite of passage for young men.[4] The three friends bond with each other over the course of the party, but they don't establish any meaningful relationships with the women at the party. At the end of the film Thomas does apologize for his behavior to Kirby, the young woman on whom he has a crush. But this is not enough to redeem the rampant misogyny on display for most of the film. And, just like Ferris Bueller, the boys get off relatively lightly for their destruction of so much in the neighborhood. As we have seen, Thomas's dad is perversely proud of his son and Thomas is voted "most likely to succeed" by his classmates. Ferris's sister would be furious that they get away with so much.

As we saw with *10 Things I Hate About You*, even in films where the protagonists are women, there are limited ways in which they express their identities. Their expressive individualism is nearly always centered on a man. In *John Tucker Must Die* the entire plot of the film is organized around attempts of four young women to humiliate a boy, for whom they all have romantic feelings. Carrie, Heather, and Beth are each dating John Tucker simultaneously. They are unaware of his betrayal, however, because they each are part of a different social clique in high school. The new girl to the school, Kate, discovers John Tucker's lies and agrees to help Carrie, Heather, and Beth in their attempt to get their revenge by humiliating him. In a rare moment of critical insight Kate is critical of their obsession with John Tucker: "You are either obsessed with destroying him or obsessed with dating him. Either way it's always all about him." She is right. Even though the film is ostensibly about the power of four young women to take charge of their lives, the film is ultimately centered on John Tucker and his relationship with the protagonists. In the end the four women "succeed" in getting John Tucker to promise never to lie again. But that only means he tells his girlfriends that he's dating other women. Beyond their obsession with John Tucker, we never learn much else about the four young women.

Easy A is another film in which there is a strong woman protagonist. There are some important messages in the film about how young women suffer from a cultural double-standard about sex: They are damned if they do have sex, damned if they don't. Nonetheless, the action of the film revolves not around the full identity development of a complex young woman but, rather, around her development in relation to men. While she is critical of the demeaning roles women are asked to play in society, the main character Olive ultimately desires the attention of a boy to make her life complete. It shouldn't surprise us much that Olive's model of a relationship comes from high school films. She asks:

Whatever happened to chivalry? Does it only exist in '80s movies? I want John Cusack holding a boom box outside my window. I want to ride off on a lawn mower with Patrick Dempsey. I want Jake from *16 Candles* waiting outside the church for me. I want Judd Nelson thrusting his fist in the air because he knows he got me, just once. I want my life to be like an '80s movie.

By contrast, Seth and Evan in *Superbad* are not defined by their relationship to women. Seth and Evan are best friends. The development of their expressive individualism revolves around their friendship and their anxiety about having to separate from each other when they go to college. In part, it is a standard boys-coming-of-age story. Seth and Evan predictably bring alcohol to a party in the hopes of having sex with women. In this respect, *Superbad* epitomizes the degrading ways in which young men relate to women in many suburban school films. Seth, in particular, degrades women throughout the film. In anticipation of the party and its potential for sex, Seth admonishes Evan for his timidity, "Stop being a pussy for once and we can fucking fuck some girls already. . . . [Y]ou know when you hear a girl saying, 'oh, I was so shit-faced last night, I shouldn't have fucked that guy.' We could be that mistake!" The crude pursuit of sex and the demeaning language used to objectify women illustrate the ways some teen boys try to prove their masculinity to each other.[5] The misogyny in the film notwithstanding, it's the relationship between Seth and Evan that is the real story in the film. *Superbad* is a surprisingly tender story about the close friendship between two boys. In this way, it illustrates how young men in suburban school films are more likely than young women to express their identities outside of a heterosexual romantic relationship. For instance, after Seth "saves" Evan from the police who broke up the party they have this tender exchange:

Evan: I can't believe you saved me. You saved me. I owe you so much. I love you. I love you man.

Seth: I love you. I LOVE you. I'm not even embarrassed to say it. I love you.

Evan: I'm not embarrassed. Why don't we say that every day? Why can't we say it more often?

Superbad raises many questions about masculinity and the ways in which its depiction in Hollywood films might be changing.[6] Nevertheless, *Superbad* still reproduces many tired themes that are typical in suburban school films—young men objectify women and pursue sex as a rite of passage and as a way of reaffirming the norms of traditional heterosexual masculinity. In addition to such pursuits, however, young men in the suburban school films also have the space to develop and express their identities as friends, athletes, or students. They have multiple ways to express their individuality. Young women in these films, even when they are the protagonists, tend to pursue love as a way of fulfilling their identities. Even when they have other interests and friendships, their characters are not fully developed until they have established a relationship with a young man.

Social Class, Symbolic Deviance, and Adolescent Identity

In these suburban school films rebellion against the expectations of parents, peers, and teachers helps middle-class youth define themselves as individuals and teaches them how to express their emerging adult identities. For the middle class in general, youth is often understood as a time when boundaries are tested, personal exploration is encouraged, and wild-oats sowing and mistakes are expected. A bit of independence, nonconformity, and rebellion is seen as healthy for the developing middle-class adolescent. As the father of high school rebel Morgan Hiller in *Tuff Turf* tells his son, "I expect you to make mistakes. That's what life is all about, for Christ's sake. How else are you going to learn who you are and what you believe in?"

As we have seen repeatedly in this chapter, students directly challenge the authority of school officials and consciously break the rules in order to discover and protect their own identities and interests. In some of the suburban school films the journey to find an identity is expressed by fulfilling an adolescent fantasy to actually destroy the school. One or more students destroy or attempt to destroy their high school in *Class of Nuke 'Em High*, *Rock and Roll High School*, *Heathers*, *Rock and Roll High School Forever*, and *Elephant*.[7] More commonly, however, the adolescents in these films rebel or deviate only mildly by engaging in casual sex and illicit drug use.

Casual sex between students is depicted in many of the suburban school films. For instance, Veronica and J.D. sleep together shortly after meeting each other in *Heathers*. Luke and Leigh Ann have sex when they are not *Teaching Mrs. Tingle*. The pursuit of sex (and love) is central to the plot of *Fast Times at Ridgemont High*. There are, in fact, too many instances of casual sex to mention. However, one movie in particular stands out as an example of how sex is treated in high school films that feature middle-class suburban young men—*American Pie*.

American Pie created a sensation when it was released in 1999 (perhaps because of its depiction of a young man having intercourse with a homemade apple pie), but it really is not that different from any number of teen sex comedies. In many ways it harkens back to *Porky's*, the 1981 film from Canada. *Porky's* is another sex comedy that created a stir (perhaps because of its infamous "shower scene" of high school girls after gym class). Both *Porky's* and *American Pie* open with a scene of the main character, an adolescent male virgin, in bed with an erection, only to be disturbed by a parent entering his room. Each movie traces the desperate attempts of the main character to lose his virginity, and each movie concludes with his long-awaited sexual initiation. It is significant that these two popular teen sex comedies are bookended by scenes of an adolescent boy's parent entering his room while he is sexually aroused and the boy ultimately losing his virginity. While based in high schools, these films are not about schooling. Instead, they are about an adolescent rite of passage as middle-class boys develop a sexual identity apart from their parents.

In the case of *American Pie* the shame of still being virgins in their senior year is too much for five sexually frustrated young men to bear. The main character, Jim, exclaims after one particularly bleak party that ended without sex for any of his friends, "You know we're all going to college as virgins. You realize this don't you? I mean, they probably have special dorms for people like us." The five friends create a pact to lose their virginity by the day of their graduation in three weeks. As Jim's friend Kevin proclaims, "We all get laid before we graduate. . . . This is our very manhood at stake. No longer will our penises remain flaccid and unused." To cement their collective goal they offer a toast, "To the next step!"

Having agreed that the night of the prom provides their best chance at success, the five friends focus their amorous energies on that evening. They are all success-ful. Jim has sex with his date, a sexually aggressive "band geek." Kevin finally has sex with his girlfriend. Finch has sex with the mother of his high school nemesis, Stifler. And while Oz doesn't say if he "went all the way," he did spend an intimate night with his new girlfriend and he reports that they are "falling in love." In the final scene the five friends once again offer a toast. Once again they say, "To the next step." This time, however, they are toasting their future lives after high school. They are toasting the transition to adulthood, to which their loss of virginity was a symbolic rite of passage.

Casual drug use, too, is often depicted in suburban school films. Jeff Spicolli is stoned in every scene in which he appears in *Fast Times at Ridgemont High*. The five students in Saturday detention in *The Breakfast Club* overcome their differences and bond together as they get high on marijuana in the school library. In *Never Been Kissed* Josie Geller is an awkward twenty-five-year-old newspaper reporter posing undercover as a high school student. She has trouble fitting in until she breaks out of her shell after eating a pot-laced brownie. In *Clueless* drug use is frequently referred to, but a distinction is made between recreational drug use and drug abuse. As the character Cher explains, "It is one thing to spark up a doobie and get laced at parties. But it is quite another to be fried all day." In *Dazed and Confused* the students *are* fried all day.

The students in the suburban school films take lots of drugs and have lots of casual sex (or, at least, try to have lots of sex). But rather than being punished for such deviation from social norms and laws, they are rewarded for it. As the promotional material for *Fast Times at Ridgemont High* states, "Only the rules get busted" at Ridgemont High School. In *Risky Business* Joel is rewarded with admission to Princeton University for his business skills as a pimp. By consciously rejecting the rules, these students are distancing themselves from adult authority, celebrating their autonomy, and experimenting with their new identities. In many of these films drug use and casual sex are depicted as developmental signposts about what it means to be an adolescent in transition to adulthood. This particular understanding of youth, however, is very much dependent upon the social class of the adolescent.

While use of drugs is treated as a rite of passage in the suburban school films, it is likely to get the students in the urban school films kicked out of school, arrested, or killed. While the students in the suburban school films race to lose their virginity and are celebrated by audiences when they do so, casual sex often results in pregnancy and dropping out of school for the girls in the urban school films. (It should be noted that among the suburban school films, sex does result in a pregnancy in *How to Deal* and *Juno* and in pregnancy and abortion in *Fast*

Times at Ridgemont High and *The Last American Virgin*.) Such freedom to express oneself without fear of punishment is a luxury not permitted poor urban youth, for whom a different standard of behavior is very often applied. Such deviance on the part of poor urban youth is not treated as permissively as it is for middle-class suburban youth, either in Hollywood films or in real life. While Hollywood (and Americans generally) thinks adolescents have a "get-out-of-jail-free" card, they are implicitly speaking about suburban middle-class youth. The "deviance" of poor urban youth is taken much more seriously than the youthful "mistakes" of suburban middle-class youth.

This asymmetric reaction to deviance by middle-class and lower-class adolescents is well recognized in the sociological literature. William J. Chambliss's classic article "The Saints and the Roughnecks" describes this dynamic well.[8] For two years Chambliss observed two groups of adolescent boys in Hannibal High School. The "Saints" were a group of eight young white men from upper-middle-class families. They were good students with college plans, they were involved with school activities, and they happened to be the most deviant kids in school. The Saints regularly skipped school, got drunk, drove recklessly, played dangerous pranks, and vandalized property. Their reputation in town, however, was that they were obedient boys, good students, and youth leaders. For the most part the Saints had access to cars and were careful to commit their deviant acts out of town in order to preserve their upstanding reputations. If they were pulled over by the police, the Saints were always polite and deferential. On the few occasions when they were caught acting delinquently, the community at large understood the boys' actions as the sowing of their wild oats—harmless fun for young middle-class men with promising futures.

The community at large, however, did not treat the adolescent "Roughnecks" with such leniency. They were a group of six lower-class white boys at Hannibal High School who also acted deviantly. The Roughnecks would drink, fight, and shoplift. Without access to their own automobiles, however, the Roughnecks would commit such delinquent acts in Hannibal, with greater visibility than the Saints' delinquency. While the Saints actually engaged in more delinquent acts than the Roughnecks, it was the Roughnecks who had the reputation in the school and in town as criminals and gang members with bleak futures. The police assumed that the Roughnecks were criminals with bad attitudes, and the Roughnecks confirmed their suspicion by acting defiantly when questioned by the police.

Because of their location in the social hierarchy, the Saints were labeled as "good kids" despite their deviant acts. These acts were not enough to relabel the Saints as delinquents. Indeed, six of the Saints graduated from college and are living the bright futures others had predicted for them. The Roughnecks, on the other hand, did not enjoy the privileges afforded to the Saints, nor did they experience bright futures. Their lower social class status made them suspicious to the middle-class residents of Hannibal, and their subsequent acts merely served to cement their label as delinquents. Their deviant acts were not viewed in light of their *adolescence*, but were seen by the school, by the police, and by the community at large as definitive statements about their worth and merit as *lower-class* adolescents.[9]

A similar dynamic is at work in these high school films. When the students of lower socioeconomic status act deviantly (drugs, fighting, sex), they are condemned and treated as serious violators of middle-class expectations. When the students of middle- and upper-middle-class status act deviantly (mostly drugs and sex, but sometimes fighting), their actions are excused, ignored, or treated as normal expressions of adolescence.

The Paths to Adulthood: Social Class and Adolescent Strategies to Independence

Social class differences affect not only perceptions of deviance, but also perceptions of students' relationship to school and their transition to adulthood. In her 1989 book *Jocks and Burnouts: Social Categories and Identity in the High School*, Penelope Eckert argues that American high schools are often organized around two dominant social categories of students: the "Jocks," whom she defines as students who are involved in school activities, cooperate with school authorities, do well academically, and largely come from the middle classes, and the "Burnouts," students who reject the school, have an antagonistic relationship to school authorities, struggle academically, and largely come from the working and lower classes:

> Studies of adolescents in school frequently isolate as two dominant categories those who share the goals of the school and those who form a counter-school culture. . . . This basic division into pro- and anti-school categories is a social process common to virtually all public schools, and it generates and institutionalizes differences among adolescents on the basis of responses to the school.[10]

Since students from the middle classes are more likely to attend a four-year college than their working-class counterparts, their adolescent years are extended longer, and they remain dependent upon adults for a longer period of time. Middle-class students are dependent upon adult "sponsorship" to get into college and to reproduce their middle-class lives. They are also dependent upon the school for most of their social relationships. Jocks, therefore, identify closely with the school for both personal and professional reasons. Burnouts, however, are less dependent upon the school for access to both future jobs and social networks. Lower-class students are less likely to have parents who have been to college, are less likely to attend college themselves, and tend to assume adult responsibilities (full-time work, marriage, children, etc.) much earlier than students from the middle classes. Burnouts, then, are more likely to reject the school and to resent the authority that it has over them.

Eckert argues that middle- and lower-class students pursue different strategies of transition to adulthood. The middle-class Jocks tend to accept the legitimacy of adult authority, cooperate with that authority, and negotiate for their own adult autonomy within the framework of that authority in the high school. The lower-class Burnouts, however, tend to demand adult autonomy on their own terms:

> Burnouts seek freedom in absence of adult supervision and view school activities as one more sphere of control. They view the freedoms dispensed within this sphere as vestiges of childhood patterns, because they are acquired at the cost of submission.[11]

To the extent to which the urban school films feature troubled poor and work-ing-class students (similar to Eckert's Burnout category) and the suburban school films feature privileged students from the middle classes who do well in school (somewhat resembling Eckert's Jock category), Hollywood inverts Eckert's thesis about social class and adolescent transitions to adulthood. In poor and urban high schools Hollywood asks Burnouts to become Jocks and to cooperate with the school in an attempt to attain utilitarian independence. In middle-class suburban high schools Hollywood asks Jocks to become Burnouts and to express their identities free of adult authority. While in reality poor youth become independent earlier in life, the films suggest they should be dependent longer. While in reality middle-class students delay their adulthood until after graduation from college, the films suggest they should assert their independence while still in high school.

The yardstick Hollywood uses to measure "adulthood" varies between the urban and suburban school films. Adulthood is defined as the attainment of educational and occupational *independence* in the urban school films (utilitarian individualism) and as the attainment of an adult *identity* in the suburban school films (expressive individualism). In the urban school films the students are criticized when they express themselves as individuals (by deviating from the norm, leaving school, having sex, getting pregnant, doing drugs, and so forth). Hollywood's lesson is that they should delay such adult identities. They are asked not to leave school, but to be more dependent upon it; to not yet focus on work, but to finish school first; to avoid sex and drugs; and to obey authority and conform to middle-class standards. Adulthood in the urban school films implies getting the skills and credentials one needs to support oneself and to be a responsible middle-class adult.

In the suburban school films, however, the students are tired of being adoles-cents and of being dependent upon adults. They feel suffocated by their dependence on the school and their parents. They long to "grow up"—to get out of school, to be in a relationship, to experiment with sex and drugs, and to explore their identities. They don't believe in the skills and credentials the discredited adults are offering them. They take their middle-class lives for granted. Earning a living is not the primary concern facing them as soon-to-be adults. Rather, adulthood in the sub-urban school films means finding and expressing your identity as an individual.

Conclusion: The Cultural Contradiction of Individualism and Conformity

Just as the urban school films reflect a middle-class fantasy that the problems in urban schools can be rectified by a middle-class savior and the adoption of middle-class values by poor urban students, the suburban school films reflect a middle-class fantasy that suburban adolescents can avoid the stultifying effects of American middle-class life if they discover who they are as individuals and learn to express themselves despite pressures to conform. The mythic fantasy in the urban school films is that conformity to adult middle-class expectations is a prerequisite for independence. The fantasy in the suburban school films is that *nonconformity* to adult expectations is a prerequisite for group acceptance.

For instance, in *Pump Up the Volume* the iconoclastic "Hard Harry" becomes beloved by a student body that ignored the well-behaved Mark Hunter. Despite his multiple transgressions during his day off from high school, Ferris Bueller is idolized by the entire school (with the exception of Mr. Rooney). In *Teaching Mrs. Tingle* Leigh Ann Watson is publicly honored as the valedictorian and given a free pass to college despite her crimes. John Moxon does things his own way and becomes a beloved local hero in *Varsity Blues*. In *Heathers* Veronica Sawyer makes time for friendship with the outcast Martha Dumptruck, but she still gets the powerful red scrunchie. The five detainees from *The Breakfast Club* will say hello to each other in school on Monday. They are now, as it were, members of the same club. Furthermore, they are members of a club that includes us, the audience. We, too, identify with and accept the student-heroes. Hollywood's fantasy tells the audience that J.D. in *Heathers* was wrong to be cynical. Heaven is *not* the only place that different social types can get along. Just as the lone teacher-heroes in the urban school films are ultimately beloved by their students, the lone student-heroes in the suburban school films are ultimately beloved by the students in all of the school's social cliques. Nonconformity, ironically, fosters social acceptance.

As Kai Erikson has noted, cultures always have contradictory potential. Cultures exist along an "axis of variation" in which "the idea and its counterpart become natural partners in the cultural order of things."[12] Drawing upon the work of Tocqueville, Robert Bellah and his co-authors specifically note the contradictory tendency in American culture between individualism and conformity. This tension is particularly strong among members of the middle class, who search for meaning and identity in their individual achievements. However, the meaning of their achievements (and, by extension, the understanding of their self) is measured by how their achievements stack up against those of others. Expanding upon Schneider and Smith's work on the middle-class culture of individualism, Bellah et al. write:

> Middle-class individuals are thus motivated to enter a highly autonomous and demanding quest for achievement and then left with no standard against which achievement is to be measured except the income and consumption levels of their neighbors, exhibiting anew the clash between autonomy and conformity that seems to be the fate of American individualism.[13]

Americans, however, are uneasy living with such contradictory tendencies in their culture. Perhaps the anxiety that is the hallmark of the new middle class in postindustrial America attempts to find some resolution in the fantasies found at the movies. The middle-class student-heroes of the suburban school films resist conformity and struggle to assert their individuality and independence. What these student-heroes in the suburban school films have accomplished is what many middle-class Americans implicitly long for—escape from a world of status competition, envy, and conformity. They seek refuge in a world of cooperation, mutual admiration, and free expression. In many ways these suburban school student-heroes have found the meaningful relationships and sense of belonging that is the fantasy of middle-class Americans who long for a return to the structure and values of a close-knit community, as symbolized by the ideals of small-town America.[14] It is fittingly ironic, however, that the small-town ideal that many middle-class Americans long for is *not* based on the acceptance of individual difference and free expression. The small-town ideal, as much as modern consumer culture, suburban sprawl, or the bureaucratic office, requires conformity to achieve acceptance. It is simply one of the many contradictions of American culture that the meaningful relationships and sense of belonging that Americans long for happen to challenge the ideals of individualism and free expression that they also hold dear. It is also one of the many contradictions expressed (and cinematically resolved) in high school films.

Notes

1. See, for instance, *Cry Baby, Crazy/Beautiful, Grease, Valley Girl, Some Kind of Wonderful, The Karate Kid, The Breakfast Club, Say Anything, She's All That, Can't Buy Me Love, Prom,* and *10 Things I Hate About You.*
2. Coleman, James S. 1961. *The Adolescent Society.* New York: Free Press.
3. Bernstein, Jonathan. 1997. *Pretty in Pink: The Golden Age of Teenage Movies.* New York: St. Martin's Griffin.
4. *The To Do List* appears progressive because it flips the script and is about a young woman's rite of passage to have sex with men without any romantic entanglements. However, the film spends much of its energy ridiculing the main character. For instance, when her top falls off after jumping in the pool she is mercilessly teased for having small breasts. It's hard for Hollywood to avoid misogyny.
5. See Pascoe, C. J. 2007. *Dude, You're a Fag: Masculinity and Sexuality in High School.* Berkeley: University of California Press; and Kimmel, Michael. 2009. *Guyland: The Perilous World Where Boys Become Men.* New York: Harper Collins.
6. I have written about *Superbad* and masculinity elsewhere. See Bulman, Robert, with Nicole S. McCants. 2008. "Enlightened Teenage Masculinity." *Contexts: Understanding People in Their Social Worlds* (summer), pp. 68–69.
7. In *Over the Edge* (1979) students attempt to destroy their junior high school. Also, the school is destroyed in *Carrie* (1976), but it is not included in this sample since I exclude horror films. One of the characters in *I Love You, Beth Cooper* asks, "Who wouldn't want to blow up their school?"
8. Chambliss, William J. 1973. "The Saints and the Roughnecks." *Society* 11, no. 1: 24.
9. Such unequal application of social sanctions upon "deviant" adolescents is still true today. In the films as well as in reality the deviance of white middle-class suburban adolescents is often evaluated in the context of their youth, while the deviance of non-white poor urban youth is often evaluated in the context of their race and class. For instance, in 2000 Californians overwhelmingly passed Proposition 21, the Gang Violence and Juvenile Crime Prevention Act. It allows prosecutors much more discretion to circumvent the juvenile justice system and to charge juvenile offenders (as young as fourteen years old) as adults and to sentence them to adult prisons. By leaving the decision to charge youthful offenders as adults up to the discretion of the prosecutor, the potential for the unequal application of justice is heightened. Even before Proposition 21, poor and non-white youth were much more likely to be charged with crimes than middle-class white youth. And when charged with similar offenses, non-white youth are at least twice as likely to be charged as adults than white youth. (Nieves, Evelyn. 2000. "California Proposal Toughens Penalties for Young Criminals." *New York Times* [March 6]; and Huizinga, D., and D. Elliott. 1987. "Juvenile Offenders: Prevalence, Offender Incidence, and Arrest Rates by Race." *Crime and Delinquency* 33: 206–223.) The supporters of Proposition 21 maintained that the juvenile justice system would remain in place to rehabilitate those youth who could be "saved." However, they used racially and class-coded words to make the distinction between those who could be saved (and treated as juveniles) and those who were beyond hope (and punished as adults). As

former California governor Pete Wilson wrote in an op-ed piece in the *San Francisco Chronicle*, "The objective of the proposition is to focus the juvenile justice system's resources on those who can be saved while protecting the public from members of vicious street gangs who are both willing and capable of random, senseless violence" (quoted in Nieves). When polled, California voters were much more likely to support the initiative when it was described as punishment for "gang-related felonies such as home-invasion robbery, carjacking, witness intimidations and drive-by shootings" than when it was described as an initiative that would "increase penalties, change trial procedures and require reporting" for juvenile felonies (Nieves). The strategic use of language that was likely to invoke in the minds of voters images of offenders who are poor non-white urban youth (*gangs, home-invasion robbery, drive-by shootings*) helped ensure its passage.

10. Eckert, Penelope. 1989. *Jocks and Burnouts: Social Categories and Identity in High School*. New York: Teachers College Press, pp. 21–22.

11. Ibid., p. 165.

12. Erikson, Kai T. 1978. *Everything in Its Path: Destruction of Community in the Buffalo Creek Flood*. New York: Simon and Schuster, p. 82.

13. Bellah, Robert N., Richard Madsen, William M. Sullivan, Ann Swidler, and Steven M. Tipton. 1985. *Habits of the Heart: Individualism and Commitment in American Life*. New York: Harper and Row, p. 149. They draw upon Schneider, David M., and Raymond T. Smith. 1973. *Class Differences and Sex Roles in American Kinship and Family Structure*. Englewood Cliffs, NJ: Prentice Hall.

14. Bellah et al., p. 282.

six

Challenging the Culture of Privilege

Class Conflict in the Private School Film

The [private] school—rather than the upper-class family—is the most important agency for transmitting the traditions of the upper social classes, and regulating the admission of new wealth and talent. It is the characterizing point in the upper-class experience. In the top fifteen or twenty such schools, if anywhere, one finds a prime organizing center of the national upper classes.[1]

—C. Wright Mills, *The Power Elite*

You go to one of the best schools in the country, Rushmore. Now for some of you it doesn't matter. You were born rich and you are going to stay rich. But here's my advice for the rest of you—take dead aim at the rich boys. Get them in your cross-hairs and take them down. They can buy anything. But they can't buy backbone. Don't let them forget that.

—Herman Blume in *Rushmore*

"Take dead aim at the rich boys." That is exactly what Hollywood does in the elite private school films. In the urban school films Hollywood depicts a class struggle between the morally challenged urban poor and their virtuous middle-class saviors. In the suburban school films middle-class students struggle with each other and their adult nemeses in an attempt to find their true selves. In the private school films the issue of social class once again emerges as a central theme. This time, however, it is poor, working, and middle-class students who do battle with the pompous power elite. Other scholars have noted that Hollywood's view of the wealthy is generally negative and has been growing more negative over the past twenty-five years.[2] The depiction of the upper class in these elite private school films offers support for this observation.

Nearly all of the schools in the elite private school film sample are boarding schools. As Peter Cookson and Caroline Persell argue in *Preparing for Power: America's Elite Boarding Schools*, the boarding school is an institution that is about much more than a formal education. Parents who send their children to a boarding school expect more than what the school has to offer in the classroom. The boarding school is, in many ways, what Goffman called a "total institution."[3] That is, nearly every aspect of boarding school life is controlled. There are few areas of life in a boarding school where a student can escape watchful eyes. Nearly everything—the curriculum, mealtimes, bedtimes, dress, and so on—is strictly regulated. As Cookson and Persell note, there is a hidden curriculum at work here: "Students discover that power and pain are inseparable and that to a large degree the price of privilege is the loss of autonomy and individuality."[4] The loss of individuality is an important step in the socialization into elite culture. The elite boarding school is not there to serve the individual student but to help create an upper-class community. As C. Wright Mills writes in *The Power Elite*:

> What holds the upper class together is not only wealth and power, but shared beliefs and shared lives. A sense of collective identity, however, does not develop naturally; it must be forged out of actual encounters.[5]

In many ways this function is seen as offensive to members of the middle class. It favors collective identity over that of individual identity. It favors the school over the family. It fosters a belief in the entitlement of the privileged. And it makes cracking the glass ceiling of the American upper class all the more difficult for individuals from more humble origins. It is no wonder, then, that the elite private school films condemn the privilege of the upper classes and feature individual heroes from the working and middle classes who deserve the rewards of their labor, not those who effortlessly inherit such rewards.

This chapter shows that in the elite private school films the importance of academics once again enters the picture. Unlike the suburban public school films in which academics were mostly absent, learning is an important element of the private school films. Unlike the urban public school films, however, academics are *not* the key to success or happiness in the private school films. Rather than offering salvation to troubled youth, the high expectations of academic success are often considered *burdensome* to the wealthy students. In the elite private school films the upper class is depicted as morally bankrupt and focused only on superficial measures of status. The heroes of the films are individual representatives of non-elite social classes who exhibit individuality, integrity, well-roundedness, and academic merit. These middle-class values help to defeat the upper-class culture of privilege in these films. I argue that the elite private school films reflect dual aspects of American culture. On the one hand they echo the urban school films to the extent that social institutions are ultimately shown to be fair and meritocratic—that success in America is open to all, not just the privileged. On the other hand, they express some of the themes of the suburban school films—specifically, the idea that there is more to life than narrow academic achievement and the pursuit of social status. Ultimately, you must figure out who you are and be true to yourself.

The Catholic and Christian school films (smaller in number), however, do not resemble the elite private school films. As I will explain later in this chapter, the characteristics of the Catholic and Christian school films depend upon the social class characteristics of the students depicted. For the most part, these private religious school films resemble the suburban public school films—middle-class students struggle against the school and adult society in order to discover and express their authentic selves. However, if the students in the film are mostly poor, then the film is more likely to resemble the urban public school films, with a middle-class teacher "saving" the students from a culture of poverty.

"Just Because You Are Accepted, Doesn't Mean You Belong"[6]

So states the promotional material to *School Ties*, the 1992 film (set in 1959) that epitomizes Hollywood's treatment of elite private schools. In *School Ties* David Greene is a working-class Jewish boy from Scranton, Pennsylvania. He is a successful student and a football hero at his local public school, where he has led his team to the state championship. Saint Matthew's Academy, an elite private boys' boarding school, recruits David for his senior year to play quarterback for their struggling football team. David accepts the scholarship and leaves his family and friends in gritty and industrial Scranton to live at Saint Matthew's in serene and bucolic New England. His parents are proud of him—they want him to take advantage of the tremendous educational opportunity and possibly to gain admission to Harvard University. David is not expected, however, to leave his past behind. His father urges him to remember where he comes from: "You show respect and get to Temple . . . no excuses." Yet David is reluctant to reveal that he is Jewish in such a blue-blooded Protestant environment where there are no other Jews and anti-Semitic comments are uttered routinely by students.

David is in awe as he first enters the grounds of Saint Matthew's—it is, to him, an entirely other world. It is overwhelmingly populated by white, Protestant, wealthy, and privileged students. He is impressed by the lush green lawns, the church steeple, the majestic old brick buildings, the elegantly dressed students, the expensive automobiles, the sporting dogs, and the air of casual sophistication that permeates the grounds. While drinking in the rarefied atmosphere he incredulously asks the football coach, "Jesus, this is a high school?"

Indeed, it is a high school, but an exceptionally elite high school. Saint Matthew's has produced two American presidents and is considered to be a "pipeline to Harvard." All who work and study at Saint Matthew's are well aware of the school's elevated status. Headmaster Bartram addresses the students on the first day of school:

> Welcome to the finest preparatory school in the nation. . . . You, my boys, are among the elite of the nation and we strive here at Saint Matthew's to prepare you for the heavy responsibilities that come with favored position.

One of the students who is quite comfortable with his favored position in life is Charlie Dillon. He is, as he proclaims himself, a big man on campus. He comes from a wealthy family, and several family members are prestigious alumni of Saint Matthew's. His older brother had been a star football player at Saint Matthew's and is now a successful student at Harvard and a new inductee into the Saint Matthew's football hall of fame. Had it not been for the last-minute recruiting of David Greene, Charlie would have played quarterback for Saint Matthew's in his senior year. Charlie is dating (or claims to be dating) the well-pedigreed Sally. However, Sally, who says she is "just friends" with Charlie, falls in love with David. The pressure to succeed academically, athletically, and socially is overwhelming to Charlie. Without Sally and without glory on the football field, Charlie feels a sharp loss in status, one that is made more painful in the shadow of his successful older brother.

At an alumni party to celebrate Saint Matthew's victory on the football field over their archrival (thanks to David much more than to Charlie), Charlie serendipitously learns that David is Jewish. Eager for revenge, Charlie soon spreads the word to the other students and to Sally, aware that such a revelation would shock the wealthy, conservative, and socially insulated Protestants and turn the tide of admiration away from his Jewish rival. As a result of this news Sally breaks up with David and his friends ostracize him. Some are disgusted that a Jew lives among them; others feel betrayed that David hid the truth from them.

The success of his revenge upon David notwithstanding, Charlie is still anxious about his chances of getting into Harvard. To improve his odds he cheats on a history test. David witnesses Charlie consult a crib sheet during the exam. After class the teacher finds the sheet on the floor and announces that if the violator does not confess the whole class will fail. He leaves it to the members of the class to come to a resolution on the matter. David approaches Charlie in private and tells him that if he doesn't confess, he will turn Charlie in. Instead, Charlie turns the tables on David and announces to his classmates that it was *David* who cheated. It is his word against David's. Charlie hopes that the old-boy network and anti-Semitism will work in his favor.

Charlie's privileged position seems at first to pay off. The class votes to clear Charlie of the charges and to indict David. The decision, however, is not unanimous. Several students have begun to realize that their rejection of David was bigoted and irrational. With his conscience bothering him, one of these students, Rip, informs the headmaster that he, too, saw Charlie cheat. As a result, David is redeemed and asked by the headmaster to remain at the school despite the awkward situation. David agrees to stay, but he is not happy about how he has been treated by the students or the administration. He tells the headmaster, "You used me for football. I'll use you to get into Harvard."

Charlie is expelled from the school. Not even his family connections to the school can protect him. Charlie, however, knows that his privileged position in society is likely to be preserved regardless. As Charlie is leaving campus on his final trip home, David sees him in the backseat of his father's luxury car. Charlie rolls down the window to speak to David:

Charlie: You know something—I'm still going to get into Harvard. In ten years no one will remember any of this. But you'll still be a Goddamn Jew.
David: And you'll still be a prick.

In *School Ties* the classroom drama of history exams and the hope of admission to an elite college animate the plot. Success in these academic matters, however, is not the climax of the film as it was in the urban school films. In fact, the single-minded pursuit of academic success and the high social status that results is considered somewhat dangerous. The pressures to achieve lead to disastrous results for Charlie. Furthermore, Charlie's smug upper-class entitlement, anti-Semitism, and unethical behavior leave his character with few redeeming qualities. On the other hand, David, the proletarian hero, remains true to his faith, exhibits personal integrity in the face of an unjust attack, and honestly earns his success in both football and academics.

School Ties is not the only elite private school film with these themes. Nearly all of the elite private school films (but not the Catholic or Christian school films) feature academic content, a concern that a narrow focus on academics is burdensome, the moral bankruptcy of the rich, a working- or middle-class hero, and a celebration of the middle-class values of individualism, well-roundedness, merit, and personal integrity.

Academic Matters

Despite the academic focus, the heroes of the elite private school films are not teachers, as they were in the urban public school films. The heroes of the elite private school films are almost always students—working- or middle-class students in particular. These students have trouble blending into the exclusive world of the elite private high school. They must overcome the prejudices of the privileged and prove that they belong. They often do so by demonstrating their academic qualifications.

In *Finding Forrester* Jamal Wallace is a poor African American student from a single-parent household in the Bronx. He plays basketball with his friends and brings home Cs from his local public high school. However, he studies in secret, has test scores through the roof, and reads and writes at every possible moment he has free. The public school authorities take notice of his astronomically high test scores, and an elite private school in Manhattan, Mailor-Callow, offers him a full academic scholarship (and they wouldn't be disappointed if he decides to play basketball for them as well).

The school is a bit snobby, with a pompous and condescending writing teacher, Robert Crawford. Mr. Crawford is suspicious of Jamal. Mr. Crawford does not believe that Jamal's high-quality work is his own. He can't conceive that a poor black basketball player could write so well: "He's a basketball player! From the Bronx!" Nonetheless, the writing is Jamal's. His academic achievements are authentic, but they are not because of the efforts of the school. Jamal does have a mentor, but he is not a schoolteacher.

Jamal has serendipitously struck up a friendship with William Forrester, a famous author who wrote a best-selling novel many years ago and never wrote another (heavy shades of J. D. Salinger). William Forrester is an eccentric man who lives alone and suffers from agoraphobia. William helps Jamal with his writing, and Jamal helps William interact with the outside world again. With William Forrester's permission, Jamal uses the title of an old Forrester short story to help him get started on a story of his own. William, however, urges Jamal never to reveal their friendship to anyone. Jamal uses the story to enter a writing contest at school. Mr. Crawford, recognizing the title, accuses Jamal of plagiarism. Jamal keeps his promise to William and does not tell Mr. Crawford that he had permission to use the story's title.

Jamal's story is disqualified from the school's writing contest. The school authorities, nervous that Jamal will be athletically disqualified, offer Jamal a deal—if he wins a key play-off game, they will drop the charges against him. Disgusted with the moral bankruptcy of the school, Jamal misses two key free throws, deliberately losing the game. On the day the stories in the contest are to be read aloud at the school, William Forrester unexpectedly shows up. His rare public appearance and dramatic reading to the crowd impress Mr. Crawford. William Forrester then announces that the story he read that day was not his own, but Jamal's:

> I spoke here today because a friend of mine wasn't allowed to. A friend who had the integrity to protect me when I was unwilling to protect him. His name is Jamal Wallace. . . . I helped him to find his own words by starting with some of mine and in return he promised never to say anything to anyone about me.

Mr. Crawford is humiliated as the school trustees go over his head and award the writing prize to Jamal. Jamal receives a standing ovation from his peers.

At first it would appear that this film has much in common with the urban school films. There is an academic focus, and a poor student is apparently saved by a white middle-class mentor (William Forrester). There are, however, important differences. The school and the teacher are discredited. The school is depicted as an elite institution that values status much more than it values learning. The school sees Jamal primarily as an athlete who can bring glory to the school on the basketball court. Mr. Crawford does not believe Jamal deserves to be at the elite school. As a result, the school and Mr. Crawford lose their authority in Jamal's eyes and in the eyes of the audience. Regardless, Jamal doesn't need the school to have a bright future. Jamal is not dependent upon the school, Mr. Crawford, or even upon William Forrester. In fact, just the opposite is true.

As an underprivileged, black, and academically gifted student from a social world far removed from that of the elite school, it is *Jamal* who has the lessons to teach. The school eventually learns these lessons and changes as a result. Mr. Crawford's humiliation symbolizes this transformation. In many ways, Jamal is the savior of both the school and of William Forrester. Only after he develops a friendship with Jamal does William emerge from his shell and reconnect with the things and people that matter to him in life. Jamal enters the world of the rich, the famous, and the elite and leaves it a better place. It was William who was lost, not Jamal. After all, the title of the movie is *Finding Forrester*, not *Finding Jamal*.

The Burden of Academic Achievement

There is another important difference between the treatment of academics in the urban public school films and the elite private school films. While academic achievement was the celebrated goal of the urban public school films, it is often considered an oppressive burden in the elite private school films. Academic and occupational success is considered to be important in the private school films, but only if they are pursued in balance with other life goals and only if they are personally meaningful. The narrow focus on academic and professional achievement often results in tragedy.

For instance, in *Dead Poet's Society* the Welton School is "the best preparatory school in the United States." Neil Perry is the son of a strict, demanding, and status-conscious father who has aspirations that Neil will become a successful medical doctor.[7] Neil, however, would like to pursue his own interests in and out of the classroom. He has an interest in exploring a career in the theater. He enjoys poetry. He looks forward to serving as the assistant editor of the school yearbook. His overbearing father, however, insists that Neil drop all extracurricular activities and devote himself entirely to his rigorous academic schedule: "After you finish medical school and you're on your own, then you can do as you please. Until then you do as I tell you. Is that clear?"

Neil auditions and wins the lead in a local production of *A Midsummer Night's Dream*. Neil has never been happier than he is in the theater. He shines as an actor. His father watches his dazzling performance on opening night, but he still disapproves of the path Neil has chosen: "I've made a great many sacrifices to get you here, Neil, and you will not let me down." He withdraws Neil from Welton, takes him home, and intends to enroll him in military school. Distraught, Neil kills himself with his father's handgun. Rather than blaming Neil's suicide on the intense pressures, high expectations, and narrow restrictions that parents and teachers put on the students, the school responds to Neil's suicide by firing the only humane teacher it has, the iconoclastic Mr. Keating, whose only sin was to encourage his students to follow their hearts.

In *School Ties* the intense academic pressure also results in tragedy. Not only is the pressure a catalyst for Charlie Dillon to cheat on his history test, but it also causes the nervous breakdown of another student, McGivern. McGivern is from a family that has had five generations attend Princeton University. The pressure to follow his family's footsteps is enormous. His chances of admission to Princeton, however, seem to rest on his French grade. Unfortunately, the demanding French teacher, Mr. Cleary, treats McGivern harshly in French class. McGivern rhetorically asks his friends, "When the guy from Princeton says they might be willing to accept a C in French and you are failing French, then life is pretty much over, don't you agree?"

During an oral exam in French class Mr. Cleary ridicules McGivern's hesitant French. McGivern knows the material, but his nerves in the face of Mr. Cleary's criticism cause him to perform poorly. To escape the humiliation, McGivern runs out of the classroom in the midst of his exam—his future admission to Princeton apparently doomed. He does not return to the dorm that night. Instead, he returns to the classroom and repeatedly recites the French assignment. His friends search the campus and find him in the classroom, half conscious and muttering in French. He is taken away in an ambulance, never to return to school.

The urban public school films treat academic achievement as a panacea to the problems of poor students. The suburban school films, on the other hand, tend to ignore academics entirely or to treat academic achievement with hostility. The elite private school films tend to strike a middle ground. Academic success is valued, but not if achieving it requires the exclusion of other life experiences. The heroes of the elite private school films reject the solitary focus on achievement and express themselves in opposition to the expectations of elite society. At the same time, the poor, working-class, and middle-class students in the elite private school films recognize that an elite private education is valuable because it can help them to become upwardly mobile. They are both expressive and utilitarian individuals.

The Art of Getting By is unique in that the role of the spoiled rich kid and the meritorious middle-class outsider is wrapped up in the same character. George is a senior at the Morgan School in Manhattan. He is disaffected and disinterested in school. His parents seem to live privileged lives and George comes across at times as a spoiled whiner. He doesn't do his homework and doesn't care about school. He is in trouble at school for smoking and he is only one mistake away from expulsion—from throwing away the opportunity of an elite education. He even rejects his art class, the class where he has the most promise and interest. He has the talent, but he doesn't do the work because it feels empty without meaning. His art teacher urges him to complete his work so he can graduate: "I want one, ONE meaningful work from you. Look in the mirror. Listen to your gut and make an image that speaks to the real you—what you care about, what you believe." George doesn't see the point. Early in the movie he explains his disinterest in school by ruminating on a paraphrased quotation by Orson Welles,

> I read this quote once when I was a kid. "We live alone, we die alone. Everything else is just an illusion." It used to keep me up at night. We all die alone. So, why am I supposed to spend my life working, sweating, struggling? For an illusion? Because no amount of friends, no girl, no assignments about conjugating the pluperfect or determining the hypotenuse is going to help me avoid my fate. I have better things to do with my time.

But George is not like the disaffected youth of urban school films who reject learning and the school altogether until they are "saved" by a teacher-hero. George sees value in learning, but not in what the school has to offer or in the way the school judges him. He wants more authentic, personal, and meaningful experiences. He routinely cuts school, but he does so with thought and intentional purpose. He has rules for cutting school. "Rule number one: Cutting school is fun. 2. Cut rarely to preserve the specialness. 3. Do something culturally rewarding with your time to earn it morally." *To earn it morally.* Even as someone who has completely rejected the institution of the school and the achievement ideology George acts in ways consistent with the Protestant ethic. He's a utilitarian individual underneath his rebellious exterior.

Unlike the students in the suburban school films who find their true identities apart from the school, George ultimately finds himself through his academic work. But there is no savior who shows him the way. George develops his own capacity for utilitarian success with personal integrity. As the end of the year approaches and George's graduation is in jeopardy he changes his attitude dramatically. In addition to having his heart broken by a girl (a fellow rebellious smoker), his parents experience severe financial hardship and get a divorce. Suddenly, George is no longer living such a privileged life. These events seem to affect George and he becomes motivated to graduate. Perhaps he wants to impress the girl who broke his heart. Perhaps he feels compelled to finish school because his family is in financial distress. Whatever the reason, he miraculously (and somewhat unrealistically) completes a whole year's worth of school work in just three weeks. It is in his art class that George excels the most, and it is in this class that George finds his voice. George impresses his art teacher by drawing a touching image of the object of his affection. In that one assignment George strikes a balance between achievement and personal expression. Impressed by his sudden work ethic, the principal of the school proudly tells George as he receives his diploma, "Anything is possible."

George rejects the mindless focus on academics that most teachers at the school ask of him. However, rather than finding his identity away from the academic side of school, he is able to find a way to express himself in the context of the school. In this way he both rejects the burden of academic achievement and uses the school to express his identity. His compromise allows him to benefit from the school credential while hanging on to his integrity. He is an expressive and utilitarian individual. Plus, he gets the girl in the end.

While the non-elite protagonists of the elite private school films heroically express both their utilitarian and expressive selves, members of the elite are consistently depicted as morally bankrupt antagonists. There is little redemption for the rich in these films.

The Moral Bankruptcy of the Rich

Just as adults were either the fools or the antagonists in the suburban public school films, it is the rich who are portrayed as fools or enemies in the elite private school films.[8] Charlie's anti-Semitism and lack of integrity in *School Ties,* Mr. Crawford's racist suspicions of Jamal in *Finding Forrester,* and the school's heartless response to Neil's suicide in *Dead Poet's Society* only begin to explore this theme. Another example of the bankruptcy of the rich in elite private school films can be found in 2002's *The Emperor's Club.*

Mr. Hundert teaches the history of Western civilization at the prestigious Saint Benedict's Academy for boys. He is fond of saying that "a man's character is his fate." He uses countless examples from the ancient Greeks and Romans to prove this point. Sedgwick Bell is a new student at Saint Benedict's Academy. He is the rich and privileged son of a U.S. senator. Sedgwick is an impetuous and immature brat who is unenthusiastic about learning. He goofs off in class, plays practical jokes on others, believes that winning is all that matters, and introduces pornographic magazines to the other boys. He frustrates and fascinates Mr. Hundert, who approaches Sedgwick's education as a personal challenge.

Mr. Hundert goes to Washington, DC, to meet with Sedgwick's dad and to discuss Sedgwick's attitude problem. After their meeting, Sedgwick's dad calls Sedgwick to tell him to get his act together. As a result, Sedgwick begins to take his studies more seriously. He begins to study in earnest for the annual Mr. Julius Caesar contest—a Saint Benedict's tradition in which the top three students in

Mr. Hundert's Western civilization class wear togas and compete against each other on the topic of Roman history. Sedgwick improves his academic performance significantly, and Mr. Hundert is proud of his progress. After the final qualifying quiz to narrow the contestants down to the top three, Sedgwick is just one point shy of qualifying. Mr. Hundert sacrifices his own values of integrity and character by changing Sedgwick's grade so that he is among the finalists—edging out the meritorious Martin Blythe, whose father won the Julius Caesar contest years ago.

Sedgwick shocks Mr. Hundert by cheating during the final contest. He had taped cheat sheets to the inside of his toga. Mr. Hundert catches Sedgwick cheating toward the end of the contest but keeps the information private (Sedgwick's father and other dignitaries are in the audience). Mr. Hundert resolves the situation by asking Sedgwick a question that he knows only the other remaining contestant, Deepak Mehta, will know. Deepak becomes Mr. Julius Caesar.

After this episode Sedgwick returns to his juvenile behavior and poor academic performance. Mr. Hundert is disappointed in Sedgwick and ashamed of himself for having believed in him. As it turns out, Sedgwick did not require good grades, academic accolades, glowing recommendations, or even "character." Sedgwick's future was already guaranteed. As Mr. Hundert explains, "Although his father's influence guaranteed him a place at Yale, it was with a profound sense of failure that in the spring of 1976 I handed Sedgwick Bell his diploma."

Twenty-five years later Sedgwick Bell becomes the CEO of one of the biggest corporations in the United States. He promises to make the largest-ever single donation to Saint Benedict's if, and only if, the recently retired Mr. Hundert agrees to officiate a rematch of the Mr. Julius Caesar contest in order to "recover his academic honor." Mr. Hundert would like to think that Sedgwick has reformed his ways. He attends the event and hosts the contest. Sedgwick seems to do quite well and is on his way to victory when Mr. Hundert once again catches him cheating—this time via a high-tech earpiece and a classics graduate student in the back of the room feeding him the answers. Once again, Mr. Hundert doesn't blow Sedgwick's cover. Instead, he asks a question that he knows neither Sedgwick nor the confederate graduate student will know the answer to (about an obscure ruler who was the subject of Mr. Hundert's very first history lesson). Deepak knows the answer, and he is once again crowned Mr. Julius Caesar.

Sedgwick Bell accepts the defeat graciously, but then announces to the crowd that he is running for the U.S. Senate and that educational excellence will be his platform. Mr. Hundert is disgusted with Sedgwick's hypocrisy. He is angry and embarrassed that as one of his students, Sedgwick acquired no noble virtues or principles. He tells Sedgwick, "I failed you as a teacher. . . . [A]ll of us at some point are forced to look at ourselves in the mirror and see who we really are." Sedgwick, however, has no interest in or capacity for self-reflection. He responds to Mr. Hundert not as the senatorial candidate whose platform is educational excellence, but as the smug and entitled rich jerk who has had his whole life handed to him on a silver platter: "Who gives a shit about principle and your virtues? I live in the real world."

Sedgwick Bell may have become a rich and successful businessman and politician, but as far as his high school history teacher is concerned, he is a morally bankrupt failure. The *true* value of an education, according to these elite private school films, is found in the honorable pursuit of knowledge. Otherwise, utilitarian success is nothing but an empty victory.[9]

Revenge of the Middle Class: The Triumph of Well-Roundedness, Integrity, and Merit

Rather than celebrating narrow academic achievement and the maintenance of high social status, it is a virtue in these elite private school films to exhibit balance by being a well-rounded human being, to exhibit integrity by being true to one's self, and to exhibit merit by earning rewards rather than inheriting them or cheating. These middle-class values defeat the culture of privilege that corrupts the upper class.

Well-Roundedness

The hero of *Rushmore* is Max Fischer, the son of a barber who is at the elite Rushmore Academy on an academic scholarship. Max is a precocious young man who loves Rushmore, has many diverse talents, and develops a friendship with Herman Blume, a rich and unhappy industrialist who was quoted at the beginning of this chapter. Herman Blume has two spoiled and bratty sons who also attend Rushmore Academy. He dislikes his own children and admires Max because Max has the passion for life that Blume is lacking—a passion that money and privilege can't buy.

Despite his passion for life and for Rushmore, Max is "one of the worst students in the school," as the headmaster says. The reason is that Max has many interests and pursues them all with gusto. He is the exaggerated picture of well-roundedness. He is the school newspaper publisher, yearbook editor, French club president, model UN member, stamp and coin club vice president, debate team captain, lacrosse team manager, calligraphy club president, founder of the astronomy society, fencing team captain, junior varsity decathlete, second choral choirmaster, kung fu club yellow belt, trap and skeet club founder, Rushmore beekeepers president, Yankee racer founder, Piper Cub club flier, backgammon club president, alternate on the wrestling team, and director of the Max Fischer Players.

Max's academic performance suffers as a result of his involvement in so many diverse activities. In fact, Max is put on "sudden-death academic probation" and is eventually expelled from school. Whereas in the urban public school films such a "failure" would have demanded drastic reformation of the student to focus on his studies, in *Rushmore* the expulsion serves as a sign of Max's salvation—only after leaving Rushmore does Max truly find and become comfortable with his true identity. At first, Max was devastated by the expulsion because he thought that Rushmore was his life. But by the end of the movie Max realizes that there is meaning to life beyond Rushmore (and Herman Blume realizes there is meaning to life beyond money). Blume's conventional "success" is starkly contrasted with Max's "failure." Yet Max is the role model and hero of this film.

Max transfers to the local public high school, Grover Cleveland. There he continues his hyper-involvement in many different activities and begins to improve his grades (to an average of C–). He produces his most successful play, *Heaven and Hell*—a Vietnam War epic and a tribute to Herman Blume, a Vietnam veteran. He also begins dating a public school student, Margaret Yang. Max comes to terms with who he is and what he wants out of life. While at the elite Rushmore Academy, Max was overly conscious about his status in relationship to the other students. He lied and told people his dad was a brain surgeon. After attending Grover Cleveland he proudly introduces his dad as a barber. The message is that you don't need to pretend to be someone you are not—you can find and express yourself and find love wherever and whoever you happen to be. You should follow your heart and not be dependent upon any particular "Rushmore." Furthermore, there is much more to school, and to life, than academic or occupational success. Max's dad is a happy man who loves his life and his job. Before he met Max, Herman Blume was a successful yet miserable capitalist. Max may not be the best student, but he finds meaning and satisfaction in living a creative and balanced life.[10]

Integrity

In addition to living a well-balanced life, these elite private school films extol the importance of personal integrity. Being true to one's self is much more important than "success." The students who exhibit the most integrity in these films are the middle- and working-class students who challenge the culture of privilege in the elite private schools. They become the triumphant heroes of these films when they are able to defeat the rich antagonists with their personal integrity.

In *Scent of a Woman* Charlie Simms is a smart kid from a humble family in Oregon. His mom and stepdad manage a convenience store. He is on an academic scholarship, the Young American Merit Scholarship, to one of the most prestigious preparatory schools in the country, Baird. While Charlie is at the school because of his own merit, it is hinted that the wealthy students are there thanks to their parents' legacy, connections, and financial donations. Most of the rich kids at Baird go to Harvard after graduation as a matter of course. As a financial aid student, Charlie is not a full member of the club. His non-elite status is a stigma among the students at the school, and his pompous and arrogant "friends" condescendingly flaunt their wealth, as this exchange illustrates:

George: You goin' home to fucking Idaho for Thanksgiving?
Charlie: I'm from Oregon.
Harry: Charlie, how do you feel about skiing the white bosom slopes of Vermont?
Charlie: How much?
Harry: $1,200 . . .
Charlie: $1,200 is a little rich for my blood, Harry. [Charlie walks away]
George: What'd you do that for? You know he's on aid.

Harry: On major holidays it's customary for the lord of the manor to offer drippings to the poor.

Harry and his rich friends pull a stunt embarrassing the headmaster and damaging his new car, an expensive Jaguar. Charlie and George were serendipitously in a position to see who was responsible for the stunt. The headmaster asks them both for information, but they both claim not to know who was responsible. The headmaster talks to Charlie alone. He subtly threatens that if Charlie does not name names, he will withdraw a special recommendation he has made on Charlie's behalf to the Harvard admissions committee and he will face possible expulsion. Charlie has the Thanksgiving weekend to come to a decision. The school judiciary committee will hold a public meeting to settle the matter on the Monday after the holiday.

George is particularly intent on keeping Charlie from talking. As a rich kid George knows the code—that rich guys don't rat each other out. He's not sure, though, if Charlie will play by their rules. He tries to make the situation clear to Charlie:

George: You're on scholarship from Oregon. At Baird! You're a long way from home, Chas.

Charlie: What's that got to do with anything?

George: I don't know how it works there. But how it works here—we stick together. . . . [A]bove all, never leave any of us twisting in the wind.

Charlie: What does that have to do with me being on scholarship?

George: I'm just trying to bring you up to speed, kid.

Charlie is not comfortable telling tales on his fellow students. But he's also not sure if he is a part of the "we" that George speaks of. He fears that the rich guys will stick together and sacrifice him, the commoner. Nevertheless, he doesn't want to be a snitch. He has too much integrity. Charlie goes away for the Thanksgiving weekend to take a part-time job caring for a blind army veteran, a colonel named Frank. Over the weekend Frank helps him talk through his ambivalent feelings and discover his identity and values (and Charlie helps Frank to embrace life and abort a planned suicide attempt). Charlie confirms his decision not to sell his soul in order to buy his future into Harvard.

Meanwhile, the rich and morally bankrupt George is preparing to sell his soul. George's rich father is putting pressure on George to name the culprits. George goes back on his pledge to keep quiet. In the public disciplinary hearing, George, with his father by his side, indicts his friends without much conviction. Charlie is needed to confirm the suspects. He does not do so. He is about to be kicked out of school for covering up a crime when Frank unexpectedly shows up as Charlie's advocate. Frank gives a rousing speech on Charlie's behalf that convinces the committee to let Charlie off the hook:

If you think you are preparing these minnows for manhood, better think again! Because I say you are killing the very spirit this institution proclaims it instills.

What a sham! . . . [T]he only class in this act is sitting next to me and I'm here to tell you that this boy's soul is intact. It's non-negotiable. . . . [H]e won't sell himself out to buy his future. That's called integrity!

Neither Frank nor Charlie is from the elite social world that sustains Baird. As a middle-class outsider, Frank attacks the hypocrisy of the school—that George, with his deep-pockets father, can remain in school even though he sacrificed his integrity and sold out his friends, while Charlie, who has so much more to lose, maintained his integrity and refused to sell his soul. Frank says that this personal integrity is the leadership quality the school should be promoting, not the self-interested moral bankruptcy of wealthy snitches who protect themselves at the expense of others.

In lieu of a father with elite connections, Charlie relies on Frank, a middle-class outsider, to make his case that integrity matters. The wealthy, Frank reveals, have no soul. Members of the middle class, however, do what is right, even at the expense of their own interests. Integrity triumphs over the corrupt old-boy network.[11]

The Triumph of Merit

In addition to living a well-balanced life full of integrity, the non-elite student-heroes of these elite private school films exhibit academic merit. While their rich peers may fall back on the social connections and the privileges of their families to get through school, the poor, working-class, and middle-class heroes rely upon their own honest talent and effort for their scholarly accomplishments. We have seen evidence of this already in several of the films discussed thus far in this chapter. *School Ties* offers yet another illustration of the value of merit and how Hollywood treats it as morally superior to the inherited "success" of the privileged classes.

Before Charlie Dillon learns that David Greene is Jewish, the two have a heart-to-heart conversation about life in the elite world of Saint Matthew's. After McGivern has a nervous breakdown and leaves campus in an ambulance, David is stunned. He had never imagined that a student could have such a negative and emotional response to a failing grade. The rich and privileged Charlie responds with an explanation of the way things are for him and his friends from elite families:

Good grades, the right schools, right colleges, right connections—these are the keys to the kingdom. None of us ever goes off and lives by his wits. We do the things they tell us to do, then they give us the good life.

David, as an invited guest to this elite world, is still in disbelief. He does not feel the external pressure that Charlie feels. He wants to get into Harvard, but his life is not depending upon it. Charlie respects David for his authenticity and his down-to-earth attitude: "I envy you . . . because if you get what you want you'll deserve it and if not, you'll manage. . . . You are who you are. That's really what draws people to you, David."

This exchange captures much of what these elite private school films are all about—Charlie, from a rich family at an elite school with a bright future, is envious of a working-class kid from Scranton. The envy that Charlie feels is because he knows that David *deserves* the success he's had. David (as a student and as a football player) is entirely responsible for his achievements in life. Charlie, on the other hand, cannot be certain that the same is true for him. Charlie is riding a wave that his family set in motion long ago. His "success" is the result not of his own talents and effort but of his lineage.

Charlie's cynical attitude about the entire process of elite socialization in which he is enmeshed echoes the lesson that several of these elite private school films teach. The education of these wealthy students is not about integrity, not about following your heart or living by your own wits. The elite boarding school experience is merely a step along the path of upper-class "success" that has been predetermined by those who came before. With Charlie's defeat and humiliation at the end of the movie, Hollywood is expressing another fantasy of the middle class—that meritorious individuals can break into the upper class and that the undeserving rich will suffer the consequences of their unethical behavior. Furthermore, Charlie's admiration for David reveals something else that is at the heart of these elite private school films. Not only does David deserve the success he has achieved, but he is comfortable with who he is. Charlie is envious that David has an independent identity he can be proud of. Charlie may be rich, but he is lost. David, however, is both academically successful (a utilitarian individual) and comfortable with himself (an expressive individual).

The Anomaly of the Catholic School Film

Roughly 10 percent of American schoolchildren attend some sort of private school. About half of all private school students are enrolled in Catholic school. Nevertheless, Hollywood's imagination seems to be more stimulated by the elite private boarding school (only 1 percent of all private school students are enrolled in such schools) than any other type of private school.[12] Still, there are a handful of Catholic school films (*Heaven Help Us, The Trouble with Angels, Sister Act 2, Girls Just Want to Have Fun, The Chocolate War, The Craft, The Dangerous Lives of Altar Boys*, and *Assassination of a High School President*) and one Christian school film (*Saved!*) in the sample. These private religious school films, however, are of an entirely different type than the elite private school films.

This may be because a very different sort of student enrolls in private religious schools than in elite private schools. Catholic school students are predominantly from the middle class. The average Catholic school student has parents who have only somewhat higher incomes and educational attainment levels than the average public school student. While there is significant racial and class diversity among Catholic school students, the very poor and the wealthy are underrepresented.[13] The Catholic school students in Hollywood's stories are also largely from the middle class.

Although they are technically "private" schools, the religious schools in Hollywood films are rarely the setting for academic drama or a conflict between social classes. Because of the predominant middle-class composition of the students in the religious school films, these films are reminiscent of the suburban public school films in which student-heroes oppose the authority of the school in their efforts to find themselves and express their identities apart from their parents and peers.[14] In the rare instance, however, when a religious school film depicts an urban school that serves poor students, the plot more closely resembles the public urban school films, with a teacher-hero saving the students from a culture of poverty. In order to illustrate how the social class of the students (and not necessarily the public or private nature of the school) determines how Hollywood chooses to tell high school stories, we will examine two typical examples: *The Dangerous Lives of Altar Boys* represents the middle-class suburban Catholic school film, and *Sister Act 2* represents the urban lower-class Catholic school film.

The Dangerous Lives of Altar Boys

Francis Doyle and Tim Sullivan are the altar boys who live such "dangerous lives." They are best friends in a suburban Catholic school. With two other friends they aspire to create an original comic book, *The Atomic Trinity*. The archnemesis of the superheroes in *The Atomic Trinity* is their strict and mean geometry teacher, Sister Assumpta, or, as they prefer to call her, "Nunzilla."

Neither Tim nor Francis has a healthy home life. Tim's parents are divorced, and both are alcoholics. Tim is a bright but rebellious teenager. Francis's parents fight most of the time. He, too, is rebellious, and the two of them get into lots of trouble at school. Just as in the suburban public school films, the parents of the students are mostly absent, and the school officials are either antagonists or fools. For instance, in contrast to Sister Assumpta's cruelty, Father Casey is mostly submissive and ineffective, without much moral authority. He is bored and indifferent to his job. He gives bland and generic advice to students without any appreciation for the actual problems they face. When Francis goes to him for advice about sin, the priest gives him platitudes and empty assurances that he will "do the right thing." Father Casey even consults a Magic 8 Ball for guidance.

Without legitimate guidance from adults, Tim and Frances organize mischief in order to express their dissatisfaction with the school and their lives in general. For instance, they steal the statue of Saint Agatha, the school's holy mascot. Sister Assumpta is furious. She suspects Tim and Francis stole it, but she can't prove it. The two boys have an even more ambitious prank in mind, however. They want to steal a cougar from a local zoo and put it in Sister Assumpta's office.

Francis, however, begins to doubt the feasibility of the cougar plan and complains that Tim only acts out in such rebellious ways because he is bored. In response Tim says, "At least I'm doing something. What do you do, Francis?" Indeed, what *does* Francis do? This is the major question that the movie confronts. As in most of the suburban public school films, this movie is about a middle-class teenager's angst and coming of age. He struggles to make sense of life and to find himself somewhere within the confusion. The movie is not about learning. It is not about class conflict (all of the characters are solidly middle class). It is about confused middle-class youth and their search for adult identity.

Where this film differs slightly from most of the suburban public school films, however, is in its darker tones.[15] Francis's search for identity is deeply existential and not nearly as superficial as that of most of the characters in the suburban public school films. For instance, while walking back from a reconnaissance trip to the animal park, Tim and Francis come across a dying dog that has been hit by a car. Francis says, "Someone has to help it! They have to come get it." Tim, angry at Francis's faith in others, says emphatically, "There is no '*they.*' *We* are 'they'!" Tim knows that it is he who must make decisions and take responsibility. No one (no school authority or family member) will either rescue the dog or rescue Francis or Tim. Tim knows that it is *he* who must take action.

Later Tim and Francis return to the zoo to carry out the theft of the cougar. After successfully sedating the cougar, Tim bravely enters the cage. However, he is unaware that there are two cougars in the zoo's display. The second cougar emerges from a den and attacks and kills Tim. Francis speaks at Tim's funeral, held at the school's church. It is Francis who brings meaning to this tragic event—not the nun, the priest, or Tim's family. Francis rises above the shallow morality of the school and the adult authorities to speak the truth about Tim and about life. This event has forced Francis to find himself and to grow up. As in the suburban public school films, however, he needed no adult guidance to do so. In fact, he had to overcome adult obstacles to find and express his true self.

Sister Act 2

By contrast, in *Sister Act 2* the depiction of the Catholic school takes on the unmistakable characteristics of the urban public schools in Hollywood's imagination. As with *The Dangerous Lives of Altar Boys*, it is not the private-ness or the Catholic-ness of the school that makes its mark on the film. Rather, the film's plot takes its cue from the socioeconomic characteristics of the students in the school. Just as with the urban public schools, *Sister Act 2* takes place in an impoverished inner-city school that serves a predominantly poor and nonwhite population. And, as in the urban public school film, the hero is a middle-class adult outsider who is new to teaching. Over the course of the film the students learn from their teacher-hero the value of hard work, middle-class values, and the virtue of following your dreams.

The teacher-hero is "Sister Mary Clarence," an imposter nun. She is actually a Las Vegas headliner. However, she leaves her lucrative career in order to help her nun friends (see *Sister Act 1*) solve the problems in the Catholic high school they operate in San Francisco, Saint Francis Academy. The nuns, new to education, are trying, as they say, "to do good in the 'hood." Doing good, however, is proving harder than they had bargained for. The students are out of control, loud, disobedient, and apathetic inner-city kids. Mr. Crisp, the administrator for the archdiocese, wants to close the school for financial reasons. "It is worth more as a parking lot than a school," he explains to the principal, a well-meaning but ineffectual priest. Only Sister Mary Clarence, it seems, can save the students and save the school.

Sister Mary Clarence is assigned to teach the music class. After encountering the hostility of the students, however, she almost quits. The ungrateful students ignore her, ridicule her, and play pranks on her. She is, nonetheless, persistent. "You must have faith," she is told by another teacher. Sister Mary must have watched many of the urban school films discussed in chapter 3, because she decides that there is only one strategy to pursue—to get the students to care about education and to exercise a work ethic. She preaches to her students, "If you don't have an education you don't have anything. . . . If you want to be somebody, if you want to go somewhere you better wake up and pay attention." In addition to inspiring her students, Sister Mary helps the other nuns to clean up the school (literally and figuratively). All that was needed, apparently, was a new coat of paint and some new attitudes.

The students begin to absorb Sister Mary's lessons and start to believe in themselves. As a result, the student choir dramatically develops very polished musical skills. The other nuns are so impressed that they enroll the choir in an all-state music competition. They travel to the competition, but the students momentarily lose faith in their own abilities after seeing the quality of the competing choirs. Sister Mary gives them an inspirational pep talk, and they end up winning the contest unanimously. The board of trustees is so impressed that they decide not to close the school after all.

Once again, a middle-class teacher-hero combats the educational establishment, overcomes administrative obstacles, is able to "get through" to students suffering in a culture of poverty, and teaches the students the middle-class values and attitudes they need in order to achieve academic success—a feat that no one else had been able to achieve previously. The fact that this is a private Catholic school is barely relevant to the story. The fact that the students are poor and in need of salvation, however, is all that Hollywood needs to know in order to structure the plot.

Inequality, Education, and American Culture

As the elite private school films suggest, the United States is a deeply unequal society. About 30 percent of the adult population in the United States has a four-year college degree. Nearly half of all income earned in the United States goes to only 20 percent of the population. Even more dramatically, approximately 42 percent of *all* the wealth in the United States (property, savings, stocks, bonds, and so forth) is owned by just 1 percent of the population.[16] Americans, however, tend to accept such social class inequality without questioning its legitimacy. While Americans do not believe in equality of outcomes, they do believe strongly in equality of opportunity. That is, as long as all individuals, regardless of social background, have equal opportunity to prove themselves in school and on the job market, then the resulting unequal outcome of educational attainment, income, and wealth is considered to be fairly determined.[17] For instance, in a 2012 international survey, 58 percent of Americans agree *somewhat* or *strongly* that the rich deserve their wealth. This figure is the same in Canada. Only Australians are more likely to believe that the rich in their country deserve their wealth (61 percent). By contrast, only 31 percent of the French believe the rich deserve their wealth.[18]

However, Americans can be particularly offended if they believe that the system is not fair. If poor people encounter blocked opportunities, for instance, Americans of all social classes believe the obstacles should be removed. By the same token, Americans are outraged if it is perceived that the privileges and social status of the wealthy are not earned in a fair contest. Despite the general acceptance of inequality, there is a strain of populism in the American character that is suspicious of "fat cats" and the power they wield in the country. In a 2011 poll, 77 percent of a random national sample believed that the rich have too much power and influence in the United States and 61 percent believe the economic system in the United States unfairly favors the wealthy.[19] Americans do not have much patience for those who benefit from unfair advantages and they are quick to criticize if those who work hard are not rewarded. The legacy of the work ethic remains strong.

The attitude of the average American toward the extremes of inequality in the United States can perhaps best be described as ambivalent.[20] Such ambivalence does not result in political attempts to redistribute income as has been the case in many other industrialized nations. In part this is because average Americans like to think that someday perhaps they, too, may be rich. In a random national poll taken in 2003, 51 percent of young Americans aged 18 to 29 believed it was either *somewhat likely* or *very likely* that they would someday be rich.[21] If one is not born rich, however, how is this likely to happen? Through hard work in school, of course.

The institution of the school figures prominently in both Americans' acceptance of economic inequality and their commitment to equality. According to a 1998 Gallup poll, 63 percent of Americans believe that wealth should be more evenly distributed in the population. However, only 16 percent of Americans believe that the answer is in providing more job opportunities for the poor. Instead, 67 percent of Americans believe the answer to income inequality is to provide better education and job training.[22] If the school is the key to upward social mobility, however, Americans have a peculiar relationship to it.

On the one hand, as utilitarian individuals, Americans believe that academic success in school is required to climb the socioeconomic ladder. Economists speak to the utilitarian individualism of the American character when they explain that schooling is a rational path to achieve success in the competitive marketplace.[23] The purpose of schooling, in effect, is to build "human capital," specific skills to be used in the job market, so that the national economy can function smoothly and the individual can experience upward mobility.[24] Schooling is a competitive race and the point is to finish first, as Benjamin Franklin would have certainly advocated. The primary purpose of school is not intellectual stimulation, but to provide a practical means of upward mobility in a market economy. The government should provide equal opportunities for all students, but it is up to individual students to take advantage of such opportunities. If they fail, they deserve their poverty.

On the other hand, Americans understand education as much more than a tool to achieve utilitarian ends. As expressive individuals, Americans also see the school as a place where human growth occurs and where creativity and self-expression are encouraged. School is not just an institution to measure achievement, but also a place to experience personal growth and celebrate human dignity and diversity. Americans see school as an institution where students discover their own identities, their relationship to others, and their relationship to society.[25]

In other words, there is an expressive function to schooling as well as a utilitarian function. These two functions, however, are often at odds with each other. Schooling in the United States is seen both as a private commodity to be consumed by individuals who hope for social mobility in the marketplace and as a public good that fosters citizenship, community, free expression, and democracy in civil society.[26] As we have seen in previous chapters, Hollywood helps Americans to resolve this tension by emphasizing different educational functions depending upon the social class of the student. In the urban school films the utilitarian function of the school is celebrated. In the suburban school films the educational setting is more of an arena for the expressive function. In the case of the elite private school films the school has both an expressive *and* a utilitarian function.

The elite private school films reflect a belief that success in school and happiness in life should be the result not of *ascribed* characteristics (inherited characteristics rooted in one's group membership, such as race, class, or gender) but of *achieved* characteristics (the hard work and talent of individuals). Sociologists have long debated whether achievement has replaced ascription as the process through which individuals attain educational and occupational status in the United States. There is some evidence that through the twentieth century, the role of ascription has declined in relation to individual achievement.[27] Perhaps this is one reason why nearly half of the elite private school films in this sample are period pieces that depict an earlier era when the privileges of membership in the upper class could be asserted without having to legitimate them through individual hard work and effort.

Despite the historical trend in favor of achievement, however, the ascribed characteristics of race, class, and gender continue to play a powerful role in determining the educational and occupational success of individuals in the United States. Therefore, I argue that Hollywood's depiction of the meritorious student-hero in the elite private school films reflects another middle-class fantasy—a projection of the ideal that hardworking individuals with integrity, regardless of their social background, do not need privileged connections to elite networks in order to become upwardly mobile. This fantasy reflects a deep desire to believe that the system *is* fair—that, despite the deep chasm between the "haves" and "have nots" in this country, we nevertheless *do* live in a meritocracy; that schools and employers accurately evaluate individual ability and fairly promote students and workers on the basis of their objective performance; that achievement is earned, not inherited; and that those who try to subvert this principle of fairness are rightly punished.

There is a tension in the elite private schools between the material value of an elite education and the resentment of such an education by those individuals normally denied access to it. These films resolve such tension both by emphasizing the utilitarian value of an elite private education (it can be an avenue of upward social mobility for meritorious members of the working and middle classes if they have access to it) and by stressing the importance of expressive individualism (there is more to life and more to school than achievement; one must be comfortable with one's self). These films suggest that access to an elite education should not be dependent upon wealth. The rich exercise their collective privilege by trying to buy access to educational status and happiness. In Hollywood's cinematic fantasy, however, the rich are doomed to fail without individuality, well-roundedness, integrity, and merit. The hero of these films is always a non-elite student who succeeds as both a meritorious academic scholar and an expressive individual. In Hollywood, achievement trumps ascription every time.

Notes

1. Mills, C. Wright. *The Power Elite*. New York: Oxford University Press, pp. 64–65.
2. Powers, Stephen, David Rothman, and Stanley Rothman. 1996. *Hollywood's America: Social and Political Themes in Motion Pictures*. Denver: Westview.
3. Goffman, Erving. 1961. *Asylums: Essays on the Social Situation of Mental Patients and Other Inmates*. Garden City, NY: Anchor Books.
4. Cookson, Peter, Jr., and Caroline Persell. 1985. *Preparing for Power: America's Elite Boarding Schools*. New York: Basic Books.
5. Mills, *The Power Elite*, pp. 64–65.
6. Quoted from the front cover of the 1998 Paramount Home Video VHS packaging for *School Ties*.
7. Some observers have claimed that Neil's parents are middle class. See, for instance, Giroux, Henry A. 1993. *Living Dangerously: Multiculturalism and the Politics of Difference*. New York: Peter Lang. Indeed, Neil says his parents are not "rich" and his father admits to having "sacrificed" for Neil's education. However, we never learn about his father's occupation. Nevertheless, the style of their clothing, car, and home suggest that the family is at least upper middle class. If not rich, Neil certainly represents the striving of the middle class to become upwardly mobile through accomplishment in elite institutions. He also represents the folly of such blind ambition if one ignores the calling of one's soul.
8. *The Blind Side* (2009) is somewhat of an exception among the private school films because the rich are only marginally vilified. The protagonist is a wealthy women, Leigh Anne Tuohy, who adopts and "saves" a poor African American boy. However, her rich friends are depicted as racist and unsympathetic to the plight of the poor. To some extent the movie resembles an urban school film in which a privileged hero saves an underprivileged student. However, it shares with the private school genre a focus on academic merit, integrity, and the achievement of a poor student who takes advantage of his opportunities in a wealthy institution despite the doubt and opposition of some at the school.
9. For instance, in 2003's *Igby Goes Down*, Igby is a smart but troubled teen from a very rich and dysfunctional family. He spends the entire movie getting kicked out of, running away from, or avoiding enrollment in private schools. Having watched his rich father self-destruct in mental anguish, he is not interested in following the rules of the upper-class "system": "My father went through the system and the system told him what he was supposed to want. He achieved everything. And then, in his forties, he flipped." Igby, and the other heroes of these films, would rather follow their hearts and be true to themselves than find their fortunes.
10. Another lesson about living a balanced life is found in *Dead Poet's Society*. The character of the English teacher, Mr. Keating, is similar to that of the teacher-heroes in the urban public school films. But from what do these talented, intelligent, hardworking, and rich boys need to be saved? Apparently, they need to be saved from the conformity and lockstep attitude of elite society, from the drudgery of traditional learning, and from the complacency of their comfortable taken-for-granted lives. Mr. Keating urges them to expand their horizons, to live life to its fullest, to challenge accepted ways of seeing the world, and to pursue their passions, even in the face of adversity. Mr. Keating wants his students to be expressive individuals—not the elite conformists the school is molding them to be.

11. It is remarkable how similar *Scent of a Woman* is to *Finding Forrester*. In both cases the working- or middle-class student with academic gifts is not fully accepted in the elite institution. The non-elite student is at the school because of merit, but school officials attempt to exploit his lower status. A troubled and mysterious outsider enters the picture to mentor the non-elite student, who is up against overwhelming odds. In each case the mentor is an alcoholic who has had much success in life, but who has since fallen far. The mentor unexpectedly comes to the aid of the student during a public trial or contest where the lower-class student is being judged. The hero makes a speech that shames the school—that shows how the student has integrity and was willing to risk his status in order to maintain that integrity. The elite private school is discredited. The student is redeemed, and the adult hero moves on to other challenges, both having learned a lesson.

12. See Henig, Jeffrey R., and Stephen D. Sugarman. 1999. "The Nature and Extent of School Choice." In *School Choice and Social Controversy: Politics, Policy, and Law*. Stephen D. Sugarman and Frank R. Kemerer, editors. Washington, DC: Brookings Institution Press; and Cookson and Persell, *Preparing for Power*.

13. For data on Catholic school students, see Bryk, Anthony S., Valerie E. Lee, and Peter B. Holland. 1993. *Catholic Schools and the Common Good*. Cambridge, MA: Harvard University Press.

14. This is also true in the case of the one private Christian school film, 2004's *Saved!* As in most of the suburban public school films, *Saved!* is characterized by the lack of attention to academic work, the heroism of students, the corruption of adult authorities, and the defeat of the popular kids by the social misfits and outsiders. Also, the drama predictably culminates the night of the school's prom, when the true natures of the various characters are finally revealed.

15. *River's Edge* and *Over the Edge* are also darker depictions of the struggles adolescents go through. *River's Edge* in particular is unique among the suburban public school films: It depicts apathetic, amoral, and emotionally numb teens who help to cover up the murder of a friend by another friend. Although it focuses on junior high school students, *Over the Edge* also depicts disaffected and violent youth who rebel against the adult authorities in their suburban town.

16. See Marger, Martin M. 2002. *Social Inequality: Pattern and Processes*. Second Edition. Boston: McGraw Hill; and Wolff, Edward N. 2012. *The Asset Price Meltdown and the Wealth of the Middle Class*. No. w18559. National Bureau of Economic Research.

17. Hochschild, Jennifer. 1981. *What's Fair? American Beliefs About Distributive Justice*. Cambridge, MA: Harvard University Press.

18. Globescan. "Public Remains Concerned over Wealth Inequalities: Global Poll." July 5, 2012. www.globescan.com.

19. Pew Research. Center for the People and the Press. December 15, 2011. www.people-press.org.

20. See Hochschild, *What's Fair?*

21. Gallup Poll. March 11, 2003. www.gallup.com.

22. Gallup Organization. 1998. "Have and Have-Nots: Perceptions of Fairness and Opportunity—1998." Gallup Special Report.

23. Turner, Ralph. 1960. "Sponsored and Contest Mobility and the School System." *American Sociological Review* 25: 855–867.

24. Becker, Gary S. 1975. *Human Capital: A Theoretical and Empirical Analysis with Special Reference to Education*. Chicago: University of Chicago Press.

25. Dewey, John. 1966. *Democracy and Education*. New York: Free Press.

26. Carnoy, Martin, and Henry M. Levin. 1985. *Schooling and Work in the Democratic State*. Stanford: Stanford University Press.

27. Hurn, Christopher. 1993. *The Limits and Possibilities of Schooling*. Boston: Allyn and Bacon.

[seven]

The Cultural Distinctiveness of the American High School Film

Using Our Sociological Imagination to Understand Hollywood Films

Hollywood films have as much to teach us about our selves and our society as any other cultural artifact that Americans produce and consume. There are layers upon layers of cultural meaning just beneath the celluloid surface of the motion picture. Movies are big business and they are art. But that is not all that they are. They are, in a sense, modern-day folktales. They are the mythical stories that we tell ourselves about who we are and what we believe. As such, motion pictures are social documents that map the terrain of our culture. Films emerge out of the imagination of an artist and the office of a businessperson and find their way into our neighborhoods and into our lives. We watch films, read about them, talk back to them, love or hate them, laugh and cry to them, tell our friends about them, argue about them, remember or forget them, and compare them to other films and to our own life experiences. Our collective reaction to films helps to create film genres that are thick with cultural meaning and that play themselves out again and again until they no longer resonate with a sizable audience.

C. Wright Mills taught us to exercise our "sociological imaginations."[1] He explained that to do sociology, one must understand the intersection of biography and history. That is, our individual biographies, the unique lives that we experience, are in very important ways influenced by the time and the place in which we live. We are not alone. The social, historical, cultural, and geographic landscape is as much a part of us as we are a part of it. Mills taught us to see our lives not as disconnected and isolated, but as a part of this larger matrix. Our "personal troubles" are not just our own. Personal troubles are in important ways also "public issues." For instance, a student who drops out of high school may experience dropping out as a very intimate, personal, and unique experience. Yet the problem of dropping out exists as a social issue that is much larger than any particular personal troubles. There are social forces (low quality schools, poverty, the labor market, cultural expectations, etc.) that make dropping out more or less likely for some students. Our individual lives are not disconnected from the larger cultural and structural forces that are outside of our immediate experiences. To recognize our connectedness to the larger social world of which we are inevitably a part is to exercise our sociological imagination.

In much the same way, I have tried to understand Hollywood films as existing within this matrix. Films are more than individual expressions of an artistic vision. They are more than a businessperson's investment. Films exist in a social context. They both are shaped by and in turn shape the social world in which they are embedded. Films are not produced in cultural isolation, nor are they consumed that way. They are social products and must be analyzed as a part of the social world.

The purpose of this book has been to examine carefully one type of modern-day folktale—the American high school motion picture—and to help make sense of its multiple and often contradictory messages in the rich and complicated milieu of American culture. Films are fantasies, but they are fantasies that are firmly grounded within a specific social and cultural context. Applying a sociological imagination to the analysis of films helps to make sense of the relationship between art and society.

What is immediately clear in this study is that there is no one single genre called the high school film. There are multiple subgenres of the high school picture, each with its own particular set of messages and meanings. The urban public school film, the suburban public school film, and the elite private school film each tell a very different story about individualism, inequality, education, and adolescence. Together, however, they speak volumes about the mysteries and contradictions of American culture.

As Kai Erikson has noted, cultures are filled with contradictory potential.[2] This is as true of American culture as it is of any other. Americans, for instance, hold contradictory beliefs about individualism, inequality, education, and adolescence. Americans believe that the individual is more powerful than society, yet we as individuals are dependent upon community. Inequality is considered to be both a social problem and a social necessity. Education is treated as both oppressive and emancipatory. Adolescence is viewed as both threatening and promising. The American high school film is just one lens through which we can get a glimpse of how Americans struggle with these contradictions.

Anthropologist Claude Levi-Strauss argued that myths are a way of reconciling cultural contradictions.[3] The structure of the myth is such that two opposing positions eventually find a compatible resolution. I agree with other sociologists who have studied film that movies are the myths of the contemporary world.[4] They are the medium that a culture uses to tell stories about itself to itself. In a small way Hollywood's representation of reality helps Americans to reconcile some of the contradictory elements within their own culture. For its part, the American high school film genre struggles to reconcile contradictory cultural beliefs about autonomy and dependence, individuality and conformity, and equality and inequality.

The urban school film, for instance, struggles to reconcile independence and dependence. These films feature poor students who suffer in a culture of poverty. The students do not believe in the achievement ideology or the ethic of hard work. These urban students are largely apathetic, violent, and hostile to school authorities. Most of the teachers and administrators have lost hope that any of these students can be successfully educated. Not everyone has lost hope, however. An idealistic teacher new to the school and often new to the profession believes that he or she can "get through" to these "at risk" students. After rejecting traditional methods these teacher-heroes are able to touch the lives of the poor students and to open their eyes to the possibilities waiting for them in the middle-class world. After enduring several crises and having their faith tested, the teacher-heroes transform these students from culturally impoverished pessimists into optimistic young people with middle-class values and aspirations. The urban high school movies tend to end happily as the students finally begin to achieve some level of academic success. While the teacher-hero encourages the students to transcend their poverty—to become utilitarian individuals—they are ironically placed in a position of dependence upon the teacher-hero in order to achieve their middle-class goal of independence.

The suburban school film, on the other hand, struggles to reconcile individuality and conformity. While middle-class adults are predominantly the heroes of the urban school films, middle-class adolescents are consistently the heroes of the suburban school films. The suburban school films feature mostly middle-class students who struggle with their parents, families, and peers as they try to figure out who they are and what they want out of life. In contrast to the urban school films, there is almost no academic content to the suburban school films. Instead, these students take their academic achievement (and future occupational achievement) for granted. The adult authorities in the suburban high school films are not wise educational guides who usher adolescents into adulthood. Instead, these adults are often antagonists who interfere with the freedom and expressive individualism of the middle-class teenager. These suburban school films end happily when the teenage hero is able to assert his or her identity in opposition to the world of conventional middle-class adults or is able to defeat the culture of popularity that governs the peer relations at their high school. Ironically, the students who oppose conventional institutions end up achieving conventional success, and the students who defeat the culture of popularity inevitably become the most popular students in school.

For its part, the elite private school film struggles to reconcile equality and inequality. The elite private school film is more likely than the suburban public school film to feature academic content. Unlike the urban public school film, however, academic achievement is not depicted as a strategy that leads to emancipation and independence. Instead, it is often considered to be a burden for upper-class students, who are under the pressure to legitimate and maintain their social class status. The heroes of these private school films are working- or middle-class students who enter the privileged world of the elite boarding school and teach their own lessons about academic merit, personal integrity, and the importance of living a balanced life. The antagonists are always members of the wealthy class. The working- or middle-class heroes of the elite private school films walk a tightrope between the lessons of the urban and suburban school films. On the one hand, they defeat the culture of privilege of the school as they assert their claims of equality, express their individuality, and resist the pressures of conformity in elite society. On the other hand, they exercise their academic talent and benefit from the unequal utilitarian rewards that the elite institution has to offer. These private school films also end happily as the integrity of the meritorious individual triumphs over the moral bankruptcy of the elite.

As for the few private Catholic and Christian school films, they more closely resemble either the suburban or urban public school films. Since the dramatic tension in these religious school films does not revolve around upper-class students at elite schools, they have very little in common with the other private school films. The dynamic of the plots and the relationships among the characters in the religious private school films depend not upon the type of school in which the story takes place, but upon the type of students who are represented in the film. If the school is populated primarily by middle-class students, then the film tends to resemble the typical suburban public school film. If the students are primarily poor and non-white, then the film takes on the defining characteristics of the urban public school film.

These tendencies speak to much more than the dynamics of storytelling. The American film is unique because American culture is unique. A glimpse into the American cinema gives us a glimpse into the American soul. The optimism, hard work, personal freedom, faith in the individual, and belief in the ultimate fairness of the system that characterize American culture also characterize American film. In reality, Americans may not necessarily be optimistic and rugged individuals working hard in a meritorious system in which the good guys triumph against the odds. However, this is often how Americans *believe* themselves to be. This is the myth we tell ourselves.

In *A Certain Tendency of the Hollywood Cinema, 1930–1980*, Robert B. Ray argues that American films tend to resolve tension and contradictions neatly in the story:

> This reconciliatory pattern, itself derived largely from earlier American forms, increasingly became the self-perpetuating norm of the American Cinema. Movies that refused to resolve contradictory myths typically found themselves without the large audiences expected by the industry; as a result, directors of such films found themselves without chances to work.[5]

This often results in the proverbial "happy ending" of the typical American film, an ending in which the tension that drove the plot is released and the characters and themes are no longer in opposition to each other. Either one pole is eliminated or a compromise is reached between opposing sides. The audience leaves feeling content and pleased that a satisfying resolution has been reached. If, as I have argued, the contradictions in these films mirror the contradictions in American culture, then perhaps the tidy resolutions of the American films help in a small way to smooth out some of the rough patches that perplex Americans in their everyday lives.

What About Foreign School Films?
An Exploratory Examination

If I am correct that American high school films teach us something important about American culture, then we should expect to see different themes in films about high school produced in other countries. In fact, my exploratory research with a nonrandom sample of forty-two films from fifteen different countries does suggest that foreign school films may be consistently different from American school films.[6] Rather than a resolution of the contradictions in the story or within the characters, the foreign school films I have studied often end in discord. The main characters frequently fail to resolve their problems. Their futures remain clouded and their relationships to others remain troubled. Happy endings are far less common and tragic endings far more common in the foreign school films than in the American school films. Finally, and most significantly, the individual is still the focus of the foreign school film, but the individual's relationship to society is dramatically different. Rather than battling the odds and successfully changing the social world, as in the American school films, the individual "hero" of the foreign school film confronts and then tries to escape the oppressive social world. In some cases the individual is defeated. In other cases the individual is happy to have escaped. But rarely does the individual succeed in transforming the antagonistic social forces.

To illustrate this contrast, it is helpful first to look in depth at one school film that typifies many of the themes expressed in the foreign school films I have analyzed. The Japanese film *Battle Royale* (2000) depicts a deteriorating Japanese society in the near future in which 800,000 students are boycotting school. *Battle Royale* begins as members of ninth-grade "Class B" are preparing to go on their annual field trip (used to bribe the students back to school). Instead of the field trip, however, the students are gassed into unconsciousness, kidnapped by the army, and taken to a deserted island, where they are required to fight for their lives in a brutal and violent game.

The adults, in fear of the nation's youth, have attempted to reassert control over society and to quell the rising rebellion of the young by passing the draconian Millennium Education Reform Act. The abducted students of Class B are about to participate in one element of the new act, the Battle Royale. Each year a randomly selected class of students is isolated on an island with the instructions to kill each other until only one "winner" is left alive. Their host, and the contest referee, is the teacher they had in seventh grade, Mr. Kitano. While the students are gathered to learn the rules of the "game," Mr. Kitano tells them:

> This country is absolutely no good anymore. . . . [Y]ou guys mock grown-ups. Go ahead and mock us. But don't forget life is a game. So fight for survival and find out if you are worth it.

The students are each given a pack with some food and one weapon in it. All have a necklace locked around their neck that constantly monitors their location and activity. It also tells the authorities when they are dead. If they attempt to take the necklace off it detonates, killing them. If there is no winner after three days, all the students are killed. In addition to the regular class of forty students participating in the game, there are two "transfer" students—one, as it turns out, won a previous Battle Royale and the other signed up just "for fun."

Some students take to the game eagerly, killing their friends without hesitation. Others attempt to gather the students together to resist the rules of the cruel game. Still others are simply depressed about the grim situation and kill themselves. The film focuses on the character of Nanahara, an angry boy who is filled with doubt about adult society. His mother left him when he was younger, and his father killed himself. He was raised in a foster home. His heart is not in the game, but he will try to survive: "I've never really trusted adults. . . . But I'll keep fighting, even though I don't know how, until I become a real adult." More importantly, he devotes himself to defending his girlfriend, Noriko.

Nanahara and Noriko befriend Kawada, the previous winner of a Battle Royale and a viciously effective fighter. Kawada is kind to them because he, too, had devoted himself to protecting his girlfriend in his first Battle Royale. The three of them form an alliance. Kawada kills many students, but Nanahara and Noriko take refuge in a cabin through most of the battles. After much carnage, Nanahara, Noriko, and Kawada are the last three left alive on the island. As it turns out, Kawada has the ability to safely disable the monitoring necklaces. Kawada fools Mr. Kitano into thinking that he has killed Nanahara and Noriko and has once again won the contest. After the army leaves their headquarters to collect the students' bodies, the three survivors return to confront Mr. Kitano alone. Nanahara kills Mr. Kitano, and the three survivors escape the island on a boat. En route back to the mainland, however, Kawada dies of the injuries he suffered in the battle. Noriko and Nanahara return home safely only to find that they are wanted for the murder of Mr. Kitano. Fugitives from the law, they must go underground to avoid capture. The film ends with the two "winners" of the game running for their lives in civilization, just as they had run for their lives in the Battle Royale.

This is certainly not the happy ending that we have come to expect in most of the American high school films. Noriko and Nanahara are the student-heroes, but they are not victorious. Noriko and Nanahara must remain constantly on the run from the oppressive adult authorities of society. The spirit of the movie may side with the youth, but the youth do not triumph. Neither, however, do the adults. The distrust and fear that are the premise of the movie remain at the end. There is no resolution to the dramatic tension that fueled the plot. Furthermore, unlike the American school films, *Battle Royale* offers little hope for the future. We do not know what will become of Noriko and Nanahara. While they were clever enough to avoid death in the *Battle Royale*, it is not certain that they can survive back home. We last see them running away from all they know in order to stay alive.

You may have noticed a striking resemblance between this description of *Battle Royale* and the 2012 American film *Hunger Games*. The plots are nearly identical. However, in typical American fashion, the ending of *Hunger Games* is much more uplifting. The heroine, Katniss, survives the brutal game and emerges victorious along with her friend Peeta. While in *Battle Royale* the two survivors face an uncertain future as they run for their lives in an oppressive society, in *Hunger Games* Katniss and Peeta are celebrated as national heroes. Admittedly, there is a sinister shadow lurking behind their victory since the authorities sense Katniss and Peeta are a threat to national order. Nevertheless, their victory is clear-cut and satisfying to audiences, who leave the theater relieved that Katniss and Peeta will live. And while the 2014 sequel (*Hunger Games: Catching Fire*) plunges Katniss and Peeta back into an uncertain fate, *Catching Fire* sets the stage for the revolution against the oppressive state that is depicted in *Hunger Games: Mockingjay*

Part I. Such a revolution is not even hinted at in the pessimistic *Battle Royale*. While not a traditional high school film, *Hunger Games* does resemble many of the suburban school American films by celebrating the expressive individualism of an adolescent coming of age. Katniss develops her own identity as she fights the oppressive forces of adult society.

The Class, a 2008 French film, provides another illustration of the ways foreign school films tend to resolve tension differently than American films do. *The Class* is about an idealistic young teacher, François Marin, who teaches French to mostly low-income immigrant students in an urban Paris high school. Just as with Erin Gruwell in *Freedom Writers*, François Marin uses the *Diary of Anne Frank* as an example to encourage the students to tell their own stories. His success with the students is much more modest than that of Erin Gruwell. There is a high degree of racial, ethnic, and class tensions in the school that do not get fully resolved. While the students occasionally respond positively to their teacher's lessons, ultimately the cultural divide between him and the students prevents any American urban-school-style breakthrough. At the end of the school year François Marin asks the students what they have learned over the course of the year. Several of them volunteer modest achievements. But the film's closing moments feature two students who claim to have learned nothing. For instance, Esmerelda says, "I didn't learn anything." François responds, "You can't spend nine months at school and not learn anything." "I'm the living proof," she says. Incredulous, he offers, "You got something from the books we read." But Esmerelda is not impressed: "[Y]our books are shit."

While in the American school films the gulf between the teacher and the students narrows (because the students move closer to the expectations of the teacher), in *The Class* the gulf between the students and the teacher grows wider. Although several of the students report that they learned something over the course of the year, the exchange between François and the two students who feel they learned nothing is what haunts the viewer. The American urban school films, as we have seen, end resolutely with utilitarian achievements and hope for the future. *The Class* and many other foreign school films end with ambiguity and pessimism for the future: a bleak assessment of the ability of the middle class to reach and rescue adolescents from poor urban environments.

By contrast, the foreign school films highlight a particularly American cultural orientation of optimism (particularly among the American middle class) and a persistent faith in the power of the individual in the face of social institutions. In their 1991 follow-up to *Habits of the Heart* Bellah and his co-authors note that after World War II there was a particularly powerful mood of optimism in the United States. While the postwar years have certainly presented many challenges to the "American Century" and provided plenty of reasons to be pessimistic, a peculiar American optimism remains.[7] Americans have lost some faith in their institutions and politicians, yet they remain hopeful and upbeat about their personal fortunes. As Alan Wolfe found in his study of the American middle class:

> Americans are usually thought of as an optimistic people, emphasizing the positive, quick to turn away from despair. They may have become cynical and resentful toward politicians, but, by the same token, they have always been, and

continue to be, hopeful about their own prospects. . . . Optimism is so pervasive in middle-class America that many found unimaginable that "our society is going to continue to decline and decline."[8]

Such optimism does not necessarily correspond with real conditions. The optimistic and happy endings of the American school films are not very accurate reflections of American society. That is, our lives are not as tidy and happy as the lives of the characters in these high school films. However, it is noteworthy that these films, with happy endings and neatly resolved conflicts, are the stories that we choose to tell to ourselves about ourselves. That is, the *image* of who we are as Americans, how we understand ourselves to be, is reflected in the cultural products we produce and consume.

While the foreign school films tend to depict the individual at the mercy of oppressive social forces, the American school films ultimately suggest that oppressive social forces are at the mercy of the individual. Whether it is the cowboy of the urban school classroom, the expressive individual fighting against suburban conformity, or the meritorious underdog of the elite private school, the American films end with the happy triumph of the individual. The myths of American culture are echoed and reinforced in American film. These myths of the capitalist ethic, the rugged individual, the drummer who marches to his or her own beat, and the fairness of social institutions help to conceal the structural sources of inequality and oppression in society. In the American high school films the system is fair, the individual is free, and hard work is rewarded. If not, then it is the task of the heroic individual to defeat the system or to reform it. The counterexample of the foreign school films helps us to see that, rather than conforming to standard requirements of movie plots, the American high school films clearly bear the unmistakable stamp of a unique cultural view of the individual and society.

Who Has Cultural Power?

Who has the power to tell the folktales that help to smooth out some of these contradictory elements of American culture? What social groups or institutions have the power to determine the messages conveyed in cultural products such as films? Feminist scholars have persuasively argued that Hollywood films tend to privilege the view of men. They argue that the movies are told from the point of view of the male gaze. As feminist scholar Laura Mulvey writes:

> The man controls the film fantasy and also emerges as the representative of power in a further sense: as the bearer of the look of the spectator. . . . [A]s the spectator identifies with the main male protagonist, he projects his look onto that of his like, his screen surrogate, so that the power of the male protagonist as he controls events coincides with the active power of the erotic look, both giving a satisfying sense of omnipotence.[9]

While I agree with this analysis, I would extend this critique to one of social class as well. The protagonists of the American high school films, almost without exception, represent middle-class assumptions, worldviews, and interests. However, the middle-class teacher or student is not explicitly painted in class terms. Rather, these film characters are taken for granted as "normal," rational, and sensible individuals. It is *assumed* that the audience will identify with and positively relate to the protagonist. These characters express individual autonomy, a capitalist work ethic, personal ambition, a faith in meritocracy, and free expression. But these are not neutral characteristics. They are characteristics with roots in a particular social class experience and perspective. It is precisely in the taken-for-grantedness of these characteristics as "normal," in the *invisibility* of class, that the perspective of the middle class holds such power in these Hollywood stories. The power to be defined as "normal" in a culture is intimately tied to the power to conceal and legitimate inequality—to justify the exclusion of the "deviant" from the status and rewards of society. There is cultural power in the privileged gaze of the middle class—and it is even more powerful if it is not recognized as a gaze that originates from a class position. Jack Zipes has made a similar argument about the class power behind the classic fairy tale:

> All the tools of modern industrial society . . . have made their mark on the fairy tale to make it classical ultimately in the name of the bourgeoisie which refuses to be named, denies involvement; for the fairy tale must appear harmless, natural, eternal, ahistorical, therapeutic. We are to live and breathe the classical fairy tale as fresh, free air. We are led to believe that this air has not been contaminated and polluted by a social class that will not name itself.[10]

In part, the middle-class perspective of Hollywood is the result of the fact that artists and audiences are largely members of the middle class. But the reasons for this cultural hegemony go much deeper. As the producer of modern-day folktales, Hollywood has the power to represent the culture. Whether individuals in the Hollywood system are aware of it or not, they create such tales in a way that reinforces dominant cultural understandings about American life. Rather than merely representing "liberal" political positions, as Hollywood is often criticized for doing,[11] mainstream film studios actually tell folk stories that reinforce rather conservative myths of American culture, which in turn reinforce existing inequalities and support the status quo.

By extolling the power of the individual, celebrating the capitalist ethic, and advancing the myth of meritocracy, Hollywood's fantasies support a worldview that preserves class inequality: a worldview that assumes individuals have the power to change the world; that in the United States you are free to be whoever you want; that the poor are responsible for their own fate; and that those who work hard and obey the rules will be richly rewarded. It is not that the middle class has most of the power in the United States. The upper class certainly wields more economic and political power. However, it is a middle-class *sensibility* that dominates American culture. Such sensibilities protect the interests not only of the middle class, but of the wealthy as well. An emphasis on the individual work ethic and a belief in the fairness and openness of educational, political, and economic institutions serve to legitimate the wealth of the "haves" and to place the blame of failure on the "have nots."

As we have seen, the cultural hegemony of a middle-class perspective leaves its mark on all three subgenres of the high school film. The middle-class teacher-heroes of the urban school films defeat the culture of poverty and encourage utilitarian individualism among their poor students. The middle-class student-heroes of the suburban school films defeat the culture of popularity and exercise expressive individualism while maintaining their class position. The working- and middle-class heroes of the elite private school film exercise their utilitarian individualism by defeating the culture of privilege *and* exercise their expressive individualism by resisting the pressures of conformity in elite society.

Such expressions of American culture, however, are not unique to the high school film. While high school films offer us a particularly rich field in which to explore the ways our culture makes sense of education, inequality, gender, and adolescence, the dominant lessons of this study can be applied to other genres of film as well. Whether it is the Western, the crime drama, the war movie, or the science-fiction film, the mark of American culture finds its way into the Hollywood film. And Hollywood films subsequently become a part of American culture.

Since this research did not talk to American moviegoers to see how they interpret and react to these films, there is more work to be done. A reception study to see how these high school films are viewed by a cross section of Americans could test many of the hypotheses about American culture that I have proposed in this book. Do Americans in general accept the dominant ideologies as they are represented in these films? Or do American film audiences actively reinterpret the messages of these films in such a way as to challenge the dominant ideology? Perhaps different groups in society react in different ways to the three subgenres discussed in this book. Only future research that collects data directly from film audiences will be able to offer answers to these questions.

The point of this book is not necessarily to be critical of the Hollywood system for perpetuating stereotypes or inaccuracies about inequality, young people, and education. The fault does not lie solely in the hands of a few studio executives. Yes, Hollywood has the power to represent our culture, but we, as members of this culture, are also participants in its creation and re-creation. As cultural artifacts, films depend both upon producers and consumers. To understand how Hollywood makes sense of youth, education, and inequality is to catch a glimpse of how *we* as a society implicitly make sense of these things. Only by looking at our own lives and at cultural artifacts in the rich complexity of social context can we begin to unpack the mysteries and contradictions of American life. If we are to challenge these views—to engage in critical dialogue with American culture and to change it—it is necessary to exercise our sociological imagination.

Notes

1. Mills, C. Wright. 1959. *The Sociological Imagination*. New York: Oxford University Press.
2. Erikson, Kai T. 1978. *Everything in Its Path: Destruction of Community in the Buffalo Creek Flood*. New York: Simon and Schuster.
3. Levi-Strauss, Claude. 1978. *Myth and Meaning: Cracking the Code of Culture*. Toronto: University of Toronto Press.
4. Wright, Will. 1975. *Sixguns and Society: A Structural Study of the Western*. Berkeley: University of California Press; and Tudor, Andrew. 1974. *Image and Influence: Studies in the Sociology of Film*. New York: St. Martin's Press.
5. Ray, Robert B. 1985. *A Certain Tendency of the Hollywood Cinema, 1930–1980*. Princeton, NJ: Princeton University Press, p. 57.
6. Because of the limited availability of many foreign films about high school, the selection criteria for this exploratory sample were loosened somewhat to include films that featured junior-high-aged students. Also, the school is not always at the center of the plot in the foreign school films. The findings of this brief exploration are merely suggestive. To make generalizable claims would require greater attention to the specific historical and cultural traditions within each of the fifteen countries represented and a much more representative sample of the films produced by each country.
7. Bellah, Robert N., Richard Madsen, William M. Sullivan, Ann Swidler, and Steven M. Tipton, 1991. *The Good Society*. New York: Knopf.
8. Wolfe, Alan. *One Nation, After All*. 1998. New York: Viking.
9. Mulvey, Laura. 1989. "Visual Pleasure and Narrative Cinema." In *Visual and Other Pleasures*. London: Macmillan, p. 20.
10. Zipes, Jack. 1993. *Fairy Tale as Myth: Myth as Fairy Tale*. Lexington: University of Kentucky Press, p. 7.
11. Medved, Michael. 1992. *Hollywood vs. America: Popular Culture and the War on Traditional Values*. New York: HarperCollins.

Appendix A

A Guide to Conducting Social Science Research with Film

Now that you have read this book you may be curious to conduct your own research project using film as data. Perhaps your professor is requiring you to write a term paper on a question inspired by this book. Or maybe you disagree with my arguments and you want to conduct your own analysis. Maybe you are thinking about studying cinematic representations as part of your senior thesis. In any case, this appendix will briefly walk you through the steps you should complete as you conduct your own social science research project using film as data. I hope this guide is helpful to both the student in a lower division class analyzing roughly ten films for a term paper and the advanced student who may be analyzing many more.

There is no one right way to study film. Different academic disciplines take different methodological approaches to the study of film. What I propose in this appendix is a particularly "scientific" approach that I think many researchers in the social sciences could use to great effect. This approach is much different from the approach taken by most film studies scholars or others in the humanities. Each tradition has its own advantages. The advantages of the approach I outline here are that it allows for the systematic collection of data, testing of hypotheses, generalization to other cases, and the ability of other scholars to build upon or challenge the findings.

It's important to remember that even though watching movies is a fun way to collect data, it's still a social scientific endeavor. Making a social scientific argument about film is different from being a film critic. We don't just watch the films we like and we don't just write our opinions of the films we see. To study movies as a social scientist requires us to research them with the same sort of rigor and scientific methodologies we would use if we were conducting a survey or interview study. Two advantages of conducting research with movies, however, are that the data are relatively accessible to most people and no Institutional Review Board approval is needed.[1]

In order to design an effective social science research project you have to know precisely what it is you would like to learn, what other scholars have learned about the subject already, what sort of information will help you to answer your research question, how you will systematically collect that information, how you will analyze that information, and how you will present the information in a way that convinces others that you have, in fact, found an answer to your research question.[2]

What Is Your Research Question?

All good social science research begins with a well-thought-out and carefully crafted research question. Most sociologists ask either an exploratory question or an explanatory question. Which type you ask depends on how much information you have about a phenomenon before you begin the research. If you are merely curious about a phenomenon and want to know more about it before you go in a specific direction of inquiry, you are likely asking an exploratory research question. For instance, you may ask the exploratory question, "How do Hollywood films about high school depict drug use?" In this case you haven't yet thought about which variables might affect the depiction of drug use in high school films. You don't yet have a hypothesis to test. Doing exploratory research means you are collecting data inductively: You are gathering data from the ground up and, as you proceed, you may generate some hypotheses about how Hollywood depicts drug use.

You may, however, already have a hunch about what you think the answer to your research question is. Maybe some preliminary research has suggested to you that men are more likely than women to be shown taking drugs in high school films.[3] Or maybe you have conducted a review of the existing literature on the subject that suggests there may be a gender difference in the depiction of drug use. In that case, you would be asking an explanatory research question: "Are men more likely than women to do drugs in high school films?" With this explanatory question you want to know if the independent variable of gender has an effect on the dependent variable of depictions of drug use. In other words, you want to know if the gender of the character helps to explain the likelihood of drug use depiction. This sort of research is deductive research because you are starting with a hypothesis (men are more likely to be shown doing drugs than women) and you are collecting data to test that hypothesis.

In doing the research for this book I began with a very general exploratory question: "How are images of high school represented in Hollywood films?" I didn't yet have an idea about what I would find. I had no hypothesis to test. I was exploring. After inductively collecting data I began to see certain patterns in the films. I then asked an explanatory question: "Do the social demographics of the students in the films affect the ways in which Hollywood tells stories about high school?" In this case the independent variable is the social demographics of the students (their social class, race, and gender) and the dependent variable is the ways in which Hollywood depicts high school.

Conduct a Literature Review

Whether it's exploratory or explanatory research, you need to find out if others have already asked a similar research question. You should know if other scholars have already published work in books or articles that makes an argument about (using our example) the depiction of drug use in high school films. If so, you need to explain how your proposed research relates to the existing literature. Maybe there is not much work in this area and your work is breaking new ground. Maybe your research is testing the findings of another scholar. Maybe you disagree with how that other scholar collected a sample of films or how he or she interpreted the data.

Your librarian can help you to get started on the search for academic literature related to your research question. It's important to remember that as scholars we want to know what other scholars have already learned (or not) about our particular research question. Therefore, we look to a particular type of literature—the academic literature. We don't look primarily to popular books, magazines, or the work of journalists. Academic literature can be books written by scholars (usually professors in a college or university) that have been published by an academic press (often the publisher is associated with a college or university). Another source of academic literature is found in academic journals. Academic journals are special magazines that publish the research reports of scholars. One of the things that makes these articles "academic" (as opposed to popular) is that they have been reviewed by other scholars in the field and have passed a sort of quality control before they are published. This is what is meant by the term "peer review." Search for academic peer-reviewed journal articles in databases such as Sociological Abstracts or Communication Abstracts. If your question is related to the field of education you might try searching in the Education Resources Information Center (ERIC) database. If you don't have access to these databases, Google Scholar is a good option.

In many cases you might not find any academic journal articles or books about your precise research question. This does not mean you have no litera-ture to review. You need to think about how tangentially related academic literature might still be relevant to help you frame your research project. For instance, you might find research about depictions of deviant behavior in high school films, but not specifically about drug use. Perhaps you will find litera-ture about drug use in films, but not specifically in high school films. Perhaps you will find an article about the use of drugs in high school films, but the author doesn't analyze it by gender. Perhaps you will find nothing about film representations, but you find an article about gender differences in drug use in the real world. In all of these examples you can use the existing literature to help you frame your research project and to make sense of the findings.

What Is Your Hypothesis?

Before you begin collecting data you should ask yourself: "What do I think the answer to my research question will be?" Whether it's an exploratory or explanatory question you probably have a prediction about what you will find. This prediction might be based on your own experience as a moviegoer, based on preliminary research, based on your reading of the academic literature, or based on your own taken-for-granted assumptions. In any case, it's useful to be aware about what you expect to find and why. In particular, as social scientists we need to be aware of our assumptions and to guard against the temptation to design our studies and interpret our data in a way that confirms them. What makes our work social *science* is that we systematically and objectively collect data to learn something new about the social world. We need to be objective observers and be open to the possibility that our assumptions or hypotheses are wrong. Sometimes the greatest scientific findings come from being surprised by the data.

Identify the Variables

Before you watch the films to collect the data you need to be clear about what the variables are that you are looking for, how you have defined them, and how you will know them when you see them in the films. For instance, if you are asking the question, "Are athletes in high school films depicted as less intelligent than non-athlete characters?" you need to identify the independent and dependent variables. The independent variable is what you think might influence the dependent variable. In this example you want to know if the independent variable of athletic status (characters are either athletes or not) helps to predict the dependent variable of how their intelligence is depicted (some characters are depicted to be smarter than other characters). Before you begin watching films you need to answer a few conceptual questions: What do you mean by "athletic status"? Does it mean the character has to be on a high school team, or is it enough that they are shown playing a sport with friends after school? What do you mean by "intelligence"? Do you mean intelligence as it's recognized by the school in terms of grades and institutional achievement, or do you mean other sorts of intelligence that the character might exhibit apart from school? Be explicit about how you define the variables and be consistent in how you use these definitions to categorize the data.

Once you have defined what you mean by each variable you need to decide how to measure the variables. In other words, you need to decide how you will know the variables when you see them on film. If you have defined athletic status as formal membership in a high school organized sport, then what in the films will indicate to you that a character is an athlete by that definition? Perhaps images such as the character practicing with the team, playing in a game, or wearing a varsity letter will be the indicators you use to measure his or her athletic status. If you have defined intelligence as academic intelligence as recognized by the institution of the school, perhaps you will measure that by the types of classes the character is enrolled in, how teachers treat the character, or if the character receives awards (or sanctions) based on his or her schoolwork.

Because this question is concerned primarily with the depiction of athletes, some students may be tempted just to analyze the characters who are athletes. This would be a mistake that prevents you from making a convincing argument. In order to make an argument about the relationship between athletic status and intelligence in high school films you need to have information not just about the depiction of athletes in films, but about the depiction of non-athletes as well. Let's pretend you collect data about many characters who are athletes and you find that most of the athlete characters are depicted as not very bright. You can't make the argument that athletes in high school movies are depicted as less intelligent than non-athlete characters because you have not yet collected data about the depiction of intelligence among non-athletes. It is possible that non-athletes are also depicted as not very bright. Only if you have found that non-athletes tend to be depicted as intelligent can you make the argument that athletes are depicted as less intelligent.

When I began this research project I first analyzed the films that feature mostly low-income students in urban public high schools (what I call the "urban school sample"). I began to make an argument about Hollywood's representation of low-income students based on my viewing of films such as *Blackboard Jungle, Dangerous Minds, Lean on Me,* and *Stand and Deliver.* However, I couldn't make an argument that the social class of the students in the films affected Hollywood's depiction of high school until I contrasted the urban school films to a sample of films that featured public schools with mostly middle-class students (what I call the "suburban school sample"), such as *Rebel Without a Cause, Pretty in Pink, The Breakfast Club,* and *Mean Girls.* Only with this contrast could I argue that my independent variable (the social class of the students in the films) affects the ways that Hollywood tells stories about high school.

What Is the Population?

The population is the largest group of units for which you hope the findings of your research will be true. What your population is depends on the nature of your research question. If you ask the exploratory question, "How are wealthy students depicted in private school films?" the population is all private school films.[4] If you ask the explanatory research question, "Does the race of the teacher in urban high school films affect the style of teaching depicted?" the population is all urban high school films. Of course, just as you have to be precise in how you define your variables, you have to be precise in how you define the parameters of the population. For instance, you'd have to decide what characteristics constitute a film as a "private school film" or an "urban public high school film."

Once you have determined what counts as a private school film or urban public high school film, you will need to generate a list of as many of the films in your population as possible. You may need to use a variety of strategies to create this list. You may start with listing all the films you know of that fit your criteria for the population. You may also ask friends to contribute titles of films to the list. Ultimately, you'll need a more systematic way to ensure you have a list of all films in your population. Many video guidebooks and online resources, such as the Internet Movie Database and Netflix, can be very useful in this regard.

If your population is too large to get a handle on for a term paper, you may want to consider ways of limiting it. You can always modify your research question by adding other criteria. For instance, you may ask instead, "Does the race of the teacher in urban high school films from the past ten years affect the style of teaching depicted?" or "How are wealthy students depicted in the ten most commercially successful private school films?" (The Internet Movie Database has box office data for most films.) When asking a research question that limits the population so precisely it is important to have a theoretical justification for that decision. In these two cases you would want to explain why, beyond practical considerations, asking a research question about recent films or popular films is of theoretical interest.

In *Hollywood Goes to High School* I defined my population as non-horror American films that "use a high school as their primary setting or films whose plots orbit around the life of a high school or high school students." (See chapter 1 for more information about my population and sample.) I tried to analyze as many of the films in my population as possible. I do not recommend this strategy to students if the population of films is large! It is time-consuming and, inevitably, you will overlook some films from the population. I recommend choosing a sample from your population using the method described in the following section.

How Will You Select a Sample?

It is most likely that you won't have the time or resources to watch all the films in your population. This is why scientists often study a sample, or subset, of the population. How you choose the sample, however, is very important. You can't just choose the films with which you are most familiar, the ones you particularly like, or, heaven forbid, just the ones you think prove your hypothesis. To do this would introduce "selection bias" into your sample and call into question all of your findings. You want your sample to be as representative of the entire population as possible. The more representative the sample is of the population, the more likely your findings from the sample will be generalizable to (true for) the entire population.

There are different sorts of samples for different circumstances, but the best way to ensure you have a representative sample is to use a probability sampling technique like simple random sampling. Random in this case does not mean haphazard. It's a mathematical concept that means that each and every unit in the population must have an equal chance of being selected for the sample. Let's say there are 100 films in your population and you want to select a sample of 20 of those films for the study. You would number those films 1 through 100. Next, you should search for a "random number generator" online. Ask the generator to randomly select 20 numbers out of 100. Once you have the 20 randomly selected numbers, go to your numbered list of 100 films in the population and indicate which 20 films were randomly selected. Now you have your randomly selected sample of films.[5]

Take Detailed Notes

If you have twenty films in your sample you will need to watch each film very carefully and take detailed notes about each. The detailed notes you take about the films are the data you will use to construct your argument. During the first viewing take notes about everything—you never know what might later turn out to be an important part of your argument. It's best to be exhaustive in your note taking. For instance, keep track of character names, all major and minor plot developments, and details such as the sound track, the mood of the film, costumes, and other details. Richly describe each character. What are their social characteristics? Who are the heroes and villains? Pay attention to where the dramatic tension is. If it's a comedy, where are the punch lines? Write down dialogue that captures key moments in the film or that best captures the essence of the characters. You will also want to take notes that specifically address your unique research question.

As soon as you are done watching the film you should write up a few paragraphs that summarize it before you forget the details. You may want to include comments about how you think this film helps to answer your research question. You won't know what your final argument is until after you have systematically analyzed the data from all of the films, but it's a useful exercise to answer for yourself after each film where you think the data are taking you. After you have seen all of the films in the sample you may want to go back, time permitting, to watch them again. You often see and hear things differently upon a second viewing. It also provides an opportunity for you to take more detailed notes of things that have turned out to be important. An advantage of using film as data is that you can always go back to the original source as many times as you need to check the accuracy of your data.

Analyze the Data

After you have taken detailed notes of each film it's time to look for patterns in the data that help you to answer your research question. For instance, how prevalent is drug use in the films? Are the films more likely to depict men doing drugs than women? Even if the primary focus was on gender it's useful to look for patterns based on other variables as well. For instance, did you notice a pattern of drug use by the race or ethnicity of the characters? Were there any differences in how the drug use was depicted—that is, was it depicted as ominous or frivolous? Was it central to the story or marginal? Were there consequences for it? Were the consequences evenly distributed by race, social class, and gender?

Social scientists analyze large amounts of qualitative data such as detailed notes about movies with a method called "coding." Coding is a way to systematically go through all of your notes in search of patterns—to see, for instance, if there is a gender difference in drug use depiction or if the style of teaching is related to the race of the teacher and so on.

Let's say you took detailed notes on ten urban high school films. Let's pretend that five films had white teachers and five films had non-white teachers. You want to know if there is a pattern between the independent variable of the race of the teacher and the dependent variable of his or her teaching style. Create two piles of papers (or two folders or files of documents on your computer) organized by the independent variable—the notes of five films with white teachers in one pile and the notes of five films with non-white teachers in the other. Go through each pile of papers coding for every description of the teachers' teaching style. Every time you find in your notes a description of their teaching methods, curriculum, style of instruction, and so on, you highlight it. (I like to use colored highlighters—each color represents a different theme I'm coding for. This allows me to go through the same set of notes later and look for a different theme and code it a different color for easy analysis later).[6]

After you have coded for the theme of teaching style you can compare pile one (white teachers) to pile two (non-white teachers) to see if there are any differences in the way Hollywood depicts the teaching styles of each. Whether you find a difference or not, you have a research finding.

You have data from a random sample of urban high school films that the race of the teacher either does or does not seem to be related to the style of teaching depicted. That's science!

Use the Data to Build an Argument

Once you have systematically coded all of your notes in search of patterns in the data, it's time to write a paper that explains to others what you did, how you did it, and what you found. A good paper will explain your research question, discuss why it is important, place it in the context of the academic literature, explain the design of the research project (population, sample, conceptualization of variables, explanation of the methods used), and make an argument using the data to convince readers why you have come to that conclusion.

You may want to make some arguments that are based on a statistical summary of the data ($x\%$ of men in suburban school films are shown doing drugs compared to $y\%$ of women, for instance). However, in most cases the small sample sizes we use studying films precludes us from conducting much of a meaningful statistical analysis. More importantly, however, I would argue that the strength of using films as data is that it allows us to construct an argument using rich and descriptive qualitative data. As qualitative sociologists we want our samples to be representative of our population and we want to collect and analyze our data systematically. However, we don't want to reduce the richness of film to a statistical summary. We are interested in how these films reflect culture, how they reflect the often messy ways in which people make sense of social life. In reporting the findings of a study on the cinematic depiction of drug use by gender, for instance, I would want to know not just the statistical differences in drug use depiction between men and women. I'd want also to understand if there are differences in how the characters use the drugs, if there are differences in what drugs they use, if there are differences in the consequences of their drug use, if there are differences in how the drug use helps us to understand their character, and so on. Only by providing the qualitative data that describes these elements of the movie can we truly understand the complexity of the phenomenon.

Most of the data you present in your paper will be drawn from the detailed notes you have taken. You must include data from your notes to explain to the reader that your argument has empirical support. The reader can't just take your word for it. You need to provide enough evidence to convince the reader. If, for instance, you found that non-white teachers in urban high school films tend to use different sorts of pedagogies in the classroom than white teachers, be sure to give examples of each. You won't likely include every example you have from every film you watched.

When you select the examples to include in the paper make sure they are examples that are representative of the pattern you found. Don't necessarily choose the most sensational examples if they are not typical. If there are exceptions to the pattern you found, be honest about it. Your paper will be stronger if you are up front about counterexamples that don't neatly fit your interpretation of the data.

Use Theory to Explain Your Findings

It's not enough to show that you have found a pattern in the films (white teachers use different methods than non-white teachers; men use more drugs than women; athletes are less likely than non-athletes to be depicted as intelligent). You also need to explain *why* you think this pattern exists. What is the sociological explanation for the differences you observed? Sometimes this is the hardest but most interesting part of the research. It may be clear that there are differences in how social life is depicted on screen, but it's not always clear what the significance is. The interpretation of the data—the answering of the "What does it all mean?" question— introduces the need for theory. In the simplest of terms, a theory is a story that helps us to explain the patterns we see in the empirical world. In *Hollywood Goes to High School* I use Bellah et al.'s theory about American individualism to help me explain the differences I observed between urban and suburban high school films.[7] If, for instance, you are looking to explain gender differences in the depiction of drug use you may find help in the literature on the sociology of deviance or gender.

Doing research with film is great fun. The number of research questions you can ask is endless. But, just because it is fun doesn't mean that it isn't also serious business. A social science approach to the study of film requires that we think carefully about our research question, do our homework with the existing academic literature, define what we mean by and how we will measure our variables, understand the parameters of our population, choose a representative sample, take detailed notes of the films, systematically analyze the data, build an argument with the data, and explain the data with theory. But don't let the rigor scare you off. All social science research is rigorous and follows these methodological steps. One advantage of doing research with film is that it is accessible to all of us. Even better, the social scientific study of film gives us fascinating glimpses into the mysteries of our culture. Good luck with your own research projects!

Notes

1. An Institutional Review Board (IRB) is a committee on most university campuses that is charged with reviewing the proposals of all research projects that collect information from human beings. The IRB wants to ensure that all human participants know their rights and are treated ethically by the researcher. If you are administering a survey or conducting interviews, for instance, it can be quite time-consuming to obtain IRB approval before beginning the research. Fortunately for scholars who study films rather than people, the IRB review is one less hurdle to overcome.
2. It should be noted that even if your object of study is not film, the processes described here can be applied to other social phenomena as well. The scientific approach outlined here can be adapted to a wide variety of sociological research questions and methodological tools.
3. All examples in this appendix are hypothetical and presented here only for purposes of illustration. If research has been done on these questions I am not aware of their findings.
4. If you are just interested in the depiction of wealthy students in private school films, then your population is "all private school films." You will describe the ways in which wealthy students are depicted in these films. Since we are social scientists looking for patterns and trends, however, you should keep your eye out for any variation in how wealthy students are depicted *within* these private school films. For instance, are wealthy young women depicted differently than wealthy young men? If, however, you wanted to compare the depiction of wealthy students *between* different sorts of high school films, then your question is an explanatory one (i.e., Does the type of high school in the film influence the way rich kids are depicted?). In this case the population would likely be "all high school films" so that it included films about both private and public high schools.
5. While working with a large sample of films may not be feasible for most undergraduate term papers, I have found that students can write convincing papers with about ten to twelve films in their sample. In order to make this small sample representative, ask research questions that limit the size of the population (see the previous section) and/or use a simple random sample to keep the number of films manageable.
6. It is not necessary, but if you are conducting a large study you may want to consider using qualitative-data software programs such as ATLASti, NVIVO, MAXQDA, or NUDist to help you with the coding process.
7. Bellah, Robert N., Richard Madsen, William M. Sullivan, Ann Swidler, and Steven M. Tipton. 1985. *Habits of the Heart: Individualism and Commitment in American Life*. New York: Harper and Row.

Appendix B
High School Film Sample

The Suburban School Films in the Sample

Rebel Without a Cause (1955)

High School Hell Cats (1958)

High School Caesar (1960)

Splendor in the Grass (1961)

The Last Picture Show (1971)

American Graffiti (1973)

Grease (1978)

Rock and Roll High School (1979)

Fast Times at Ridgemont High (1982)

The Last American Virgin (1982)

All the Right Moves (1983)

Risky Business (1983)

Valley Girl (1983)

16 Candles (1984)

The Karate Kid (1984)

The Breakfast Club (1985)

Weird Science (1985)

Better Off Dead (1985)

Tuff Turf (1985)

Teen Wolf (1985)

Just One of the Guys (1985)

Peggy Sue Got Married (1986)

Pretty in Pink (1986)

Ferris Bueller's Day Off (1986)

Dangerously Close (1986)

Hoosiers (1986)

Class of Nuke 'Em High (1986)

Lucas (1986)

River's Edge (1986)

Three O'Clock High (1987)

Can't Buy Me Love (1987)

Some Kind of Wonderful (1987)

Permanent Record (1988)

Heathers (1989)

Say Anything (1989)

How I Got into College (1989)

Bill and Ted's Excellent Adventure (1989)

Cry Baby (1990)

Pump Up the Volume (1990)

Rock and Roll High School Forever (1990)

Buffy the Vampire Slayer (1992)

Dazed and Confused (1993)

Clueless (1995)

Powder (1995)

Mr. Holland's Opus (1995)

Angus (1995)

Foxfire (1996)

Can't Hardly Wait (1998)

The Faculty (1998)

Disturbing Behavior (1998)

Election (1999)

Varsity Blues (1999)

10 Things I Hate About You (1999)

Teaching Mrs. Tingle (1999)

She's All That (1999)

American Pie (1999)

Never Been Kissed (1999)

October Sky (1999)

Jawbreaker (1999)

Get Over It (2000)

Remember the Titans (2000)

Whatever It Takes (2000)

Ghost World (2000)

Bring It On (2001)

Crazy/Beautiful (2001)

My Horrible Year (2001)

Not Another Teen Movie (2001)

Orange County (2002)

The New Guy (2002)

The Hot Chick (2002)

Swimfan (2002)

Dumb and Dumberer (2003)

How to Deal (2003)

Freaky Friday (2003)

Better Luck Tomorrow (2003)

Radio (2003)

Blue Car (2003)

Elephant (2003)

Friday Night Lights (2004)

Mean Girls (2004)

Napoleon Dynamite (2004)

The Perfect Score (2004)

The Girl Next Door (2004)

Confessions of a Teenage Drama Queen (2004)

New York Minute (2004)

A Cinderella Story (2004)

John Tucker Must Die (2006)

Charlie Bartlett (2007)

Juno (2007)

Superbad (2007)

Twilight (2008)

17 Again (2009)

I Love You, Beth Cooper (2009)

Jennifer's Body (2009)

Easy A (2010)

Prom (2011)

Touchback (2011)

21 Jump Street (2012)

The Perks of Being a Wallflower (2012)

Project X (2012)

The Bling Ring (2013)

G.B.F. (2013)

The Spectacular Now (2013)

The To Do List (2013)

The Urban School Films in the Sample

Blackboard Jungle (1955)

Up the Down Staircase (1967)

Halls of Anger (1970)

Conrack (1974)

Cooley High (1975)

Fame (1980)

Class of 1984 (1982)

Teachers (1984)

Wildcats (1986)

Stand and Deliver (1987)

The Principal (1987)

Summer School (1987)

The Beat (1988)

Lean on Me (1989)

Class Act (1992)

Zebrahead (1992)

Just Another Girl on the I.R.T. (1992)

Only the Strong (1993)

Dangerous Minds (1995)

The Substitute (1996)

High School High (1996)

Sunset Park (1996)

187 (1997)

The Substitute 2 (1998)

Detention (1998)

Light It Up (1999)

Cheaters (2000)

Our Song (2000)

Save the Last Dance (2001)

Real Women Have Curves (2002)

Detention (2003)

Love Don't Cost a Thing (2003)

Coach Carter (2005)

Take the Lead (2006)

Freedom Writers (2007)

Precious (2009)

Here Comes the Boom (2012)

The Private School Films in the Sample

The Trouble with Angels (1966)

The Prime of Miss Jean Brodie (1969)

Our Time (1974)

Up the Academy (1980)

Taps (1981)

Class (1983)

Private School (1983)

Making the Grade (1984)

Heaven Help Us (1985)

Girls Just Want to Have Fun (1985)

The Chocolate War (1988)

Dead Poet's Society (1989)

School Ties (1992)

Scent of a Woman (1992)

Sister Act 2 (1993)

The Craft (1996)

All I Wanna Do (1998)

Rushmore (1999)

Outside Providence (1999)

Cruel Intentions (1999)

Finding Forrester (2000)

O (2001)

Donnie Darko (2001)

The Smokers (2002)

Cheats (2002)

The Emperor's Club (2002)

The Dangerous Lives of Altar Boys (2002)

Igby Goes Down (2002)

Saved! (2004)

Step Up (2006)

She's the Man (2006)

Assassination of a High School President (2008)

The Wackness (2008)

The Blind Side (2009)

The Art of Getting By (2011)

Words and Pictures (2013)

Bibliography

Ayers, William. 1996. "A Teacher Ain't Nothin' but a Hero: Teachers and Teaching in Film." In *City Kids, City Teachers: Reports from the Front Row*. William Ayers and Patricia Ford, editors. New York: The New Press.

Banfield, Edward. 1968. *The Unheavenly City*. Boston: Little, Brown.

Becker, Gary S. 1975. *Human Capital: A Theoretical and Empirical Analysis with Special Reference to Education*. Chicago: University of Chicago Press.

Behm-Morawitz, Elizabeth, and Dana E. Mastro. 2008. "Mean Girls? The Influence of Gender Portrayals in Teen Movies on Emerging Adults' Gender-Based Attitudes and Beliefs." *Journalism and Mass Communication Quarterly* 85, no. 1:131–146

Bellah, Robert N. 1973. "Introduction." In *Emile Durkheim on Morality and Society*. Chicago: University of Chicago Press.

Bellah, Robert N., Richard Madsen, William M. Sullivan, Ann Swidler, and Steven M. Tipton. 1985. *Habits of the Heart: Individualism and Commitment in American Life*. New York: Harper and Row.

Bellah, Robert N., Richard Madsen, William M. Sullivan, Ann Swidler, and Steven M. Tipton. 1991. *The Good Society*. New York: Knopf.

Berliner, David C., and Bruce J. Biddle. 1997. *The Manufactured Crisis: Myths, Fraud, and the Attack on America's Public Schools*. White Plains, NY: Longman.

Bernstein, Jonathan. 1997. *Pretty in Pink: The Golden Age of Teenage Movies*. New York: St. Martin's Griffin.

Bourdieu, Pierre. 1977. "Cultural Reproduction and Social Reproduction." In *Power and Ideology in Education*. Jerome Karabel and A. H. Halsey, editors. New York: Oxford University Press.

Bryk, Anthony S., Valerie E. Lee, and Peter B. Holland. 1993. *Catholic Schools and the Common Good*. Cambridge, MA: Harvard University Press.

Bulman, Robert C. 2002. "Teachers in the 'Hood': Hollywood's Middle-Class Fantasy." *Urban Review* 34, no. 3 (September): 251–276.

Bulman, Robert C., and Nicole S. McCants. 2008. "Enlightened Teenage Masculinity," *Contexts: Understanding People in Their Social Worlds*, (Summer) 7: 3, 68–69

Burbach, Harold J., and Margo A. Figgins. 1993. "A Thematic Profile of the Images of Teachers in Film." *Teacher Education Quarterly* (spring): 65–75.

Carnoy, Martin, and Henry M. Levin. 1985. *Schooling and Work in the Democratic State*. Stanford, CA: Stanford University Press.

Chambliss, William J. 1973. "The Saints and the Roughnecks." *Society* 11, no. 1: 24.

Chennault, Ronald E. 2006. *Hollywood Films About Schools: Where Race, Politics, and Education Intersect*. New York: Palgrave.

Chubb, John E., and Terry M. Moe. 1990. *Politics, Markets, and America's Schools*. Washington, DC: The Brookings Institution.

Coleman, James S. 1961. *The Adolescent Society*. New York: Free Press.

Coleman, James, et al. 1966. *Equality of Educational Opportunity*. Washington, DC: U.S. Government.

Considine, David M. 1985. *The Cinema of Adolescence*. Jefferson, NC: McFarland and Co.

Cookson, Peter, Jr., and Caroline Persell. 1985. *Preparing for Power: America's Elite Boarding Schools*. New York: Basic Books.

Corbett, Dick, Bruce Wilson, and Belinda Williams. 2002. *Effort and Excellence in Urban Classrooms: Expecting and Getting Success with All Students*. New York: Teachers College Press.

Crane, Diana. 1992. *The Production of Culture: Media and the Urban Arts*. New York: Sage.

Dalton, Mary. 1999. *The Hollywood Curriculum: Teachers and Teaching in the Movies*. New York: Peter Lang.

Dalton, Mary. 2010. *The Hollywood Curriculum: Teachers in the Movies*. Second Revised Edition. New York: Peter Lang.

Darling-Hammond, Linda. 1997. *The Right to Learn: A Blueprint for Creating Schools That Work*. San Francisco: Jossey-Bass.

Denby, David. 1999. "High School Confidential: Notes on Teen Movies." *The New Yorker* (May 31): 94–98.

Denzin, Norman K. 1991. *Hollywood Shot by Shot: Alcoholism in American Cinema*. New York: Aldine de Gruyter.

Deschenes, S., David Tyack, and Larry Cuban. 2001. "Mismatch: Historical Perspectives on Schools and Students Who Don't Fit Them." *Teachers College Record* 103, no. 4: 525–547.

Dewey, John. 1966. *Democracy and Education*. New York: Free Press.

Doherty, Thomas. 2002. *Teenagers and Teenpics: The Juvenilization of American Movies in the 1950s*. Philadelphia: Temple University Press.

Durkheim, Emile. 1973a. *Moral Education: A Study in the Theory and Application of the Sociology of Education*. New York: Free Press.

Durkheim, Emile. 1973b. "Individualism and the Intellectuals." In *Emile Durkheim on Morality and Society*. Chicago: University of Chicago Press.

Durkheim, Emile. 1973c. "The Dualism of Human Nature and Its Social Conditions." In *Emile Durkheim on Morality and Society*. Chicago: University of Chicago Press.

Durkheim, Emile. 1984. *The Division of Labor in Society*. Translated by W. D. Halls. New York: Free Press.

Eckert, Penelope. 1989. *Jocks and Burnouts: Social Categories and Identity in High School*. New York: Teachers College Press.

Ehrenreich, Barbara. 1989. *Fear of Falling: The Inner Life of the Middle Class*. New York: Harper Press.

Emerson, Ralph Waldo. 1883. "Self Reliance." In *Essays*. Boston: Houghton, Mifflin, and Co.

Epstein, Joyce L. 1987. "Parent Involvement: What Research Says to Administrators." *Education and Urban Society* 19, no. 2: 119–136.

Epstein, Joyce. 1996. "Perspectives and Previews on Research and Policy for School, Family, and Community Partnerships." In *Family–School Links: How Do They Affect Educational Outcomes?* A. Booth and J. Dunn, editors. Mahwah, NJ: Lawrence Erlbaum Associates.

Erikson, Kai T. 1978. *Everything in Its Path*: *Destruction of Community in the Buffalo Creek Flood*. New York: Simon and Schuster.

Farber, Paul, and Gunilla Holm. 1994a. "Adolescent Freedom and the Cinematic High School." In *Schooling in the Light of Popular Culture*. Paul Farber, Eugene F. Provenzo Jr., and Gunilla Holm, editors. Albany: State University of New York Press.

Farber, Paul, and Gunilla Holm. 1994b. "A Brotherhood of Heroes: The Charismatic Educator in Recent American Movies." In *Schooling in the Light of Popular Culture*. Paul Farber, Eugene F. Provenzo Jr., and Gunilla Holm, editors. Albany: State University of New York Press.

Farhi, Adam. 1999. "Hollywood Goes to School: Recognizing the Super-teacher Myth in Film." *The Clearing House* 72, no. 3: 157.

Feldman, Shirley S., and Glen R. Elliott, editors. 1990. *At the Threshold: The Developing Adolescent*. Cambridge, MA: Harvard University Press.

Fine, Michelle. 1991. *Framing Dropouts: Notes on the Politics of an Urban High School*. Albany: State University of New York Press.

Foley, Douglas E. 1990. *Learning Capitalist Culture: Deep in the Heart of Tejas*. Philadelphia: University of Pennsylvania Press.

Franklin, Benjamin, 1941. *The Autobiography of Benjamin Franklin*. New York: Walter J. Black.

Gallup Organization. 1998. "Have and Have-Nots: Perceptions of Fairness and Opportunity—1998." Gallup Special Report.

Gallup Organization. 2004. "36th Annual Phi Delta Kappan/Gallup Poll" (September).

Gans, Herbert J. 1988. *Middle American Individualism: The Future of Liberal Democracy*. New York: Free Press.

Geertz, Clifford. 1973. *The Interpretation of Cultures*. New York: Basic Books.

Gibson, Margaret A., and John U. Ogbu, editors. 1991. *Minority Status and Schooling: A Comparative Study of Immigrants and Involuntary Minorities*. New York: Garland.

Giroux, Henry A. 1992. "Resisting Difference: Cultural Studies and the Discourse of Critical Pedagogy." In *Cultural Studies*. Lawrence Grossberg, Cary Nelson, and Paula A. Treichler, editors. New York: Routledge, 199–212.

Giroux, Henry A. 1993. *Living Dangerously: Multiculturalism and the Politics of Difference*. New York: Peter Lang.

Giroux, Henry. 1996. "Race, Pedagogy and Whiteness in 'Dangerous Minds'." *Cineaste* 22, no. 4: 46–50.

Gitlin, Todd. 1983. *Inside Prime Time*. New York: Pantheon.

Globescan. 2012. "Public Remains Concerned over Wealth Inequalities: Global Poll." July 5. www.people-press.org

Goffman, Erving. 1961. Asylums: Essays on the Social Situation of Mental Patients and Other Inmates. Garden City, NY: Anchor Books.

Grant, Peggy A. 2002. "Using Popular Films to Challenge Preservice Teachers' Beliefs About Teaching in Urban Schools." *Urban Education* 37 (January 2002): 77–95.

Hall, Granville Stanley. 1904. *Adolescence: Its Psychology and Its Relations to Physiology, Anthropology, Sociology, Sex, Crime, Religion, and Education.* New York: D. Appleton and Company.

Harrington, C. Lee, and Denise D. Bielby. 2001. "Constructing the Popular: Cultural Production and Consumption." In *Popular Culture: Production and Consumption.* C. Lee Harrington and Denise D. Bielby, editors. Malden, MA: Blackwell.

Heilman, Robert B. 1991. "The Great-Teacher Myth." *American Scholar* 60, no. 3: 417–423.

Henig, Jeffrey R., and Stephen D. Sugarman. 1999. "The Nature and Extent of School Choice." In *School Choice and Social Controversy: Politics, Policy, and Law.* Stephen D. Sugarman and Frank R. Kemerer, editors. Washington, DC: Brookings Institution Press.

Hill, David. 1995. "Tinseltown Teachers." *Teacher Magazine* (March) 5: 40–45.

Hine, Robert V., and John Mack Faragher. 2000. *The American West: A New Interpretive History.* New Haven, CT: Yale University Press.

Hine, Thomas. 1999. *The Rise and Fall of the American Teenager.* New York: Perennial.

Hochschild, Jennifer. 1981. *What's Fair? American Beliefs About Distributive Justice.* Cambridge, MA: Harvard University Press.

hooks, bell. 1996. *Reel to Real: Race, Sex, and Class at the Movies.* New York: Routledge.

Huizinga, D., and D. Elliott. 1987. "Juvenile Offenders: Prevalence, Offender Incidence, and Arrest Rates by Race." *Crime and Delinquency* 33: 206–223.

Hurn, Christopher. 1993. *The Limits and Possibilities of Schooling.* Boston: Allyn and Bacon.

Hutcheson, Ron. 2001. "Bush Calls for Faith-Based 'Assault on Poverty'." *Sacramento Bee* (May 21): A15.

Johnson, LouAnne. 1992. *Dangerous Minds.* New York: St. Martin's Paperback.

Katz, Michael B. 1987. *Reconstructing American Education.* Cambridge, MA: Harvard University Press.

Katznelson, Ira, and Margaret Weir. 1985. *Schooling for All: Class, Race, and the Decline of the Democratic Ideal.* Berkeley: University of California Press.

Kett, Joseph F. 1977. *Rites of Passage: Adolescence in America, 1790 to the Present*. New York: Basic Books.

Kimmel, Michael, 1996. *Manhood in America: A Cultural History*. New York: The Free Press.

Kimmel, Michael. 2009. *Guyland: The Perilous World Where Boys Become Men*. New York: Harper Collins.

Kozol, Jonathan. 1991. *Savage Inequalities: Children in America's Schools*. New York: Crown Publishers.

Ladd, Everett Carll, and Karlyn H. Bowman. 1998. *Attitudes Toward Economic Inequality*. Washington, DC: The American Enterprise Institute.

Lareau, Annette. 1987. "Social Class Differences in Family-School Relationships: The Importance of Cultural Capital." *Sociology of Education* 60: 73–85.

Lee, Valerie E. 2001. *Restructuring High Schools for Equity and Excellence: What Works*. New York: Teachers College Press.

Levi-Strauss, Claude. 1978. *Myth and Meaning: Cracking the Code of Culture*. Toronto: University of Toronto Press.

Lewis, Jon. 1992. *The Road to Romance and Ruin: Teen Films and Youth Culture*. New York: Routledge.

Lieberman, Myron. 1993. *Public Education: An Autopsy*. Cambridge, MA: Harvard University Press.

Lipsitz, George. 1990. *Time Passages: Collective Memory and American Popular Culture*. Minneapolis: University of Minnesota Press.

Macartney, Suzanne, and Alemayehu Bishaw. 2013. "Poverty Rates for Selected Detailed Race and Hispanic Groups by State and Place, 2007–2011." www.census.gov

MacLeod, Jay. 1995. *Ain't No Makin' It: Aspirations and Attainment in a Low-Income Neighborhood*. Boulder, CO: Westview Press.

Males, Mike A. 1999. *Framing Youth: 10 Myths About the Next Generation*. Monroe, ME: Common Courage Press.

Marger, Martin M. 2002. *Social Inequality: Pattern and Processes*. Second Edition. Boston: McGraw Hill.

McCarthy, Cameron, et al. 1996. "Race, Suburban Resentment, and the Representation of the Inner City in Contemporary Film and Television." In *Off White*. Michelle Fine et al., editors. New York: Routledge.

Medved, Michael. 1992. *Hollywood vs. America: Popular Culture and the War on Traditional Values*. New York: HarperCollins.

Merton, Robert. 1968. *Social Theory and Social Structure*. New York: Free Press.

Mills, C. Wright. 1956. *White Collar: The American Middle Classes*. New York: Oxford University Press.

Mills, C. Wright. 1959a. *The Sociological Imagination*. New York: Oxford University Press.

Mills, C. Wright. 1959b. *The Power Elite*. New York: Oxford University Press.

Modell, John, and Madeline Goodman. 1990. "Historical Perspectives." In *At the Threshold: The Developing Adolescent*. S. Shirley Feldman and Glen R. Elliott, editors. Cambridge, MA: Harvard University Press.

Mora, Richard, and Mary Christianakis. 2012. "'No Free Rides, No Excuses': Film Stereotypes of Urban Working-Class Students." In *Blue Collar Pop Culture: From NASCAR to Jersey Shore*. M. Keith Booker editor. Santa Barbara: Praeger

Motion Picture Association of America. 2003. "The 2003 U.S. Movie Attendance Study."

Mukerji, Chandra, and Michael Shudson, editors. 1991. *Rethinking Popular Culture: Contemporary Perspectives in Cultural Studies*. Berkeley: University of California Press.

Mulvey, Laura. 1989. "Visual Pleasure and Narrative Cinema." In *Visual and Other Pleasures*. London: Macmillan.

Natriello, G., Aaron M. Pallas, and E. L. McDill. 1986. *Community Resources for Responding to the Dropout Problem*. New Brunswick, NJ: Rutgers University Press.

Natriello, Gary, Edward L. McDill, and Aaron M. Pallas. 1990. *Schooling the Disadvantaged: Racing Against Catastrophe*. New York: Teachers College Press.

Nieves, Evelyn. 2000. "California Proposal Toughens Penalties for Young Criminals." *New York Times* (March 6).

Oakes, Jeannine. 1985. *Keeping Track: How Schools Structure Inequality*. New Haven, CT: Yale University Press.

Palladino, Grace. 1996. *Teenagers: An American History*. New York: Basic Books.

Pascoe, C. J. 2007. *Dude, You're a Fag: Masculinity and Sexuality in High School.* Berkeley: University of California Press.

Powers, Stephen, David Rothman, and Stanley Rothman. 1996. *Hollywood's America: Social and Political Themes in Motion Pictures.* Denver: Westview.

Purkey, Stewart C., and Marshall S. Smith, 1983. "Effective Schools: A Review." *Elementary School Journal* 83 (March): 427–452.

Putnam, Robert. 2000. *Bowling Alone: The Collapse and Revival of American Community.* New York: Touchstone Books.

Ray, Robert B. 1985. *A Certain Tendency of the Hollywood Cinema, 1930–1980.* Princeton, NJ: Princeton University Press.

Reed, Joseph W. 1989. *American Scenarios: The Uses of Film Genre.* Middletown: CT: Wesleyan University Press.

Riesman, David, with Nathan Glazer and Reuel Denney. 1961. *The Lonely Crowd: A Study of the Changing American Character.* New Haven, CT: Yale University Press.

Roper Poll. January 2003. "Child Tax Credit Survey."

Rosenthal, Robert, and Lenore Jacobson. 1968. *Pygmalion in the Classroom.* New York: Holt, Rinehart and Winston.

Schatz, Thomas. 1981. *Hollywood Genres: Formulas, Filmmaking, and the Studio System.* Boston: McGraw Hill.

Schlesinger, Arthur M., Jr. 1979. "Foreword." In *American History/American Film: Interpreting the Hollywood Image.* John E. O'Connor and Martin A. Jackson, editors. New York: Continuum.

Schneider, David M., and Raymond T. Smith. 1973. *Class Differences and Sex Roles in American Kinship and Family Structure.* Englewood Cliffs, NJ: Prentice Hall.

Schuman, Howard, Charlotte Steeh, Lawrence Bobo, and Maria Krysan. 1998. *Racial Attitudes in America: Trends and Interpretations.* Cambridge, MA: Harvard University Press.

Sewell, William H., Robert M. Hauser, and David L. Featherman, editors. 1976. *Schooling and Achievement in American Society.* New York: Academic Press.

Shary, Timothy. 2002. *Generation Multiplex: The Image of Youth in Contemporary American Cinema.* Austin: University of Texas Press.

Shary, Timothy. 2014. *Generation Multiplex: The Images of Youth in American Cinema After 1980.* Revised Edition. Austin: University of Texas Press.

Slater, Philip. 1976. *The Pursuit of Loneliness: American Culture at the Breaking Point*. Boston: Beacon Press.

Smith, Dorothy. 1987. *The Everyday World as Problematic*. Boston: Northeastern University Press.

Steele, Claude. M. 1997. "A Threat in the Air: How Stereotypes Shape the Intellectual Identities and Performance of Women and African Americans." *American Psychologist* 52: 613–629.

Swidler, Ann. 1986. "Culture in Action: Symbols and Strategies." *American Sociological Review* 51: 273–286.

Thomas, W. I. 1928. *The Child in America: Behavior Problems and Programs*. New York: Knopf.

Thomsen, Steven R. 1993. "A Worm in the Apple: Hollywood's Influence on the Public's Perception of Teachers." Paper presented at the Southern States Communication Association and Central States Communication Association joint annual meeting, Lexington, KY, April 15.

Thoreau, Henry David. 1960. *Walden*. New York: Signet.

Tocqueville, Alexis de. 1945. *Democracy in America*. Translated by Henry Reeve. New York: Vintage Books.

Trier, James D. 2001. "The Cinematic Representation of the Personal and Professional Lives of Teachers." *Teacher Education Quarterly* (summer): 127–142.

Tudor, Andrew. 1974. *Image and Influence: Studies in the Sociology of Film*. New York: St. Martin's Press.

Turner, Frederick Jackson. 1985. *The Frontier in American History*. Malabar, FL: Robert E. Krieger Publishing.

Turner, Ralph. 1960. "Sponsored and Contest Mobility and the School System." *American Sociological Review* 25: 855–867.

Varenne, Herve. 1977. *Americans Together: Structured Diversity in a Midwestern Town*. New York: Teachers College Press.

Vera, Hernan, and Andrew M. Gordon. 2003. *Screen Saviors: Hollywood Fictions of Whiteness*. Lanham, MD: Rowman and Littlefield.

Weber, Max. 1985. *The Protestant Ethic and the Spirit of Capitalism*. Translated by Talcott Parsons. London: Counterpoint.

Wells, Amy. S., and Todd S. Serman. 1998. "Education Against All Odds: What Films Teach Us About Schools." In *Imaging Education: The Media and Schools in America.* Gene Maeroff, editor. New York: Teachers College Press, 181–194.

Willis, Paul. 1981. *Learning to Labor.* New York: Columbia University Press.

Wilson, William Julius 1987. *The Truly Disadvantaged*: *The Inner City, the Underclass, and Public Policy.* Chicago: University of Chicago Press.

Wilson, William Julius. 1996. *When Work Disappears.* New York: Knopf.

Wolfe, Alan. 1998. *One Nation, After All.* New York: Viking.

Wolff, Edward N. 2012. *The asset price meltdown and the wealth of the middle class.* No. w18559. National Bureau of Economic Research.

Wright, Will. 1975. *Sixguns and Society: A Structural Study of the Western.* Berkeley: University of California Press.

Yosso, Tara J., and David Gumaro García. 2010. "From Ms. J. to Ms. G.: Analyzing Racial Microaggressions in Hollywood's Urban School Genre." In *Hollywood's Exploited: Public Pedagogy, Corporate Movies, and Cultural Crisis.* Richard Van Heertum et al., editors. New York: Palgrave Macmillan, pp. 85–103.

Zipes, Jack. 1993. *Fairy Tale as Myth: Myth as Fairy Tale.* Lexington: University of Kentucky Press.

Index